Managing tomorrow today

dynamic financial management

Bill Snaith ● Jane Walker

FINANCIAL TIMES
Prentice Hall

An imprint of **Pearson Education**

London ● New York ● San Francisco ● Toronto ● Sydney ● Tokyo ● Singapore
Hong Kong ● Cape Town ● Madrid ● Paris ● Milan ● Munich ● Amsterdam

PEARSON EDUCATION LIMITED

Head Office:
Edinburgh Gate
Harlow CM20 2JE
Tel: +44 (0)1279 623623
Fax: +44 (0)1279 431059

London Office:
128 Long Acre
London WC2E 9AN
Tel: +44 (0)20 7447 2000
Fax: +44 (0)20 7240 5771
Website: www.financialminds.com

First published in Great Britain in 2001

ISBN 0 273 65067 X

British Library Cataloguing in Publication Data
A CIP catalogue record for this book can be obtained from the British Library.

10 9 8 7 6 5 4 3 2 1

Typeset by Northern Phototypesetting Co. Ltd, Bolton
Printed and bound in Great Britain by Redwood Books, Trowbridge, Wiltshire

The Publishers' policy is to use paper manufactured from sustainable forests.

About the authors

Bill Snaith BA, MSc, CEng, MBCS is the Director of Medium Enterprise Development, in the Foundation for SME Development at the University of Durham. He has combined his extensive business experience with his knowledge of management development to design and deliver specialist courses aimed at the managers in growing and entrepreneurial businesses. Bill's career has also involved the management, design and implementation of information systems in large and small organizations. His Masters degree in Business Project Management, has developed the idea of the business as a total system, an approach at the heart of dynamic financial management.

Jane Walker BSc, MBA is a freelance consultant specializing in the development of medium-sized businesses and their managers. She has 20 years' business experience including management within large, medium and small sized businesses. In the last ten years she has forged links with many academic institutions to bridge the gap between academia and management practice. Her earlier career, which included auditing company accounting and financial analysis with a major multinational company, has helped her see the world of finance from both the practitioner's and the business manager's points of view.

Preface

Managing Tomorrow Today represents a new approach in managing the day-to-day financial performance of businesses and makes finance more relevant to business management.

The dynamic financial management (DFM) techniques within *Managing Tomorrow Today*, seek to excite the reader, reduce the fear and provide a route-map to allow the more entrepreneurial manager to keep their *finger on the pulse* of a fast-moving business.

The development of DFM has been shared by the many businesses we have worked with over a 15-year journey. We have been fortunate to get to know so many businesses through our associations with a number of influential organizations including the Foundation for SME Development at the University of Durham, UK, the Small Business Unit at Curtin University, Perth, Western Australia and the Business Development Centre at Manchester Business School.

Who should read this book?

This book will help company owners and directors of smaller and medium-sized businesses, profit centre managers, business unit managers or senior managers within a large corporation or charity. It has been designed for anyone with responsibility for the financial performance of a business or part of a business. DFM provides the *cockpit* to help the entrepreneurial manager in *Managing Tomorrow Today*.

Further help

We cannot of course respond to everyone who may want to discuss their business, but we can offer a web site for discussion and sharing of experiences at www.dfmuk.com

Contents

Introduction

What is it all about?

Welcome to *Managing tomorrow today – dynamic financial management*. This book will teach you how to better manage your business using information that will already be available to you. The tools and techniques introduced will be new to you. They will open up whole new aspects of controlling your business and easily enable you to 'keep your finger on the pulse'.

Do you struggle to understand the relationship between accountancy jargon and your business activities? Are you still looking for that magical book that will contain the secret to understanding financial reports and what they mean to your business? Look no further. This book is not magical, but it does contain some secrets that will easily give you the knowledge, skills and understanding to improve your business performance by adopting dynamic financial management tools and techniques.

Whether you are a company owner, director, business unit manager, profit centre manager, or senior manager within any size of organization or charity, this book will provide you with enough information to ascertain how you are performing today and even where you might be heading tomorrow.

The dynamic financial management tools and techniques introduced relate as easily to profit, surplus or contribution measurement. You will not have to learn about standard accountancy, but you will learn enough to be able to control and communicate the performance of your business to professionals and understand more than they do about the financial aspects of *your* business.

This book is about managing your business; it is not yet another book about standard accounting practices. It will not therefore involve you in the mundane 'How to produce a profit and loss' or 'How to calculate your liquidity ratio'. These skills are useful. However, no one then tells you how to interpret such information back into the everyday operational business decisions you have to make. We all pay a lot of money for standard accounting reports to be prepared by professionals. Typically, these reports land on your desk and are not put to enough use because they take too much time to read or are clouded in jargon.

Even worse, they may be badly presented using a standard format that is inappropriate to your business.

But hang on a minute – this is *your* business and you want to know how you are performing *today*. Is there anything that you should be doing, and what will be the effects of those proposed actions on *tomorrow's* performance? You need to move away from the traditional approach to finance – waiting until tomorrow to discover the results of today's actions – into the arena of the *dynamic* manager – managing tomorrow today.

This book will teach you how to focus on the numbers you need and how to use them to your advantage – to design your future.

There are many questions managers need to ask every day:

- Are we doing OK?
- Should we drop our prices in order to increase sales?
- Why are we so busy and yet don't seem to be making enough money?
- Should we drop that old product?
- Should we take on that new order or project?
- Can we afford that new machine?
- Is our stock too high?

These are all valid questions and standard accounting reports may contain the information you need to understand the problem. They will not, however, supply an easy answer. Of course, if you ask the professionals who have prepared these reports, they are often reluctant to commit themselves, saying: 'It's your decision! It's up to you!'

In that case it is *you* who should have the information you need and the skills and knowledge, tools and techniques, to utilize that information. That is exactly what this book will provide you with.

So, please read on and learn how to understand and improve the performance and control of your business – to manage tomorrow today, to design your future.

Bill Snaith and Jane Walker

www.dfmuk.com

part one

Managing today

1

Introduction to part one

Every action in your business will affect your financial performance. It is not surprising therefore that managers make many decisions with reference to the financial information that is said to reflect this performance. But this information is usually taken from standard accounting reports that many managers do not fully understand. This means that the decisions are, in fact, made without fully understanding the information and without appreciating the consequences of those actions.

We believe that the most useful financial information is concise, accurate and timely. However, traditional accounting reports may have a number of limitations. They are often received well after the relevant period because many businesses, especially smaller ones, rely upon professionals to collate the necessary information and then produce the reports. They are often produced too infrequently for you to really be able to keep your finger on the pulse of the business. This means that crucial decisions about the future of your business are based on what is information about the past. With the speed of change in business today we need information *now!* – *dynamic* information, that *changes* with your business.

You are the one who knows your business. And it is you who should know the dynamic indicators that really reflect your performance. In fact, you should know the value of these dynamic indicators on a day by day basis. But how?

Ask yourself, what was your income last year, last month, last week, yesterday, and what will it be today and tomorrow? You should know the answer to these questions, and similarly with other dynamic indicators of your business. That's why dynamic financial management concentrates on both today *and* tomorrow.

Dynamic financial management does not rely upon standard accounting reports. It simply uses a number of 'dynamic indicators'. It also uses tools and techniques that provide a guide to your current performance and an illustration of probable future performance. They indicate where action may be needed to realign performance to expectations – designing the future.

To maximize the power of dynamic financial management you will first have to be able to answer some fundamental business questions:

● Question 1: How can a business be measured and then monitored?

● Question 2: What should be measured and monitored in a business to truly understand what is going on?

● Question 3: What should be measured and monitored in *your* business to truly understand what is going on?

● Question 4: By how much does a figure have to vary from a target before you act (or even panic)?

● Question 5: What options are available to keep your business in shape?

These questions, and more, will be fully answered in this book. They are introduced in *Chapter 1: The dynamic landscape* to raise awareness of what may be appropriate measures and monitors for you and your business. We are not talking about 'paralysis by analysis'; indeed, this is the opposite of the dynamic financial management philosophy.

Dynamic financial management is about capturing the appropriate information and applying the appropriate time and effort to understand the financial aspects of the business, yet ensuring that you have the necessary and sufficient detail to converse meaningfully with all of the stakeholders of your business.

Pilots have a saying: *'When you're flying at night you have to trust the instruments.'* The dynamic financial management tools and techniques included in this book will present you with the instruments you need to read to make your business really fly!

And there's more. These techniques will not only allow you to monitor your business in a new and dynamic way but also facilitate the management of other stakeholder views of your business. Every business has other stakeholders; even in the single-person business the bank will be keen to view your progress. And what business or department does not have some sort of customer?

Using dynamic financial management means you are always ready to answer vital questions from these stakeholders. If their measures mean anything, it is probably worthwhile monitoring them anyway.

The way forward

Managing tomorrow today is what dynamic financial management is all about. It is about you enjoying a successful business – now and into the future.

Success comes from knowing where you are today and where you want to be. To do this we need to bring in the new – to move away from the traditional financial reports, into the dynamic financial management indicators designed for managers who manage at the sharp end. We are not damning the old approach, just putting it into perspective.

We need to introduce the tools and techniques of dynamic financial management to understand and act upon the indicators of your business. This requires a new way of thinking and a new language to support this thinking. Yes, we know you are busy, but stick with it – time invested today *will* reap benefits tomorrow.

chapter 1

The dynamic landscape

This chapter will describe the terrain of the dynamic landscape. It is not entirely smooth – there are hills to climb, but then of course there are valleys where you can freewheel. *The dynamic landscape* describes the principles upon which our tools and techniques used throughout the book are built. The power of these techniques may not be immediately obvious until later chapters. Read this first chapter carefully to get your bearings – if you can navigate the dynamic landscape you can control the future of your business.

Any book looking at a new approach to an old subject needs to be set in context. The introduction has brought in the philosophy of dynamic financial management. But where do you go from here? As a way of helping you to work your way through the book we are going to address the questions raised in the *Introduction to Part One* using the fundamental concepts of dynamic financial management. In brief, these concepts are about monitoring your business using a small set of dynamic indicators. But which indicators should you use? Well, those appropriate to *your* business of course, and we believe we have identified eight dynamic indicators that traverse the full terrain of any business. For ease of reference, the questions from the *Introduction to Part One* are:

- Question 1: How can a business be measured and then monitored?

- Question 2: What should be measured and monitored in a business to truly understand what is going on?

- Question 3: What should be measured and monitored in *your* business to truly understand what is going on?

- Question 4: By how much does a figure have to vary from a target before you act (or even panic)?

● Question 5: What options are available to keep your business in shape?

To answer any of these questions requires the use of some sort of financial jargon. And typically, it is at this point that most people have problems with finance or accounting. They get lost in the jargon. Not only is the jargon complex, but everyone seems to use different words for the same things, or even the same words for different things!

For this book we wanted to simplify things. But the irony is that in order to do this effectively, we wanted to create our own language. This may at first seem contradictory. However, it is for a good reason and we will clearly define our terminology as we progress. At the back of the book, there is a glossary of the terms we use. On balance we feel this is far easier and better than giving yet another alternative definition of existing financial jargon.

Now, back to the five questions. In this chapter we will use these questions as a way to start using the language and as a sort of route map for the rest of the book. Answering these questions will help show how dynamic financial management will help you to improve the performance of your business.

Question 1

How can a business be measured and then monitored?

Some of the concepts we will cover in answering this question are basic and are probably already familiar to you. However, as with any subject the language used is important and we will therefore take it step by step to introduce our language into these concepts.

Let's start by looking at measuring and monitoring activity. Ask most managers what is the traditional measure of performance and the answer will be profit – the difference between the value of sales (your income) and the total costs of your business:

Sales – Costs = Profit (or Loss)

Is sales a good word with which to measure activity? If you manage a department of a business you may think you do not manage 'sales'. If you are a business unit manager or a department manager you will manage 'budget and actual' or 'income and contribution'. If you are in a non-profit organization perhaps you manage 'income and surplus' (or 'deficit'). If you are an owner-manager you will manage 'sales and costs'. Whichever words are used in your business it is basically about 'money in', 'money inside' and 'money out'.

Knowing these three numbers is vital, but are they sufficient to know everything about how your business is performing?

Let's return to the equation above but start using the language of dynamic financial management:

Income – Costs = Contribution (positive or negative)

Does this tell you how your business is performing? No, it is just the same as before but now expressed in our language. We need further clarification to measure performance.

You cannot yet answer efficiency questions such as 'What are your costs if you sell another ten items tomorrow?' or 'What would your contribution be if you put up your price by 5 per cent and volume remained the same?' Efficiency and effectiveness are additional measures of performance. Efficiency is 'doing things right' and effectiveness is 'doing the right things'. To be able to judge which are the right things to do and whether you are doing them well or not you need to be able to further analyze your business.

These are more detailed questions and so you need more detailed analysis of your figures, especially your costs. There is an endless list of such questions about your costs that you should be able to answer with ease, but you either do not have the information at present or you cannot interpret the available information appropriately. Or maybe you are unsure about the nature of costs inside your business. You know which account code they have been charged to, but is this enough to understand how these costs react to the actions you take within your business?

To begin to interpret your business in more detail, you therefore need to break down your costs into what we call *dynamic costs* and *static costs*. Each of these is fundamentally different in nature and will have a fundamentally different impact on your business. Again, similar concepts may have been used (or misused) in more traditional management accounting. But to avoid any confusion over the terminology, we have developed our own language with specific definitions associated with this:

- dynamic costs vary with the *activity* of the business, for example, the time spent on a project, or the materials used in production;
- static costs are regular costs that occur even if there is no activity, for example, rent and rates on your premises, or salaries. Static costs are often *lumpy* in that they change in big steps rather than in direct relation to activity, for example, recruiting one more person will increase your static costs in one step.

Dynamic and static are key terms in dynamic financial management. *Dynamic* reflects figures that change constantly due to the level of activity and the decisions made within the organization, they are fluid. *Static* refers to looking at the business at a moment in time – freezing the shot.

Looking back at the contribution calculation we can now identify two types of contribution using the language of dynamic financial management as follows:

Income – Dynamic Costs = *Gross Contribution*

And then:

Gross Contribution – Static Costs = *Dynamic Net Contribution*

Or, as a very simple dynamic contribution statement, the arithmetic can be illustrated as follows:

	£
Income	100
– Dynamic Costs	60
= *Gross Contribution*	40
– Static Costs	30
= *Dynamic Net Contribution*	10

Your dynamic costs are directly related (proportional) to your activities and as such the better you are at those activities, the lower your dynamic costs. The gross contribution, therefore, is a measure of how *efficient* your activities are.

The dynamic net contribution is a measure of how *effective* your activities are, i.e. how well you have used the resources of your business. It is the 'bottom line'. For example, the salaries of your management team are a static cost. Are all of your managers working on the *effective* use of resources in their department?

So already we can measure and monitor a little more of your business. We have also introduced some of the language we want to use throughout the book. Standard accounting terms often do not seem to relate to your business activity and decisions, your dynamic landscape; we think the language of dynamic financial management does.

We can now predict the dynamic net contribution (the effectiveness of your business) under different circumstances, for example, if income were to increase by 50 per cent (yes!), then taking the table above and changing the income accordingly, we get:

	£
Income	150
− Dynamic Costs	90
= Gross Contribution	60
− Static Costs	30
= Dynamic Net Contribution	30

Notice that the dynamic costs vary with the activity of the business, so they have also increased by 50 per cent, but of course the static costs have remained the same (you may feel this is unrealistic and we too will challenge this later in the book). We now make a dynamic net contribution of £30.

So far, this seems quite easy, but unfortunately life is more complicated than that. Businesses often confuse activity with money. In reality, the effects of some activities occur immediately, but others take some time to be reflected in your results. The effect of this delay is that part of your business actually exists in what we call the *time warp*.

As we mentioned at the beginning of this chapter, when most managers are asked to comment on the financial performance of their business they talk about profit. Managers need to adopt a more holistic approach to the financial management of their business. They need to understand and monitor the effects of this time warp. Take income and debtors for example. Income is the value of your activities for the period measured. Debtors (the money customers owe to you) reflect income frozen in a time warp – you have not yet received the income from a sale but you will get it at some time in the future. This concept will be fully explored later.

Chapter 2: What are dynamic indicators? will ensure you look at the business in a holistic manner. Not only are we concerned with the dynamic contribution statement, we are also concerned with something we are going to refer to as the DNA statement. The DNA statement looks after the day-to-day management of the time warp. It will look at the money that is constantly being imprisoned and released from your dynamic net assets (DNA). These are the movements in stock, debtors and creditors as a response to the activity and management of your business. The DNA statement will be represented as follows:

	£
Stock	50
+ Debtors	100
− Creditors	75
= Static Net Assets	75

Why static net assets? Because these values are a snapshot at a moment in time. They become dynamic only when comparing one period with another. But let's stop there with the DNA statement. As mentioned, the detail behind this will be discussed in *Chapter 2: What are dynamic indicators?*

To complete the answer to Question 1: How can a business be measured and monitored?, there is only one other piece of terminology to introduce in order to complete the picture of your dynamic landscape – dynamic cash movement. No business would be well measured and monitored if there was not some way of looking at cash, and dynamic financial management brings this into the frame by constantly monitoring the dynamic cash movement.

So what is the answer to Question 1, or more importantly, where will I find the answer within this book? *Managing tomorrow today* is all about the analysis of your business – how to measure and monitor performance – and then how to improve the results of your business. *Chapter 2: What are dynamic indicators?* will introduce all the measures, *Chapter 3: What are dynamic targets?* will introduce the standards against which to monitor your performance, and *Chapter 4: Dynamic decisions* will show you how to improve that performance.

We have only just begun. There are four more fundamental questions to consider.

Question 2

What should be measured and monitored in a business to truly understand what is going on?

Having discussed what should be measured via the dynamic contribution statement, the DNA statement and dynamic cash movement, we now need to look at how we can understand these. This book will not attempt to explain the standard accounting reports and as such will assume you have some basic knowledge of the contents and terminology of such reports. There are already many books around that offer explanations of these standard reports.

We appreciate that standard financial reports have their uses and are appropriate to certain situations, but they are far too involved and therefore too time consuming for our techniques. These reports contain information that is fixed in time, *historical* information. As soon as data is collected in preparation for the compilation of these reports, it is frozen in time, and therefore out of date. A business is a dynamic system with moving parts that continuously interact. The future of a business cannot therefore be analyzed using historic information alone. The future of your business will not wait for standard reports to be produced by your accountants – you need to know now so that you can act.

So what do you measure and monitor to truly understand what is going on in a business? Our answer to this question is going to revolve around a number of issues:

- making numbers dynamic;
- the influence of time;
- making measures comparable;
- looking at the gaps between expected performance and real performance;
- managing tomorrow today;
- using income as the anchor point for all indicators.

Making numbers dynamic

It is the dynamic indicators that you must truly understand in order to appreciate what is going on in your business. We have a standard list of measures that we will use to monitor your business. *Chapter 2: What are dynamic indicators?* and *Chapter 5: You are not alone* detail how to choose your own dynamic indicators. But first we want to discuss what type of information, which figures, should be considered as dynamic indicators.

If you are aiming at a moving target, you aim for the future position. It is the same in business. Every decision changes the position of the business. Every decision therefore changes the future. Dynamic financial management uses indicators that aim for the future.

In dynamic financial management we relate all the information together in a holistic way. This means that when one part of the business changes, the effects can be seen dynamically throughout the analysis. Numbers in isolation mean nothing. We need more than numbers, we need relationships between all of our dynamic indicators. As an illustration, take the figure below extracted from a standard accounting report:

302,657

Is this number good or bad? There is no way to tell. At present it is an isolated piece of data. What is it, a count of something, say stock in hand, or a value? We have no way of knowing. What, then, if we add a monetary sign:

£302,657

Is this any better? There is still no way to tell. What if it is a salary? Do you think it is good or bad? Now you might have a view, but you still need more information about this piece of data to be able to decide. What if it is a salary for a week (pretty good!) or the predicted salary for the next 30 years (oh dear!)?

It seems that a number alone tells us nothing, it is an isolated piece of data. But relate it to other things such as value, time, or indeed other measures, and it comes alive, it becomes much more significant, more meaningful and therefore immediately more useful, more powerful – it becomes dynamic.

So, a dynamic figure has more interest and power than an isolated figure. A dynamic figure can be related to other figures and therefore its effect can be seen throughout the organization. It is dynamic information that we use to analyze your business. By relating figures together we gain some cohesion in the measurement of business performance, the parts operating together – affecting each other. If we gain cohesion from dynamic analysis, we must also gain greater control. If by changing one figure we can predict the effect on the rest of the business, we are managing the whole business and not reacting to the performance of each part individually. This is dynamic management, and will definitely lead to improved business performance.

Case study

Take a management meeting where the MD is discussing the business plan for next year. The sales last year were £1,000,000 and the dynamic costs were £600,000. The MD asks the sales director what she expects to achieve next year. She knows she could reach £1.4 million but says £1.2 million to be safe. The MD asks the production manager what the dynamic costs will be for this projected sales level. He knows he could maintain costs at 60 per cent of sales, which is £720,000, but says £780,000 to be safe. Now, when this plan is implemented and budgets are set, we see the lack of cohesion in the business. When sales reach £1.5 million, the sales director is a hero, but naturally the production costs were 60 per cent of this figure, which is £900,000 – well over budget – so the production manager looks bad. Where is the synergy, the cohesion in this? Who wins?

What a business needs is measures of performance linked together dynamically so that if one piece of the business stretches, the rest of the business displaces proportionately to accommodate the change.

The influence of time

Cohesion and control help to bring numbers into perspective, they bring them together and make them comparable. But dynamic financial management goes further than this – it brings the past, present and future into perspective. To manage from the past is *reactive* planning, from the present it is *active* planning, and managing for the future is *proactive* planning. Bringing the past, present and future together is dynamic planning, it is using the dynamic nature of your business to your advantage – putting you ahead.

You can manage the interaction of figures (past, present and future) if you understand how they are linked dynamically. This also facilitates a faster response to dynamic trends that are easily apparent with our techniques. You design your future.

Table 1.1 shows how the past, present and future interact in your business. How you respond to information is your preferred planning orientation:

Table 1.1 ● Interaction between past, present and future on your business

Orientation	Past	Present	Future
Reactive	✔	✘	✘
Active	✘	✔	✘
Proactive	✘	✘	✔
Dynamic	✔	✔	✔

This is by no means a new concept – it has been used in systems dynamics for years[1] – but it is perhaps new to financial management. What we need is a comparable way to measure a business over all these time frames.

Making measures comparable

As an example, let us return to the figure we extracted from a standard statement

£302,657

What if this is your debtors figure? Customers owe you £302,657 – is this good or bad, is it too much? To answer these questions, first take your income figure of, say, £900,000. Now calculate your debtors figure as a percentage of your income figure:

$$\frac{302,657}{900,000} \times 100 = 33\%$$

What if we know your credit terms are 60 days. Is 33 per cent good or bad? The first question you need to ask is: 'What is the income of £900,000?' Is it a

1 Ackoff R.L. (1981) *Creating the Corporate Future*, Wiley.

year's income, a month's income, or maybe even a week's income? Whatever the answer, your debtors are 33 per cent of it.

If it is a year's sales, then 33 per cent of the year's sales (four months) is still tied up in debtors. This is not good. Your credit terms are 60 days (two months), so your debtors are taking twice as long to pay you as they should. How could we show this as a comparable measure? Two months equates to 17 per cent of a year, which means you should have roughly the equivalent of 17 per cent of your annual income held in your debtors figure. If your current debtors figure is 33 per cent you know immediately that it is actually 16 per cent more than it should be.

What does this mean in money terms? Sixteen per cent of £900,000 is roughly £150,000. So now you know you have overdue debtors to the value of £150,000 – oh dear! To repeat the question: Is this good or bad? You know the answer immediately. With this simple new technique you can now do some mental arithmetic, say, in a meeting.

Case study

If your sales director in the US boasts about annual sales being $1,200,000, simply ask what the current debtors figure is. For a 30-day credit term, the answer should be 30/365, of $1,200,000, which is $100,000 (8.5 per cent). If the sales director says the debtor figure is $201,483, she should be taken to task for having approximately $101,483 more of our money out there – remember, a sale is not a sale until the money is in the bank. It is worse still for your cash flow if the commission has already been paid to your salesforce and you have not yet received the money. What decisions would you now make? …

Looking at the gaps between expected performance and real performance

What we have done so far is used debtors, one of the dynamic indicators, and calculated it as a percentage of the income figure. We then calculated a target figure by referring to the driver for debtors which is your credit period. This target was also expressed as a percentage of the income figure. You can now continually monitor your debtors by comparing the actual figure against your target figure – looking at the gap between them.

So the debtors gap is simply the gap between the actual debtors figure and the target debtors figure:

Debtors Gap = Actual Debtors – Target Debtors

In dynamic financial management, gaps, like most of our monitors, are expressed as a percentage of income – we will refer to these as Gap%.

$$\text{Gap\%} \ = \ \frac{\text{Gap Value}}{\text{Income}} \times 100$$

In the earlier example our actual debtors were £302,657 while the target (our credit terms) was £153,000 (17 per cent of £900,000). The debtors gap would have been:

	£	%
Debtors Gap	Actual Debtors – Target Debtors	Actual Dr% – Target Dr%
	£302,657 – £153,000	33.63% – 17.0%
	= £149,657	= 16.63%
AND	£149,657 / £900,000	£900,000 * 16.63%
	= 16.63%	= £149,657

In *Chapter 3: What are dynamic targets?*, you will become very familiar with the terms gap and Gap% and the power they give to your decision making. Indeed, you will discover much quicker ways of getting to these key figures – information you need, when you need it.

Managing tomorrow today

But wait a minute. The examples we have used are looking at annual figures. If you wait a year to realize you have a debtors gap, your business might not survive – this is hardly dynamic financial management. When is your tomorrow? Is it next year? Is it next month? Or is it, in reality, the next day: *tomorrow*. Dynamic financial management works around any time period – the one appropriate to your business. Dynamic managers do not simply wait for tomorrow to see the consequences of today; they manage tomorrow today.

Using income as the anchor point for all indicators

Going back to the original question, 'What should be measured and monitored in a business to truly understand what is going on?', the most important message is that all dynamic indicators are interrelated and dynamic. We have illustrated the use of one dynamic indicator and suggested that there are many candidates for inclusion in your list.

What makes these figures dynamic? Let us start by looking at the common driver – income. Whether your income is your sales value generated, your budget allocation, or your donations received, your income figure is driven by the activities of the business. Or you could look at it the other way round – your income drives the level of activity you can undertake in your business; you can only do what you have enough income to do. So income, in whatever form is appropriate to you, is the one common measure for all businesses.

In fact, income is the anchor point for all our dynamic tools and techniques. Everything you measure in a business can, and should, be related to its income figure. By calculating each dynamic indicator as a percentage of the income figure, it is possible to see the relationship – the dynamic relationship – between all the dynamic indicators and also the ripple effects throughout these indicators of any decisions or changes made.

A single anchor point enables a view of the business that shows where parts are stretching or shrinking, like pieces of elastic all fixed to one point. We illustrate this changing shape of your business using a *radar chart* and this is introduced below as a way to answer the third question. Using the concept of gaps, the radar chart clearly shows both the positive and negative gaps, representing the stretching and shrinking of your business activities.

In conclusion to Question 2, it may be useful to look at where the answers will come within the book.

- Making numbers dynamic will be addressed in *Chapter 2: What are dynamic indicators?*
- The influence of time is a concept that permeates the whole book but is perhaps most dramatically demonstrated in *Chapter 4: Dynamic decisions.*
- Making measures comparable is addressed in *Chapter 3: What are dynamic targets?*
- Looking at the gaps between expected performance and real performance is initially developed in *Chapter 3: What are dynamic targets?* while the ways of closing the gaps are explored in *Chapter 4.*
- Income as the anchor is a fundamental concept that permeates the whole of this book.

Question 3

What should be measured and monitored in your business to truly understand what is going on?

This question is phrased slightly differently than the last. We are now talking about *your* business. So what is the difference? In the last question we said the dynamic indicators could be different for individual businesses. Having said that, we *will* use a set that should be common to most businesses. Whatever your dynamic indicators are, the techniques are the same. This question will focus on the impact of the way you measure and monitor your business. Dynamic financial management believes this impact should be very visual and easy to interpret.

We advocate three main tools with which you should monitor any business:

1   Radar chart of dynamic indicators.

2   The dynamic breakeven graph.

3   The dynamic cash graph.

Together these will incorporate all the time frames we have discussed – the past, the present, and the future – and will look at the business as a whole using a combination of information from the dynamic contribution statement, the DNA statement and the dynamic cash movement. Let us look at each of these in order to see exactly what they are helping you to monitor.

Radar chart of dynamic indicators

As we have said, there is a common set of dynamic indicators that will suit most businesses and these are therefore a good place to start. For example, the dynamic indicator for stock will be:

$$\text{Stock\%} = \frac{\text{Stock}}{\text{Income}} \times 100$$

To demonstrate the use of the radar chart we are going to use the common dynamic indicators defined below. These terms may feel unfamiliar to you at the moment but will quickly become part of the language you will use to dynamically manage your business. They will be explained in detail in the next chapter but for the moment we will concentrate on how we might present them in a stimulating and visual manner. Our eight dynamic indicators are shown in Table 1.2.

Table 1.2 ● **The eight dynamic indicators**

Dynamic indicator	Meaning
Dynamic net contribution% **DNC%**	The money left from your income after all costs (dynamic and static) have been deducted. In a business this indicates the potential cash from each sale that could be invested back into your business.
Dynamic net assets% **DNA%**	This indicates the money you have imprisoned in the time warp of your business. Dynamic net assets show the movement in the money tied up in this time warp.
Dynamic cash movement% **DCM%**	A product of the dynamic net contribution plus or minus dynamic net asset movement. This indicates the net amount of money you have imprisoned or released from the time warp and money generated from DNC.
Breakeven gap% **BeGap%**	Breakeven income is the amount of income you need to cover all your costs – to make neither a negative nor a positive DNC. Breakeven gap is the difference between your income and the breakeven income. Breakeven gap% is the breakeven gap as a percentage of income. It indicates how safe your current income level is – how much above or below breakeven you are.
Gross contribution% **GC%**	Income less dynamic costs. It indicates the efficiency of your organization, how well you are able to control your dynamic costs or your income stream.
Stock% **Stock%**	This is made up of raw materials in manufacturing businesses, work in progress in manufacturing and service organizations, and finished goods in manufacturing and retail organizations. This indicates the money invested in stock but still imprisoned in the time warp of your business and is the first of three strands building up your DNA.
Debtors% **Dr%**	Debtors are people who owe you money. This indicates the money from income still in the hands of your customers and therefore imprisoned in the time warp of your business and is the second strand of your DNA.
Creditors% **Cr%**	Creditors are the people to whom you owe money. This indicates the future money you need to release from your time warp, and is the third, and last, strand of your DNA.

These last three indicators are the strands of DNA but may not be appropriate in all organizations. If they are not applicable to you, just use those that best reflect your own DNA structure.

So what is a radar chart? It is a chart that shows several values on different axes. Arranging the dynamic indicators around a radar chart gives you the shape of your business. Figure 1.1 is used as an illustration only.

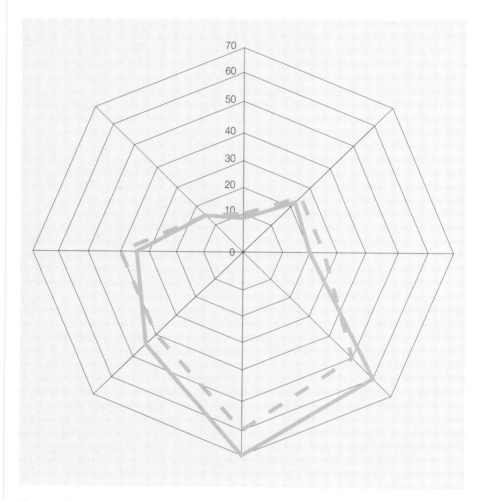

Fig 1.1 ● Radar chart example

The radar chart shows the changing shape of your business in all eight dynamic indicators, comparing performance across periods or against targets. The radar shows all the operational elements of your business – your contribution (GC%, BeGap% and DNC%), the strands of your DNA (Stock%, Dr%, Cr% and DNA%) and your cash (DCM%).

We have already introduced the contribution statement, which is certainly a good measure of the effectiveness of today's activities but this is not the only measure of a business. We have also introduced the concept of the time warp –

how activity today is often confused with money today. We can now say this in a different way – the *contribution* today is confused with the *cash* today.

Cash In ⟶ **Cash Imprisoned** ⟶ **Cash Out**

Cash is often imprisoned within your business – within the time warp – and it is an analysis of this time warp – the dynamic net assets – that shows the amount of cash held in this prison.

Later, we need to understand the relationship between something we will refer to as static net assets and the DNA%. This will be examined and explained fully in the next chapter.

The radar chart gives you an effective and visual measure of the strands of your DNA (Stock%, Dr% and Cr%), but how can you manage their performance? If your debtors are higher than expected, i.e. you have money from your customers tied up in the time warp, you may be tempted to delay payments to your creditors to compensate. We do not think this is dynamic management. And yet these compensating gaps can give the false impression that your static net assets are well managed. This is why DNA% is such an important measure.

The final piece of the radar is the DCM%. This is the 'cash out' bit of the equation. How much cash have you released from the time warp this month? Again this will be discussed in detail in the next chapter but, briefly, the way this is calculated is as follows:

Dynamic Cash Movement = Dynamic Net Contribution – Dynamic Net Assets

Again for the radar graph, this dynamic indicator will be stated as a percentage of income:

$$DCM\% = \frac{DCM}{Income} \times 100$$

Remember that DNA is the movement of cash in or out of the time warp, so DCM is a mixture of the contribution we have made plus or minus any money released or imprisoned in the time warp this period.

The radar chart is only one way of pictorially representing the interactive nature of your business and its performance. We will introduce you to two more – the dynamic breakeven graph and the dynamic cash graph.

The dynamic breakeven graph

We believe that one figure every business should know is the breakeven income – the income point at which you make neither a positive nor a negative dynamic net contribution: your dynamic net contribution is zero. Breakeven is the base camp you need to reach before starting to climb the mountain.

The dynamic breakeven graph compares your actual income figure with the breakeven income figure. In fact, it does more than this: it shows trends in both, allowing you to compare the past with the present and predict and manage the future – dynamic analysis.

Breakeven sales or breakeven income is a figure that has been used in management accounting for many years and has a standard calculation. For this you need to know your static costs which we will refer to as 'SC' and your gross contribution percentage which we will refer to as 'GC%'.

First we need to know how to calculate the GC%. As with all dynamic indicators in dynamic financial management, all percentages are of income.

$$\text{Gross Contribution \%} = \frac{\text{Gross Contribution}}{\text{Income}} \times 100$$

Then, breakeven income

$$\text{Breakeven Income} = \frac{\text{Static Costs}}{\text{GC\%}}$$

For example:

	€
Income	150.00
– Dynamic Costs	90.00
Gross Contribution	60.00
– Static Costs	30.00
Dynamic Net Contribution	30.00

$$\text{Gross Contribution\%} = \frac{€60.00}{€150.00} \times 100 = 40\%$$

and

$$\text{Breakeven Income} = \frac{€30.00}{40\%} = €75.00$$

So this company requires an income of €75 to break even. Putting this figure back into the simple contribution statement from above can prove this. The dynamic costs react dynamically with the income level so they will reduce proportionately (remember that the GC% will remain at 40 per cent of the income):

	€
Income	75.00
− Dynamic Costs	45.00
Gross Contribution	30.00
− Static Costs	30.00
Dynamic Net Contribution	0.00

As we can see, the company breaks even at €75 income.

But that is today. Tomorrow this business may break even at €80 or €70. Our dynamic costs% may vary slightly, as may our static costs%, or the income could change on a month by month basis and this may impact on the GC%. To manage the business dynamically we must monitor breakeven dynamically. We must not be fooled into thinking that our breakeven will always stay the same. Monitoring your breakeven involves comparing your income and breakeven income on a regular basis. This is best done by mapping your income and breakeven figures on a graph.

Figure 1.2 shows a monthly recording of breakeven analysis. The real power of a *dynamic* breakeven graph is that you can choose your own time period for recording it – monthly, weekly, even daily, if that is important in your business.

The interpretation of this graph is one of the main issues we will discuss in *Chapter 2: What are dynamic indicators?* For the moment we can say that the business in Fig 1.2 appears to be performing well. Certainly in months 4, 5 and 6 things are improving as the breakeven gap (the difference between income and breakeven income) is getting greater. This graph actually tells you more than this and will be further explored in the next chapter.

The radar chart and dynamic breakeven graph give visual information on the past and present performance of the business, allowing you to make good management decisions about the future. The final visual image to allow you to understand the measures and monitors in your business is the dynamic cash graph.

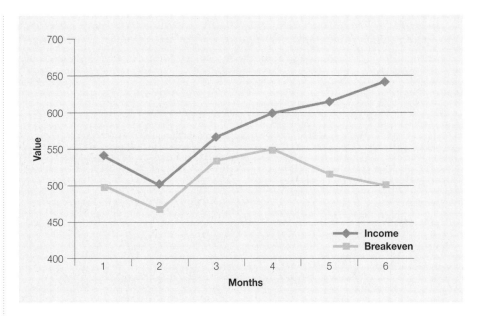

Fig 1.2 ● **The dynamic breakeven graph**

The dynamic cash graph

We can now monitor dynamic indicators at a moment in time and dynamic trends using our radar chart and dynamic breakeven graph. The dynamic cash graph involves making the leap to looking at the difference between contribution and cash. To do this we will return to the dynamic cash movement. This is the amount of cash that has been released or entrapped within your business as a result of your activities. The calculation for this could not be simpler and it emphasizes the interactive nature of dynamic financial management:

Dynamic Cash Movement = Dynamic Net Contribution – Dynamic Net Assets

where dynamic net assets are:

This Period's Static Net Assets – Last Period's Static Net Assets

Matching this to the time orientations:

	Time orientation
Dynamic Cash Movement	Tomorrow
Dynamic Net Contribution	Today
This Period's Static Net Assets	Today
Last Period's Static Net Assets	Yesterday

This is not a true cash flow and is not a replacement for the traditional cash flow forecast but, if funding and investment remain the same, it is an indication of the relative cash performance from the activities of your business on a period by period basis. We will come back to this in a later chapter.

However, we now have all the components for the dynamic cash graph. The three vital signs of a business are:

1   DNC% – an indication of the money made from your income (today).

2   DNA% – an indication of the value of money imprisoned or released from your time warp (yesterday and today).

3   DCM% – an indication of the cash impact of the two above (tomorrow).

The dynamic cash graph illustrates the trends in these on one chart, as shown in Fig 1.3. The dynamic cash graph shows whether your actions in any period have resulted in the overall generation of cash or a reduction in cash. If the DNC% is greater than the DNA%, cash has been generated. If it is the other way round, cash has been taken out of the business. Cash is the lifeblood of the business and Fig 1.3 shows the interaction of the dynamic contribution statement and the DNA statement. It brings together trends in the overall performance of the business showing whether we are generating cash inside the business to allow the business to develop in the future.

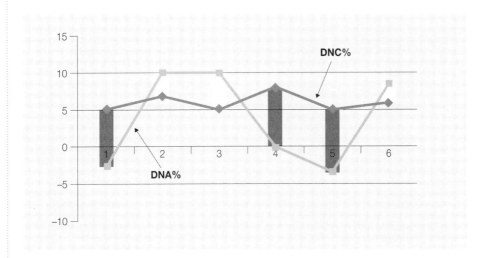

Fig 1.3 ● **The dynamic cash graph**

In summary

To conclude the answer to Question 3: What should be measured and monitored in your business to truly understand what is going on?, we have suggested the eight dynamic indicators that illustrate business performance. Once you have calculated your dynamic indicators they should tell you how you are performing. You need to be able to tell if that performance is good or bad. If it is good, could it be better? This answer has identified three visual ways of representing all the dynamic indicators of your business, showing your business performing dynamically as an integrated whole.

Once you have your dynamic indicators and you know how to produce these three charts (there will be more on this in the next chapter) you need to monitor these against a budget or target value. But how do you set that budget or target? In dynamic financial management there are techniques you can use to set appropriate targets to monitor against. This targeting provides the quick monitoring ability for all of the figures we need to be truly dynamic in business management. *Chapter 3: What are dynamic targets?* is devoted to the ways and means of making these targets appropriate to your particular business.

By overlaying the targets for each of these dynamic indicators on the same graph you can see the shape your business should be and how it shapes up at present. It is worthwhile saying that the value of the target will be closely related to the time period you are analyzing. Dynamic targets can reflect a week's activity, a month's activity, a year's activity, or any other period that is appropriate to your business.

Question 4

By how much does a figure have to vary from a target before you act (or even panic)?

Managing tomorrow today will help you identify your dynamic indicators and set appropriate targets for these. However, in reality your dynamic indicators may not always be on target. In dynamic financial management these differences are referred to as a gap, and gaps can be positive or negative, good or bad. That is what this question is about – understanding and interpreting the gaps. We are asking you to mind the gap!

Consider the dynamic breakeven we have just discussed. We can now take this analysis slightly further by considering the gap between the income and breakeven income lines. We call this the breakeven gap.

$$\text{Breakeven Gap} = \text{Income} - \text{Breakeven Income}$$

$$\text{Breakeven Gap} = \text{€}150.00 - \text{€}75.00 = \text{€}75.00$$

As with all our dynamic indicators, we can calculate the breakeven gap% as a percentage of income:

$$\frac{\text{Breakeven Gap\%}}{\text{(BeGap\%)}} = \frac{\text{Breakeven Gap}}{\text{Income}} \times 100$$

$$\text{Breakeven Gap\%} = \frac{€75.00}{€150.00} \times 100 = 50\%$$

This tells you that even if you were to lose 50 per cent of your volume you would break even. So again, the breakeven gap and BeGap% give a feeling for how far above breakeven you are operating, or maybe how far below. Remember, the breakeven gap (as all gaps) can be negative too. A negative breakeven gap would mean you had less income than required to cover your total costs (dynamic + static costs) and so your dynamic net contribution must be negative. But more than that, among many other uses the breakeven gap% tells you by how much you must increase your sales volume to reach breakeven again.

It is these gaps that we will be using to help you decide when to panic, when to act, and, sometimes, when to relax.

Looking at the radar chart, every spindle on the radar should have the actual performance of the dynamic indicator and should be compared with the target for that indicator. You will be able to see on one chart a full representation of all the gaps, in:

- DNC%
- DNA%
- DCM%
- GC%
- BeGap%
- Stock%
- Dr%
- Cr%.

What you need to be able to identify at a glance is whether that gap as shown on the radar chart is good or bad for your business – whether it was anticipated or not, whether it is a temporary blip, whether you need to take some action to close that gap, or whether you need to re-set your targets. The interpretation of these gaps will form the basis of discussion in *Chapter 3: What are dynamic targets?*

Finally, what do the gaps on the dynamic cash graph represent and when should you react or panic? Is a negative DCM% always bad? Of course not. Again we need to show you how to interpret this graph in the light of a dynamic and developing business. This will be examined in both the next chapter and in *Chapter 4: Dynamic decisions.*

Question 5

What options are available to keep your business in shape?

This final question is perhaps the key to dynamic management. Understanding the options available to you to change the shape of your business, being able to quickly calculate the effect of each of these options on all the dynamic indicators of your business, and then choosing the best option for your business – all this will give you a dynamic tool kit and you will know what values you want to measure in your business.

Can you do it? Can you readily get your hands on the required information? If not, and it is information you need for your dynamic indicators, you must set up the systems to capture that information. If it can be computerized, so much the better; if not, record it manually, there is not that much to do. With dynamic indicators we are looking to capture live information from the business, not tombstone information from your management accounts. For example, to dynamically manage your business you should, at any moment in time, know such key information as how much money you are owed (debtors) so you can calculate Dr%. Finger-on-the-pulse management is about knowing your activity and income levels on a regular basis and being able to pull together quickly the information to calculate your dynamic indicators.

Furthermore, these dynamic indicators can be used to drill down inside your business. You will have your key dynamic indicators for the business as a whole visually represented on the radar chart, the dynamic breakeven graph and the dynamic cash graph. Drilling down can also provide the same visual representations by product, by individual services or by market – whatever is appropriate for your business. You can also produce 'spin-off' radar charts representing the information needs of different stakeholders – this will be explored in *Chapter 5: You are not alone.*

Dynamic decision making

What about real business decisions that change performance? Can these be measured? Of course they can, but how? Take one of the main decisions you might face: whether to change prices. Let us assume your customers are negotiating for a price decrease. Should you do it? Will it buy you more sales? How much volume increase will you need to make it worth your while?

For the purposes of this chapter we will define 'worth your while' as 'making at least as much money as before'. This, we believe, is defined as maintaining your level of DNC%, i.e. the same proportional dynamic net contribution whatever your level of activity.

We know that if your current DNC% is 15 per cent and you reduce your prices by 10 per cent you need to increase volume by 40 per cent to maintain your DNC% at 15 per cent. We know this because dynamic decision making uses a small number of tools and techniques, tables and calculations that will show the outcomes of such decisions. These are the tools and techniques you will soon learn to use. Indeed, dynamic decision-making tools and techniques form the major part of this book.

The concepts and key questions for dynamic decision making are developed in *Chapter 4: Dynamic decisions* but the 'how to' part of this question forms the whole of *Part Two* of this book. By 'how to' we mean 'how to calculate the effect of the decisions on your business'. So long as you know the current values of your dynamic indicators, *Part Two* will enable you to calculate how each of those dynamic indicators will look after one of the following:

- changes in income;
- changes in dynamic costs;
- changes in static costs;
- improving your DNC%.

But it does more than this. Seeing what will happen is like becoming a victim of change. Dynamic financial management then goes on to consider how you can respond to those changes to get your business back into shape. Depending on the change you are faced with, you can get back into shape by:

- increasing the level of activity;
- increasing the price you charge for that activity;
- decreasing your dynamic costs;
- decreasing your static costs.

So *Chapter 4: Dynamic decisions* and the whole of *Part Two* will be looking at answering Question 5.

Summary

In this chapter we have introduced several ideas, tools and techniques that can be used to measure and monitor your business performance. While we believe these techniques are simple and easy to use, they are also very powerful and will aid dynamic decision making in any business. So far we have introduced only the concepts and a selection of tools and techniques. We have purposefully not provided some of the detail you require to apply these techniques to your business.

One of our main aims has been to introduce you to the language of dynamic financial management. The few terms we use are specific and yet are common to all of the tools and techniques we will use. This gives consistency. We also believe it will help you differentiate this from the many and varied bits of terminology used in standard accounting, where many different words are used to mean the same thing – very confusing. We have listed below the words and terms we have introduced so far. A full glossary can be found at the back of the book.

- Breakeven
- Breakeven gap%
- Dynamic breakeven graph
- Dynamic cash graph
- Dynamic cash movement%
- Dynamic costs
- Dynamic indicator
- Dynamic net assets%
- Dynamic net contribution%
- Gap%
- Gross contribution%
- Income
- Radar chart
- Static costs
- Static net assets
- Target
- Time warp.

The way forward

To use the dynamic tools and techniques of dynamic financial management well we need first to dig a bit deeper. To give you a feel for the way forward it may be useful to give a summary of what we will cover in the remaining chapters of the book.

Part one – Managing today

Chapter 2: What are dynamic indicators?	The main illustrative tools introduced in this chapter will be discussed in detail. These tools are not independent, they are interdependent, so their interactions will be examined further to increase their power.
Chapter 3: What are dynamic targets?	Forecasting, budgeting, target setting, call it what you like, most businesses work towards a goal. In a well-managed business, you must set a target against which you measure the actual performance of every dynamic indicator. Targets, introduced in this chapter, allow you to compare how well you have done with how well you needed to do. Sometimes you will do better, sometimes worse. But targets are useful only if calculated accurately. We will give you specific tools and techniques that will produce targets that accurately portray your future – your potential performance. Having chosen your dynamic indicators and calculated your dynamic targets, you can now accurately assess your performance. But of course at this stage your business shape may not look anything like your target position. So you are out of shape, but what can you do? You have to make difficult decisions inside your business to 'get fit'. So now that you are competent in the use of the dynamic tools and techniques, how do you begin to change the shape of your business? There are many different ways to get back into shape. This chapter looks at the alternatives and the pros and cons of each.
Chapter 4: Dynamic decisions	This is the heart of managing your business using dynamic financial management. Having found your

starting point from dynamic targets, it will explore the decisions available to you and the possible effects they will have on your results.

These decisions are major changes to your business, perhaps changing prices, dynamic costs, static costs, cost structures. The results from these major changes will, of course, be illustrated using all of the dynamic tools and techniques we have introduced. Dynamic look-up tables, dynamic adjuster and some simple but effective calculations will be added to your dynamic tool kit.

Chapter 5: You are not alone	While we have discussed the dynamic indicators and targets that are right for you to manage your business (or your part of the business), we recognize that there are aliens that are interested in your performance. And these aliens don't view your world in the same way that you do. Take, for example, your bank manager. He might see 'gearing' as a dynamic indicator in your business. In this chapter we will look at how you can expand your dynamic analysis to cover the needs of other stakeholders by producing separate stakeholder radar charts. These may need monitoring by you on a less frequent basis but still form part of your understanding of business performance. Stakeholders may include people external to your business but also managers of other departments in your business.
Chapter 6: Making it happen	Once you have familiarized yourself with dynamic financial management techniques you need to develop your skills to keep your finger on the pulse of the business. There is no point simply replacing your financial reporting cycle with one that uses our techniques. You need to feel confident with the techniques so that you can achieve value added finance.

Part two – Managing tomorrow

Chapter 7: Increases in your income	This chapter considers the response of your dynamic indicators to the initial impact of an increase in price. If you can put up your price you have created an area of freedom. You can afford for your volume to drop

and to invest for the future in either your dynamic or static costs.

This chapter tells you the exact impact of the initial decision and the exact magnitude of the above benefits of this decision.

Chapter 8: Decreases in your income	This chapter considers the response of your dynamic indicators to the initial impact of a decrease in price. If your price has been forced down, what are the alternative actions you can take to get your business back into shape? We look at changing volume, dynamic costs and static costs to cope with this possibility. This chapter tells you the exact impact of the initial decision and the exact magnitude of the above actions needed as a result of this decision.
Chapter 9: Increases in your dynamic costs	This chapter considers the response of your dynamic indicators to the initial impact of an increase in your dynamic costs. If your dynamic costs have been forced up, what are the alternative actions you can take to get your business back into shape? We look at changing volume, price and static costs to cope with this possibility. This chapter tells you the exact impact of the initial decision and the exact magnitude of the above actions needed as a result of this decision.
Chapter 10: Decreases in your dynamic costs	This chapter considers the response of your dynamic indicators to the initial impact of a decrease in your dynamic costs. If you can get your dynamic costs down, you have created an area of freedom. You can afford for your volume to drop and to invest for the future in either your static costs or to pass on this decrease to your customer in the form of a price reduction. This chapter tells you the exact impact of the initial decision and the exact magnitude of the above benefits of this decision.
Chapter 11: Increases in your static costs	This chapter considers the response of your dynamic indicators to the initial impact of an increase in your static costs. If your static costs have been forced up, what are the alternative actions you can take to get your business back into shape? We look at changing

volume, price and static costs to cope with this possibility.

This chapter tells you the exact impact of the initial decision and the exact magnitude of the above actions needed as a result of this decision.

Chapter 12: Decreases in your static costs	This chapter considers the response of your dynamic indicators to the initial impact of a decrease in your static costs. If you can get your static costs down, you have created an area of freedom. You can afford for your volume to drop and to invest for the future in either your static costs or to pass on this decrease to your customer in the form of a price reduction. This chapter tells you the exact impact of the initial decision and the exact magnitude of the above benefits of this decision.
Chapter 13: Meeting ever more demanding targets	If you need to improve your DNC% this chapter will look at the alternative ways of doing this – increasing price or volume or decreasing dynamic or static costs. In addition, given your existing dynamic indicators, it will tell you the value of each of the changes needed to achieve the new DNC%.

chapter 2

What are dynamic indicators?

Dynamic indicators are the interactive figures within your business that allow you to keep your finger on the pulse, keep your hand on the helm. They are the vital signs that describe the key attributes of the performance of your business. The shape you are in is measured and illustrated by these indicators.

We have introduced you to the radar chart, the diagram we use to portray the dynamic indicators of your business, and related to this are the key trend graphs of the dynamic breakeven graph and the dynamic cash graph. These separate pictures are brought together in Fig 2.1.

These diagrams are dynamic because their information interacts in the following ways:

- the eight dynamic indicators represented on the radar chart are all stated as a percentage of income – the anchor;
- the trends in this income are shown in the dynamic breakeven graph in relation to the breakeven income and so the breakeven gap;
- the gap between income and breakeven income gives an indication of your DNC;
- DNC% is one of the vital signs in the dynamic cash graph;
- to close the circle, the trends in DNC% and DNA% shown in the dynamic cash graph interact to produce the DCM% and these are all dynamic indicators in the radar chart.

The radar chart is therefore a broad examination of the present while the other two graphs give us a view of the past. Using the three together allows you to visualize and create your future – managing tomorrow today.

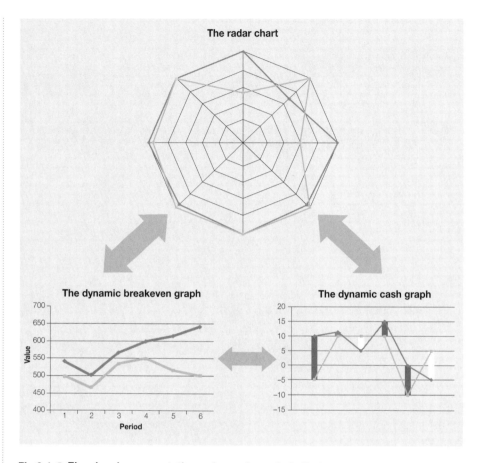

Fig 2.1 ● **The visual representations of your dynamic indicators**

We will explore each of the diagrams in turn, explain their individual function, then bring them all back together to explain their interaction.

The radar chart

The radar chart concentrates on business performance and is the hub of all the dynamic indicators we use. What figures do you select to truly represent the shape of your business? As a start we have the eight dynamic indicators we have already introduced (*see* Table 2.1).

Table 2.1 ● The eight dynamic indicators

Dynamic indicator	Meaning
Dynamic net contribution% **DNC%**	The money left from your income after all costs (dynamic and static) have been deducted. In a business this indicates the potential cash from each sale that could be invested back into your business.
Dynamic net assets% **DNA%**	Static net assets are stock + debtors – creditors. This indicates the money you have imprisoned in the time warp of your business. Dynamic net assets show the movement in the money tied up in this time warp.
Dynamic cash movement% **DCM%**	A product of the dynamic net contribution plus or minus dynamic net asset movement. This indicates the net amount of money you have imprisoned or released from the time warp and money generated from DNC.
Breakeven gap% **BeGap%**	The amount of income you need to cover all your costs – to make neither a negative nor a positive DNC. Breakeven gap is the difference between your income and the breakeven income. Breakeven gap% is the breakeven gap as a percentage of income. It indicates how safe your current income level is – how much above or below breakeven you are.
Gross contribution% **GC%**	Income less dynamic costs. It indicates the efficiency of your organization, how well you are able to control your dynamic costs or your income stream.
Stock% **Stock%**	This is made up of raw materials in manufacturing businesses, work in progress in manufacturing and service organizations, and finished goods in manufacturing and retail organizations. This indicates the money invested in stock but still imprisoned in the time warp of your business and is the first of three strands building up your DNA.
Debtors% **Dr%**	Debtors are people who owe you money. This indicates the money from income still in the hands of your customers and therefore imprisoned in the time warp of your business and is the second strand of your DNA.
Creditors % **Cr%**	Creditors are the people to whom you owe money. This indicates the future money you need to release from your time warp, and is the third, and last, strand of your DNA.

These last three indicators are the strands of DNA but may not be appropriate in all organizations. If they are not applicable to you, just use those that best reflect your own DNA structure.

Remember that these dynamic indicators are all percentages of your income figure. We will discuss the possibilities for more dynamic indicators which may be specific to your business in *Chapter 5: You are not alone*. We will look at the dynamic indicators in three parts:

1 Those leading to DNC%.

2 Those leading to DNA%.

3 DCM% as a product of DNC% and DNA%.

Dynamic indicators relating to contribution

These are:

● GC%

● DNC%

● BeGap%.

Gross contribution% (GC%)

Where does the GC% come from? We first need to know the gross contribution value and this is calculated as follows:

Gross Contribution = Income − Dynamic Costs

Remember that the dynamic costs are those costs that vary with the activity of the business. From this value we can calculate the gross contribution% as follows:

$$GC\% = \frac{\text{Gross Contribution}}{\text{Income}} \times 100$$

What does it mean? The GC% tells you the proportion of income you make on each sale after the cost to you of making that sale. Why is this a dynamic indicator? It is the difference between your income and dynamic costs and as such illustrates your business efficiency. Measuring your efficiency today is crucial to understanding how to improve the performance of your business tomorrow. Increasing your GC% by just 1 per cent can be the difference between a healthy company and a sick one.

There are only two ways to affect the GC% figure:

1 Increase your price.

2 Decrease your dynamic costs.

We will investigate both these options in *Chapter 4: Dynamic decisions*. Our techniques allow you to foresee the effects of these possible decisions.

Dynamic net contribution% (DNC%)

Where does the DNC% come from? Yet again, we first need to know the dynamic net contribution value and this is calculated as follows:

Dynamic Net Contribution = Gross Contribution – Static Costs

Remember that the static costs are those costs that do not vary with the activity of the business. From this value we can calculate the DNC% as follows:

$$DNC\% = \frac{\text{Dynamic Net Contribution}}{\text{Income}} \times 100$$

What does this mean? The DNC% tells you the proportion of income you keep after deducting the dynamic *and* the static costs of making that sale. DNC% is a measure of effectiveness: are we actually making enough out of our income? By 'enough' we mean both the volume of activity and whether that activity made a contribution. Static costs benefit from economies of scale, i.e. they are reduced as a percentage of income with a higher volume of activity. Improving your effectiveness today means generating the resources required for a better business tomorrow. Every extra 1 per cent of DNC% is money available for reinvestment into the future of your business.

There are only three ways to affect the DNC% figure:

1 Increase your gross contribution.

2 Decrease your static costs.

3 Increase your volume of activity.

Breakeven gap% (BeGap%)

The traditional way to calculate your BeGap% would be to:

- calculate your breakeven income (static costs/GC%);
- calculate your breakeven gap (income – breakeven income);
- calculate your breakeven gap% (breakeven gap/income).

The dynamic way, illustrating the full interaction of these dynamic indicators, is:

$$BeGap\% = \frac{DNC\%}{GC\%}$$

This links the three dynamic indicators of contribution.

The breakeven gap tells you how much of your income you are making a contribution from. If your BeGap% is negative, it indicates the size of the hill you need to climb to begin making a positive DNC. BeGap% is a measure of how secure your business is – it is the sensitivity and risk in your business. The bigger the BeGap% (assuming it is positive, of course), the less vulnerable you are to the fluctuations of the market place.

Again there are two main controls that will affect the breakeven gap% figure:

1 Increase your gross contribution%.

2 Decrease your static costs.

Dynamic indicators relating to net assets

Money inside your business is imprisoned in the time warp of your static net assets (SNA). In dynamic financial management we are interested in the movement in this money – the dynamic net assets. We are interested in what has happened to the SNA in the time period we are looking at. Has it grown or shrunk? Have we imprisoned cash in, or released cash from, the time warp of your business?

The DNA value can be calculated as follows:

DNA = This Period's SNA – Last Period's SNA

i.e. your DNA is the movement in your static net assets or, more correctly, the movement in the strands of your SNA – your stock, debtors and creditors. So the first step to understanding DNA is to look in more detail at the strands of your SNA.

The strands of your SNA

The strands of your SNA show exactly where the money is imprisoned in the time warp of your business. Analysis of your SNA enables you to reengineer its structure by managing the constituent parts, to release cash back into the business, to enable your business to develop.

The value of your SNA is calculated as follows:

SNA = Stock + Debtors – Creditors

This is the net cash value imprisoned in the time warp within your business. The higher the percentage, the more cash is locked away. And equally the SNA% (a percentage of the income figure) can be calculated in one of two ways:

$$SNA\% = \frac{SNA}{Income} \times 100$$

Or:

$$SNA\% = Stock\% + Dr\% - Cr\%$$

This is another illustration of the interaction of the dynamic indicators, as these strands of your SNA are all dynamic indicators in their own right. But combined they will contribute towards an additional and powerful dynamic indicator – DNA%. There are many important uses for this indicator that will be discussed later.

Before going on to discuss this in any more detail we really need to know where the strands have come from. These are:

- Stock% (Stock%)
- Debtors% (Dr%)
- Creditors% (Cr%)

Stock%
The Stock% is:

$$\text{Stock\%} = \frac{\text{Stock}}{\text{Income}} \times 100$$

What makes Stock% a dynamic indicator? It is one of the key strands of the static net assets and represents money locked inside the time warp of your business. The higher this percentage, the more cash is imprisoned, and the less freedom you have to invest in your business.

Stock comes in many forms in manufacturing, service and retail businesses. The materials a manufacturing company buys to produce its product (raw materials), partly completed products or services (work in progress), and goods ready to be sold (finished goods). The concept of stock in service industries is often overlooked, but don't write it off too soon; it is a powerful idea and we will revisit this later in the next chapter.

Debtors%
The Dr% is:

$$\text{Dr\%} = \frac{\text{Debtors}}{\text{Income}} \times 100$$

Debtors also represent cash locked up within the dynamic system of your business. And it is worth repeating: the higher this percentage, the more cash is imprisoned, and the less freedom you have to invest in your business. Debtors are the value of sales frozen in the time warp. Every sale you make on credit adds to your debtors. Every extra day taken to collect the money you are owed increases the Debtors% in the radar chart.

Creditors%
The Cr% is:

$$Cr\% = \frac{Creditors}{Income} \times 100$$

Creditors represent free cash given to you by your suppliers. It is their cash locked up within the dynamic system – the time warp – of your business. The higher the percentage, the more money you have borrowed from them. Is this a good thing? Every purchase you make on credit adds to your creditors. Every extra day you take to pay the money you owe increases the Cr% in the radar chart – money you have borrowed without the agreement of your suppliers.

Dynamic net asset%

Going back to the discussion on the structure of your DNA, this was calculated as follows.

DNA = This Period's SNA – Last Period's SNA

The DNA% is the usual calculation to make it a percentage of your anchor – income:

$$DNA\% = \frac{DNA}{Income} \times 100$$

DNA% is a percentage of the current period's income. It says, quite simply, how much cash you have released or imprisoned from the time warp as a percentage of this period's income.

How do we manage this key figure of DNA%? By managing the strands of the SNA: Stock%, Dr% and Cr%. This is why we believe these should be included on your radar chart. But they all need to be managed together. A low overall SNA% may seem to indicate that the business is managing the time warp effectively. However, you can manipulate a good SNA% for all the wrong reasons. For example, your Dr% may be too high so you compensate by not paying your creditors. The SNA% looks good, but is this dynamic financial management?

You need to focus on your DNA%. Sometimes this will be positive (imprisoning cash) and sometimes it will be negative (releasing cash). What you need to monitor is whether it is in line with your targets (we will discuss this in the next chapter).

Dynamic indicators relating to cash movement

Cash can come from two sources: straight from your contribution, your DNC, or from the cash released from your time warp, your DNA. So, DCM% is a result of two other dynamic indicators, DNC% and DNA%, again showing the interaction between all these dynamic indicators. To see the total cash movement in your business you simply perform the following calculation.

$$\text{DCM\%} = \text{DNC\%} - \text{DNA\%}$$

Stating the DCM as a percentage of income reflects the cash dynamically generated or lost within the current period.

DCM% is the result of the interaction between all the dynamic indicators in your business. It is the cash that has been generated from dynamically managing your business. It is dynamic in that it joins the past, the present and the future of your business. Cash is king! Businesses die because they lack cash. So, having cash means being in control of your future. Dynamic cash movement allows you to design your future – managing tomorrow today.

The nature of cash movement within a business can be a rollercoaster ride. The value of this indicator will therefore vary considerably from period to period. If a business is growing, its DNA% will grow with it, and DCM% will often be negative (your cash reserves are drifting into the time warp). This is not necessarily bad, but how long can you sustain this cash drain at the magnitude indicated by your DCM%?

The validity and strength of this dynamic indicator will become very apparent when we examine the power of the dynamic cash graph to look at the trends within the business, trends in DNC%, DNA% and DCM%.

Beware, however: this is not a full cash flow forecast but an appraisal of the dynamic cash flow in this period. For example, funding, investing and depreciation decisions are not adjusted for in the dynamic cash movement calculation, nor are such essential payments as tax and, in the UK, VAT.

The dynamic breakeven graph

Within the radar chart one of the dynamic indicators is the breakeven gap% (BeGap%). The dynamic breakeven graph plots actual income in comparison to breakeven income over a period of time. The difference between the two lines is the breakeven gap that represents the income above or below the breakeven point. This is a dynamic indicator because it looks at how these have changed in your business over time. A widening gap, assuming income is higher than breakeven, would suggest positive trends, a narrowing one the reverse. BeGap% shows this gap as a percentage of your actual income.

Why does the dynamic breakeven graph (Fig 2.2) give additional information over and above the radar chart? The calculation for breakeven income we used in the previous chapter was:

$$\text{Breakeven Income} = \frac{\text{Static Costs}}{\text{GC\%}}$$

An easier way to calculate this figure if you are managing straight from your dynamic indicators is:

$$\text{Breakeven Income\%} = \frac{\text{GC\% – DNC\%}}{\text{GC\%}}$$

And

$$\text{Breakeven Income} = \text{Income} \times \text{Breakeven Income\%}$$

What, then, can affect the breakeven gap? It is changes within your contribution statement that have an effect, and these changes can be either in the GC% or the SC%. What effect will each of these have on the breakeven gap?

Change		Effect	
GC%	↑	Breakeven gap	↑
GC%	↓	Breakeven gap	↓
Static costs	↑	Breakeven gap	↓
Static costs	↓	Breakeven gap	↑

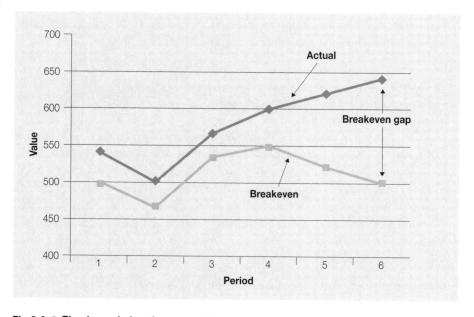

Fig 2.2 ● The dynamic breakeven graph

But remember that there are two things that can affect GC%: price and dynamic costs. Representing these in a similar format would give:

Change		Effect	
Price	↑	GC%	↑
Price	↓	GC%	↓
Dynamic costs	↑	GC%	↓
Dynamic costs	↓	GC%	↑

So GC% and static costs are key to a widening breakeven gap and the wider the gap the better.

Managing the dynamic breakeven

So, what are the key things we need to do to 'mind the gap'? The answer to this question is fundamental to your becoming 'a dynamic manager' and forms the main thrust of *Chapter 6: Making it happen*.

We will also discuss the changes you can make to your business in *Chapter 4: Dynamic decisions*, identifying the decisions available to you to change the shape of your business seen through your dynamic indicators in the radar chart, such as changing your pricing structure, changing your volumes, changing your dynamic costs, changing your static costs, or redistributing your cost structure across the business. All of these decisions can be considered and their effects appraised using our dynamic tools and techniques.

But where do you start? What needs changing and why? A deeper interpretation of the dynamic breakeven graph will give you some guiding principles. Let's start with a huge assumption about your business – that your income is higher than your breakeven. Given this situation there are a limited number of trends you can see in your dynamic breakeven graph. These are shown in Fig 2.3.

This matrix tells the dynamic manager a lot about the business, its current trends and, as we shall see in *Chapter 6: Making it happen*, the seven possible dynamic routes to success. In any business situation you have three main choices in management:

- trying to manage the internal factors – costs (the horizontal axis);
- trying to manage the external factors – price and volume (the vertical axis);
- trying to manage both at the same time – the internals and externals.

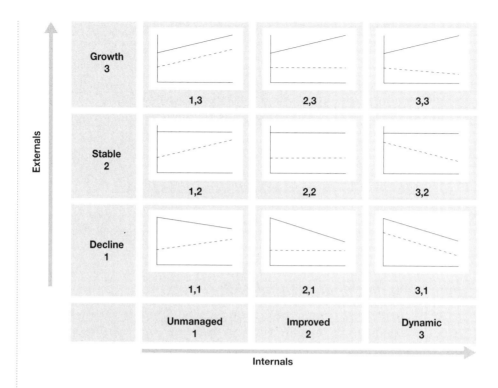

Fig 2.3 ● **The dynamic breakeven matrix**

Looking at managing the internals – the costs – when you start on the path to dynamic management you may discover that your internal systems are not being managed effectively – we have called this 'unmanaged'. What we are all aiming for is to manage these internals in a dynamic manner. In reality you are probably somewhere in between – you are looking to improve the management of costs.

Looking at managing the external factors – the price and volume – you may be facing a decline in income, due to lowering prices or a decrease in activity, or you may see income growth from higher prices or higher levels of activity. Again you are probably somewhere in between – the external environment is stable for your business (often the case for budget holders).

Your internal approach may therefore be unmanaged, improved or dynamic and the externals may be in decline, stable or in growth. These are the nine options shown in the dynamic breakeven matrix. Let's look at a few of them in a bit more detail.

Box (1,1) – a disaster scenario?

This surely requires little explanation, but simply:

Externals		Effect	
		Breakeven gap	↓
Income	Down	DNC	↓
	↓	BeGap%	↓
		Risk	↑

Income is falling and breakeven income is going up, so neither the internal factors nor the external factors are being dynamically managed, and once these lines cross, the business is making a negative dynamic net contribution. In a market that is in decline, many managers are tempted to either try to spend their way out of the decline by inappropriate marketing or lower prices hoping to create further demand. They are reluctant to accept all the evidence that the decline is terminal.

Box (3,3) – the dynamic manager

Contrasting Box (1,1) with this Box (3,3):

Externals		Effect	
		Breakeven gap	↑
Income	Up	DNC	↑
	↑	BeGap%	↑
		Risk	↓

Here the external environment is in growth and the internal factors are being managed in a dynamic manner. Control of both income growth and internal costs illustrates the good management of the dynamic manager – keeping the finger on the pulse of the business. Therefore, in this example not only is actual income going up but the breakeven income in going down – the dynamic manager is controlling the GC% and the static costs, the elements of breakeven control. So what of the other extremes?

Box (1,3) – unmanaged growth

The income is increasing but the internals are unmanaged – the costs are uncontrolled. Volume could have increased simply because of a reduction in prices.

But it looks like the volume increase has not compensated for the reduced price – the DNC% is falling (*see Chapter 4: Dynamic decisions*). This is unmanaged growth, so the impact on the business is thus:

Externals		Effect	
		Breakeven gap	↓
Income	Up	DNC	↓
	↑	BeGap%	↓
		Risk	↑

It is sometimes difficult for managers to accept this as a concept. You expect to earn more if you sell more. Indeed, if the business is not making enough contribution, the cry often goes out to 'make more sales'. This may, however, be the path to disaster. We need to be effective internally first, thus ensuring that any increase in income makes a contribution. Then we can look for growth in the business. If the business is growing and DNC% is falling, we are working harder and harder for less and less.

Box (3,1) – dynamic management of decline

This is the manager who is often likely to be given a lot of grief when actually doing a good job. Income is going down due to a declining market, but 'sales = vanity, profit = sanity' as the old adage goes. Look at the following:

Externals		Effect	
		Breakeven gap	↔
Income	Down	DNC	↔
	↓	BeGap%	↑
		Risk	↓

The only thing this manager seems to have got wrong is the income figure. But is the income figure wrong? No, it could be more money for less work. For example, in the declining market this is definitely the way to manage. And sometimes it is worthwhile saying 'no' to the possibility of increasing income in a highly competitive market. It may be better to go for a smaller but more lucrative part of the market. Income may be lower, but because the breakeven is so much lower due, perhaps, to higher margins, the DNC is significantly higher.

A word of caution

In all the boxes in Fig 2.3 we have looked at fairly simple, straight-line graphs. In reality your graph will be lumpy – more like the one in Fig 2.2 – with the gap dynamically changing in response to internal and external changes to your business.

Be careful not to overreact. The graph, because it is dynamic, will respond to any decisions you implement (*see Chapter 4: Dynamic decisions*). But businesses also have natural cycles within them that will cause fluctuations in sales, buying, costs, etc. You know your own business and should therefore have a budgeted dynamic breakeven graph (*see Chapter 3: What are dynamic targets?*). And, as with all your gaps, the differences in your breakeven gap that you need to investigate are the ones you did not predict.

The DC/SC see-saw

It is vital that you understand your existing cost structure, i.e. your DC% and your SC%. Basically you can have one of three cost structures:

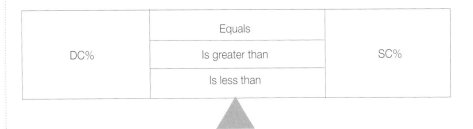

Interestingly, when DC is less than SC, things can be difficult. When the externals are in decline, static costs are hard to get rid of quickly. However, DC less than SC will be beneficial when the externals are in growth; you make proportionately more money on every extra sale.

To quickly calculate your DC% and SC% from your radar chart, use the following:

DC% = 100 – GC%

SC% = GC% – DNC%

If your cost structure is DC% = SC%, changes in breakeven gap on the dynamic breakeven are going to be difficult to interpret without a more detailed analysis of the figures behind them. However, if you have one of the other two structures, the nine principles of dynamic breakeven shown in Table 2.2 will help interpret the movements in the dynamic breakeven graph. And the more marked the difference is between your two types of costs, the more likely these laws are to apply.

Table 2.2 ● The principles of dynamic breakeven

Principle	Probable cause if: *DC*% greater than *SC*%	Probable cause if: *SC*% greater than *DC*%
1,1 Unmanaged decline	DC% is probably *up* Price is probably *down*	SC% is probably *up* Price is probably *down*
1,2 Unmanaged stable	DC% is probably *up*	SC% is probably *up*
1,3 Unmanaged growth	Price is probably *down* Volume is probably *up* DC% is probably *up*	Price is probably *down* Volume is probably *up* SC% is probably *up*
2,1 Improved decline	Volume is probably *down* Costs remain the *same*	Volume probably *down* Costs remain the *same*
2.2 Improved stable	No change in price, volume, dynamic costs or static costs	No change in price, volume, dynamic costs or static costs
2,3 Improved growth	Volume is probably *up* Costs remain the *same*	Volume is probably *up* Costs remain the *same*
3,1 Dynamic decline	DC% is probably *down*	SC% is probably *down*
3,2 Dynamic stable	DC% is probably *down*	SC% is probably *down*
3,3 Dynamic growth	DC% is probably *down* Price is probably *up*	SC% is probably *down* Price is probably *up*

So, if DC% is greater than SC%, the first place you should look for the cause of a change in the breakeven gap is your dynamic costs. Conversely, if SC% is greater than DC%, the first place you should look for the cause of a change in the breakeven gap is your static costs.

Note that for Principle 2.2, in most live businesses this situation is somewhat unlikely except as a transitional phase. In the longer term you would expect to see movement in most businesses. If this has been the trend in your business, you are probably looking for a kickstart (*see Chapter 6: Making it happen*).

The dynamic cash graph

The radar chart offers an insight into the present situation, both in terms of your expectations (the targets) and what has happened to your business (the actual figures). The dynamic breakeven graph gives an indication as to whether the business is growing or declining in terms of its income. It also gives an indication as to how well the growth or decline in income is being managed. But it does so only in terms of contribution. The final piece of the jigsaw puzzle is how well the business is managing its cash.

The dynamic cash graph combines the key indicators of DNC% and DNA% in a way that reveals the third key indicator – DCM% – all on one graph. This is vital signs monitoring if you like. It allows you to quickly see all three indicators as relative trends, effectively seeing the past and present and the future possibilities together on one chart. What we see is the combined results of our decisions and the external effects on each of these indicators as the business moves its shape. Consequently this graph can be quite volatile, but this is the nature of cash flow.

The beauty of dynamic financial management is that once the dynamic indicators are all established as a percentage of the period's income, they become directly comparable, both as a percentage and, as a consequence, as a value.

These three indicators are all truly dynamic. DNC% represents that amount of your income that you have managed to retain in your business in the current period – your dynamic net contribution. The DNA% represents the movement, or flow, of cash in and out of your time warp – your static net assets. The DCM% represents the combination of these two flows and shows the result of their interaction with each other. Sometimes this is good for the business because it generates cash, sometimes it is not so good because it absorbs cash and so requires more careful management. Whichever it is will be revealed in the dynamic cash graph.

Let us take a closer look at the graph, as shown in Fig 2.4. The interpretation of this graph is a bit more complex. Your DNC% can be positive or negative and your DNA% can be either positive or negative. Which is good and which is bad?

When it comes to the DNC% this is pretty clear – a positive DNC% is good and a negative DNC% is bad. The DNA% takes a bit more thinking about. Let us remind ourselves of the calculation for DNA:

DNA = This Period's SNA – Last Period's SNA

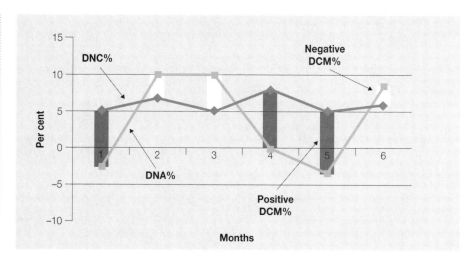

Fig 2.4 ● **The dynamic cash graph**

If this period's SNA is bigger than last period's SNA, more cash has been tied up in the SNA time warp – a positive DNA figure is bad as far as cash is concerned. On the other hand, if this period's SNA is less than last period's SNA, cash has been released from the SNA time warp. So a negative DNA is good. Let us summarize:

DNC%	Positive	=	Good for cash
DNC%	Negative	=	Bad for cash
DNA%	Positive	=	Bad for cash
DNA%	Negative	=	Good for cash

If DNA% rises this is usually a good indication that there will be more cash imprisoned in your business. Sometimes a business can compensate for this by the amount generated from its DNC%.

There is a very important point here and it is best explained by example. Let us look at a growing business. A growing business often requires investment in the strands of its SNA, most notably its stock and debtors. As a result of this, sometimes the cash outflow of the DNA% is high and the business will therefore experience a cash deficit – a negative DCM%. The point of this growth was to increase the income, increase the BeGap% and increase your DNC%. But how much DNC% will compensate for your investment in your DNA%? The answer was perhaps a mystery – until now. Dynamic financial management has an easy answer, shown below:

Relationship			Effect on DCM%
DNC%	Equals	DNA%	Neutral
	Greater than		Positive
	Less than		Negative

So, as long as your DNC% is greater than your DNA% you are growing within your cash availability. This is also clearly shown in Fig 2.4. When DNC% is greater than DNA% there is a positive DCM% and when DNC% is less than DNA% there is a negative DCM%.

So the dynamic cash graph tells us whether today's activities have generated both contribution and cash. But what about tomorrow?

Leading on from this there is another key figure that dynamic financial management can provide. It can tell you exactly what your maximum rate of growth should be if you want to be able to fund it yourself, i.e. if you want your DCM% to be zero. The only caution here is that there will be a cash time lag. We will now discuss these two points.

Calculating your maximum growth with a zero DCM%

If you are increasing your activity (your volume) this growth will mean a growth in stock, debtors and creditors – more cash will be imprisoned in the time warp of your SNA. The SNA% should stay the same but as income grows the value of the SNA will also grow. The extra cash imprisoned in your SNA in any growth period is your DNA. So we need to know at what growth rate your DNC% will continue to fund your DNA% and this relies on your knowing and maintaining your current SNA%.

Your growth percentage is:

$$\frac{\text{This Period's Income}}{\text{Last Period's Income}} \times 100$$

Table 2.3 shows how to find your maximum income growth percentage. All you need to know is your SNA% (Stock% + Dr% – Cr%) and your DNC% which are all dynamic indicators on your radar chart.

Let us use the table to look at some typical companies.

HV Car Parts Limited, a manufacturing business, has a DNC% of 5 per cent and its SNA% is 150 per cent of the current month's income. Table 2.3 shows its maximum growth percentage to be 103.45 per cent. Sales could grow by 3.45

Table 2.3 ● The dynamic look-up table – maximum growth percentage for a zero DCM%

Existing DNC%	Existing SNA% 20	40	60	80	100	110	120	130
1	105.26	102.56	101.69	101.27	101.01	100.92	100.84	100.78
2	111.11	105.26	103.45	102.56	102.04	101.85	101.69	101.56
3	117.65	108.11	105.26	103.90	103.09	102.80	102.56	102.36
4	125.00	111.11	107.14	105.26	104.17	103.77	103.45	103.17
5	133.33	114.29	109.09	106.67	105.26	104.76	104.35	104.00
6	142.86	117.65	111.11	108.11	106.38	105.77	105.26	104.84
7	153.85	121.21	113.21	109.59	107.53	106.80	106.19	105.69
8	166.67	125.00	115.38	111.11	108.70	107.84	107.14	106.56
9	181.82	129.03	117.65	112.68	109.89	108.91	108.11	107.44
10	200.00	133.33	120.00	114.29	111.11	110.00	109.09	108.33
12	250.00	142.86	125.00	117.65	113.64	112.24	111.11	110.17
14	333.33	153.85	130.43	121.21	116.28	114.58	113.21	112.07
16	500.00	166.67	136.36	125.00	119.05	117.02	115.38	114.04
18	1000.00	181.82	142.86	129.03	121.95	119.57	117.65	116.07
20		200.00	150.00	133.33	125.00	122.22	120.00	118.18
25		266.67	171.43	145.45	133.33	129.41	126.32	123.81
30		400.00	200.00	160.00	142.86	137.50	133.33	130.00
35		800.00	240.00	177.78	153.85	146.67	141.18	136.84
40			300.00	200.00	166.67	157.14	150.00	144.44
50			600.00	266.67	200.00	183.33	171.43	162.50

per cent on a month by month basis and, assuming everything else remains the same, the company could fund that growth out of its DNC% each month.

What do we mean by 'assuming everything else remains the same'? Growing by 3.45 per cent month on month would mean your sales would be 50 per cent higher at the end of a year. Could you cope with this increase in income? Have you got the capacity? Would your SC% remain the same? These are additional management issues you would need to answer before embarking on this growth strategy.

VUC Computer Services, in contrast, is a service industry with a DNC% of 10 per cent and the SNA% is 75 per cent of the current month's income. Table 2.3 shows the maximum growth percentage to be 115.72 per cent. Sales could grow by 15.72 per cent on a month by month basis and the company could fund that growth out of its DNC%. That means that within five months this business could double its income.

This means VUC Computer Services can self-fund a growth percentage of 15.38 per cent. But can it *manage* a growth of 15.72 per cent? A 15.38 per cent

Table 2.3 ● Continued

Existing DNC%	140	150	160	Existing SNA% 170	180	190	200
1	100.72	100.67	100.63	100.59	100.56	100.53	100.50
2	101.45	101.35	101.27	101.19	101.12	101.06	101.01
3	102.19	102.04	101.91	101.80	101.69	101.60	101.52
4	102.94	102.74	102.56	102.41	102.27	102.15	102.04
5	103.70	103.45	103.23	103.03	102.86	102.70	102.56
6	104.48	104.17	103.90	103.66	103.45	103.26	103.09
7	105.26	104.90	104.58	104.29	104.05	103.83	103.63
8	106.06	105.63	105.26	104.94	104.65	104.40	104.17
9	106.87	106.38	105.96	105.59	105.26	104.97	104.71
10	107.69	107.14	106.67	106.25	105.88	105.56	105.26
12	109.38	108.70	108.11	107.59	107.14	106.74	106.38
14	111.11	110.29	109.59	108.97	108.43	107.95	107.53
16	112.90	111.94	111.11	110.39	109.76	109.20	108.70
18	114.75	113.64	112.68	111.84	111.11	110.47	109.89
20	116.67	115.38	114.29	113.33	112.50	111.76	111.11
25	121.74	120.00	118.52	117.24	116.13	115.15	114.29
30	127.27	125.00	123.08	121.43	120.00	118.75	117.65
35	133.33	130.43	128.00	125.93	124.14	122.58	121.21
40	140.00	136.36	133.33	130.77	128.57	126.67	125.00
50	155.56	150.00	145.45	141.67	138.46	135.71	133.33

month-on-month growth would mean sales would double within five months. Unless the company was running well below capacity, this growth would be very difficult to manage.

The cash time lag

There is one final thing to consider when looking at the dynamic cash graph and funding your growth. You may think you can grow at a rate of, say, 25 per cent but the cash from the new growth takes time to flow into the business. For example, look at your debtors when you grow:

	Month 1	Month 2	Month 3
Income	100,000	125,000	156,250
Dr%	100%	100%	100%
Cash received this month	N/A	100,000	125,000

A Dr% of 100 per cent indicates that you receive all this month's cash from your debtors next month. So there is a one-month time lag for cash from your debtors in your business. You need to ensure that you can cover that gap for one month.

But the creditor gap will work the other way. So how can you predict the time lag for your business? There is, in fact, a common time lag for every business that is growing with a DCM% of zero. The time taken to get the cash back into your business is one *period*. If you are monitoring DNC% and DNA% on a weekly basis and you are growing within your cash means, it will take one week to get the cash back into your business. If you are growing and monitoring on a monthly basis, it will take one month, and so on.

So the growth factor table tells you your maximum growth over a certain period and also tells you it will take one period to recover the cash to cover that growth. This may only be a one-period cash gap but it needs to be planned for – you need to have some cash in reserve or you need to borrow a little more for this period.

Summary

The dynamic cash graph is the final piece of information to complete the dynamic picture of your business. This graph gives valuable information about the past trends in your business, your current situation, and the potential for the future. Using this information you can:

● see whether your business is generating cash overall – the DCM%;

● predict the DCM% for the future by managing the DNC% and the DNA% (if DNC% > DNA% you have a positive DCM%);

● you can ensure you have short-term funding in place to cover the one-period cash time lag.

Now it is over to you. We advise that you try out your figures with our dynamic indicators. Do it for your current period and prepare your radar chart to look at the shape your business is in. If you can get hold of some previous period information, start to portray the trends from this on your dynamic breakeven graph and your dynamic cash graph. We give you more advice on how to prepare this in Step 1, *Chapter 6: Making it happen.* You may want to have a quick look at this before moving on to the next chapter and starting to think about dynamic targets.

chapter 3

What are dynamic targets?

Introduction

Indicators alone are not enough. We need to monitor these indicators against expectations – against targets. This chapter sets out a methodology for creating and setting targets. Using the visual representations introduced in the previous chapter, you can then 'see' how your business is performing.

Every business uses some kind of forecasting, whether it is in your head, on the back of an envelope, or in a comprehensive business plan. We all have some idea of where we want to be, perhaps on a daily, weekly or monthly basis. We roughly know the shape we want our business to be. This is often called budgeting, or setting targets against expected performance.

Traditional planning can lead to the rather bland method of budgeting and control which says 'We have a problem in costs – reduce all of our costs by 10 per cent!'. This 'across the board' management does not take into account *why* those things have changed and therefore what the real cause of the discrepancy is. It is short-term and reactionary, and the 'problem' is likely to reoccur.

Targeting discrete figures will show individual changes in the business but will not necessarily highlight the real relationships between the business functions. Attacking one figure in isolation cannot reach the true cause of changes occurring within something as complex as a living business. So we need a better method, a set of target values that will match our interactive dynamic indicators.

Targeting has been critically labelled 'comparative statics', comparing static numbers in a business. The dynamic targets we use portray the shape we want our business to be in, and the actual dynamic indicators show us how we compare. In a well-run business the actual results will match the budgets, the targets. The dynamic indicators we use can be matched against these targets as regularly as appropriate for your business, acting as either a clarion call or as an air-raid siren warning of impending doom. The essential point is that it allows you to react *now*, before the air raid starts.

The eight dynamic indicators are listed below for reference:

- **Contribution:**
    - Gross contribution% (GC%)
    - Dynamic net contribution% (DNC%)
    - Breakeven gap% (BeGap%)

- **Static net assets:**
    - Stock% (Stock%)
    - Debtors% (Dr%)
    - Creditors% (Cr%)

- **Dynamic cash movement:**
    - Dynamic net assets% (DNA%)
    - Dynamic cash movement% (DCM%)

There are, again, a number of questions you can ask yourself when considering how to set appropriate dynamic targets: ·

- Question 1: What values could we use as dynamic targets?

- Question 2: Should I use internal or external targets?

- Question 3: How do I create my own dynamic targets?

- Question 4: How do I monitor my business against these dynamic targets?

Question 1

What values could we use as dynamic targets?

Starting to set a target can be a difficult task. How do you know what you can do? You may have had some traditional budgeting techniques inside your business, but translating these into truly dynamic indicators may be difficult.

When we come to answering Question 3 we will look at some fairly sophisticated techniques for setting targets, techniques that follow the same logic you have used in discovering your dynamic indicators. But for the moment let us just consider how you might get the process started.

In the previous chapter we introduced the visual representations of your dynamic indicators: the radar chart (p. 36), the dynamic breakeven graph (p. 44) and the dynamic cash graph (p. 52). It is important that we think dynamically about all of these, i.e. that we consider the influence of the past, the present and the future.

The radar chart captures today. It is a representation of the business at the current period in time. But it is more than this. It is a representation of where the business *is* and where we *thought* it would be. This is the idea of the two lines on the radar – one to capture the actual performance and one to show the target – and is the principle behind the gaps we talked about in the previous chapter.

The radar with one line does not really tell you much. Yet when you start on the dynamic financial management journey you may not have progressed to the detailed level of targeting. This should not take away the value of the radar however. What could you use in your business instead? We suggest one of the following:

- recalculating your existing budget – if you already have a budget, simply recalculate this as a percentage of income to produce budgeted dynamic indicators;

- history – in order to start to understand the dynamics inside your business, looking to the past will help. Your comparison for today may be a consideration of yesterday. And yesterday may be last year, last month, or whatever is most appropriate for you.

A third alternative may be to compare yourself with other players in your line of business and we will consider this under Question 2.

We still have two more visual monitors of our business to consider for targeting: the dynamic breakeven graph and the dynamic cash graph. Both are designed to show the trends in your business. It is often tempting with trends to focus on just two dimensions of time – the past and the present. To think dynamically you should also consider the future. Let us look at these two graphs separately.

The dynamic breakeven graph compares income with breakeven income. Most organizations are making some forecast of their income, so why not plot this on to the dynamic breakeven chart. You should also be able to make some prediction of both your dynamic costs and your static costs so you can produce a simple forecast contribution statement. You can, therefore, also forecast your breakeven income.

But how far ahead should you forecast, and how much history should you include on your dynamic breakeven? You know your business, you should have enough information on the graph to give you trends over a cycle of your business. For most people this will mean a year's information split down month by month; in some businesses it may be three months' information split down week by week.

The final trend graph to consider is the dynamic cash graph. This is a product of monitoring the movements in your dynamic indicators, especially the DNC% for the period, the sales growth revealed in the dynamic breakeven graph, and the changes in the strands of the SNA. As such, the targets for this graph are all calculated from the targets we have already created. Using this graph is like monitoring all the vital signs of your business, looking at historic trends, the present situation, and forecasting (targeting) for the future.

Question 2

Should I use internal or external targets?

As mentioned earlier, to begin using dynamic targeting within your business you need to decide what values are to be used as a base target. These values can be refined over time, but we need to start somewhere and this can be done in two ways:

1 by calculating your own dynamic targets from your experience as discussed in the previous section (dynamic targets, like dynamic indicators, are calculated as a percentage of the income figure).

2 by looking externally and recognizing norms in similar businesses to yours, an approach we will consider in this section.

A combination of these two methods will quickly arrive at some finely tuned targets that are right for your business, which will define the shape you want your business to be in.

By analyzing other businesses, external targets can be derived. These can then be used as a basis for tuning your own internal targets. This is a useful approach when starting out with targeting, especially if you are unsure of your business operations.

So where can you get external comparisons from? An obvious place is your competitors' accounts. It is worth knowing that in most countries, if your competitors are incorporated businesses they will have to register their annual accounts in a central location. These accounts can then be accessed by anyone who is interested. The information available from these registered accounts will depend on the requirements of each country. All we can focus on is the information you need to be able to get your hands on in order to make some kind of comparison.

The first thing to note is that published accounts may not reflect our dynamic contribution statement. You are going to have to make some guesses about their businesses. What you should get, depending on the reporting requirements where you are, is:

- a profit and loss account showing turnover (income) and costs which need to be split, using your knowledge of your business, between dynamic and static costs;
- a balance sheet, somewhere within which you should be able to extract figures for stock, debtors and trade creditors.

Your other dynamic indicators can be calculated once you know these building blocks.

Business libraries often hold general information available on businesses split into various industry sub-sections. These may contain industry averages using traditional financial ratio analysis. We will consider how we can replace these with dynamic indicators in *Chapter 5: You are not alone*.

You should also consider the type of business you operate compared to your competitors. For example, retail businesses would have a very low figure for DNA% as, in a cash business, they typically have low Dr%. You might be in the same industry but selling via the wholesale network. Your Dr% would be different to that of your competitors.

You may also feel that many of your competitors are much bigger organizations and this would influence their performance in their dynamic indicators. As we have already said, the better targets are a combination of the external and internal indicators. The external figures may give you a feel for how a business could perform, but in reality your business will perform differently.

Often the information you get on other companies is old – historic. We want our dynamic indicators to be dynamic. Again you know your business – competitor information will tell you how they performed then, they will not tell you how you should perform now. Growth in your industry sector, economic recession, interest rates, etc. will also have an effect on your ability to perform.

Question 3

How do I create my own dynamic targets?

Rather than relying on target values derived from the performance of other businesses and waiting while these are refined by your own business performance, you may prefer to start by calculating your own. This will provide an initial set of values that may be closer to the performance of your business and so take less time to 'settle down' to a true picture of the shape your business should be.

To illustrate the calculations involved, we will take each of the eight dynamic indicators in turn. We do not pretend that creating your own targets will be an instantaneous thing. It does take time and some real thinking about your business. But as we have said, 'no pain, no gain'. The setting of your own specific targets is true value-added finance.

Dynamic targets relating to contribution

These are based on the dynamic indicators of:

- GC%
- DNC%
- BeGap%.

Gross contribution% (GC%)

This is a value for which, unfortunately, there is no magic formula you can use as a guideline. However, there are a number of components that you might consider when setting the target. Gross contribution is income less dynamic costs. It makes sense to look at each of these separately.

How can you estimate your income for the next period? You might look at last year and add on a bit or take off a bit. However, we would not advocate this as the best way to look at this figure. Remember, income is the anchor point for all other indicators – if you get this wrong it will distort all your dynamic indicators. You might be thinking it questions much of what we have said so far. How can we possibly know our future income? You are right. Very few organizations can know absolutely their future income. However, there are smarter ways of guessing. If you make a smart guess and it is wrong, your investigation into the gaps will help you understand where it went wrong. If you make a wild guess and it is wrong, it is just wrong.

So how do you make a smart guess? Historic information is part of the picture, but not the final number. You need to ask yourself a number of questions about your past performance:

- What is my product/service mix?
- What price(s) do I charge?
- What was my level of activity (volume)?
- Who did I sell to?

You then need to ask yourself some questions about the future:

- Will my product/service mix change?
- Will my price change?
- Will my level of activity change?
- Will my customers change
- Are there any new opportunities I would like to exploit?

You can be as sophisticated as you like with this process, but you can start small and work up. Whatever you do when you investigate your gaps, you can relate them back to this series of questions.

The second thing to consider when calculating a target GC% is your dynamic costs. By their very definition, dynamic costs vary with the level of sales. So here is the first pointer for your targets. Again, history is a good starting point, but it is not the end of the journey. You are a manager, you manage the figures within your dynamic costs. You can therefore consider whether these will increase or decrease next year. For example, will your labour costs increase or decrease – will your employees get a pay rise? Are you intending to employ more people?

Once you have estimated your income and your dynamic costs you can calculate your gross contribution and, finally, your dynamic indicator of GC%. Let us look at an example.

A small distribution company in Western Australia is forecasting sales to start the year at $450,000 per month and increase by $10,000 every month due to a new order negotiated at the end of the previous year. The deal has been hard won. In the previous year the dynamic costs for the business had been a constant 60 per cent. The new client has negotiated a very high service level as part of the distribution deal and the impact of growing the sales with this client will be a 1 per cent reduction in the GC% every other month for the next six months. This is due to the speed of response the company has offered the client. The target for income and GC% is summarized below:

W.A. Special Distribution Services

	Month 1	Month 2	Month 3	Month 4	Month 5	Month 6
Sales	$450,000	$460,000	$470,000	$480,000	$490,000	$500,000
GC%	60%	60%	59%	59%	58%	58%

Having established our first dynamic indicator target GC%, we can start to consider the remainder. We will use this income figure to form the basis of the calculation for all the other targets for this business.

Dynamic net contribution% (DNC%)

Your dynamic net contribution calculation is gross contribution less static costs. This leaves us with only one figure to estimate – the static costs. It would be nice to say that 'in a perfect world static costs never change'. But the world is not perfect. Static costs are not static. They can change for two reasons:

● the outside world imposes a change, e.g. there is an increase in the rent of your building;

● you negotiate a change, e.g. you increase the salaries of your administrative staff.

They can even change because of a variation in the weather. Again, calculating the future value of the static costs will be a mixture of what has been – today, the current status quo – the present, and the management decisions you intend to make – tomorrow.

For the distribution company in our example, the SC% has been 50 per cent. As the income increases, the company expects to keep static costs at the same value. It hopes to become more effective.

W.A. Special Distribution Services

	Month 1	Month 2	Month 3	Month 4	Month 5	Month 6
Sales	$450,000	$460,000	$470,000	$480,000	$490,000	$500,000
GC%	60%	60%	59%	59%	58%	58%
GC	$270,000	$276,000	$277,300	$283,200	$284,200	$290,000
SC	$225,000	$225,000	$225,000	$225,000	$225,000	$225,000
DNC	$45,000	$51,000	$52,300	$58,200	$59,200	$65,000
DNC%	10%	11.09%	11.13%	12.13%	12.08%	13%

The company now has a target for DNC% improving on a monthly basis as the business becomes more effective.

Breakeven gap% (BeGap%)

By far the easiest way to calculate the target BeGap% is using the two dynamic indicators we have already set targets for:

$$\text{Target BeGap\%} = \frac{\text{Target DNC\%}}{\text{Target GC\%}}$$

If you have produced smart targets for GC% and DNC%, then using the above, you cannot fail to have a smart target for BeGap%.

The Australian distribution company can now summarize its targets of profitability as follows:

W.A. Special Distribution Services

	Month 1	Month 2	Month 3	Month 4	Month 5	Month 6
GC%	60%	60%	59%	59%	58%	58%
DNC%	10%	11.09%	11.13%	12.13%	12.08%	13%
BeGap%	16.67%	18.48%	18.86%	20.56%	20.83%	22.41%

Dynamic targets relating to net assets

These are:

- Stock% (Stock%)
- Debtors% (Dr%)
- Creditors% (Cr%)

Before getting down to detail you need to consider the time intervals you are going to use to monitor your business. Will it be weekly, monthly or annual (we hope it will not be the latter as this would hardly fall into our definition of finger-on-the-pulse management).

The time interval to use in the following equations will be:

Weekly = 7   (days in a week)
Monthly = 30   (days in a month)
Annually = 365   (days in a year)

For the purpose of our examples we have assumed you will be monitoring your business on a monthly basis. As Dr% is the easiest to set targets for, we will start with this one.

Debtors%

Not surprisingly, the Dr% reflects the amount of money you are owed by your customers in relation to your income figure. So what is a good target for this figure? An obvious starting point is your credit terms.

Sales taxes, such as VAT in the European Union, will have an impact on this figure, but let us start by ignoring this complication.

If we are looking at a one-month time period, that month equates to 30 days' income. If you have credit terms of 30 days, this would suggest your debtors should be the same as the current month's income. We have applied a debtor target calculation:

$$\text{Dr\% Target} = \frac{\text{Credit Terms Given}}{\text{Time Period}} \times 100$$

$$\text{Dr\% Target} = \frac{30}{30} \times 100$$

$$\text{Dr\% Target} = 100\%$$

Let us add an air of realism here. We will assume we give credit terms of 30 days, but we know that most customers pay within 30 to 60 days – let us say at 45 days on average. Our realistic debtors target would be:

$$\text{Dr\% Target} = \frac{\text{Credit Taken}}{\text{Time Period}} \times 100$$

$$\text{Dr\% Target} = \frac{45}{30} \times 100$$

$$\text{Dr\% Target} = 150\%$$

Now let us consider sales tax and we will use the UK Value Added Tax (VAT) rate of 17.5 per cent as an example. The income figure excludes VAT, but the debtors figure includes VAT. So the quick calculation above can result in us comparing apples and oranges. We need to state the figures in the same currency, one that includes VAT. This is actually quite simple to do:

$$\text{Dr\% Target} = \frac{\text{Credit Taken}}{\text{Time Period}} \times 100 \times \text{VAT\%}$$

$$\text{Dr\% Target} = \frac{45}{30} \times 100 \times 117.5\%$$

$$\text{Dr\% Target} = 176.25\%$$

Stock%

Any product, and some services, are made up of three component parts. The names of these components are a result of history and conventional accounting practice which developed alongside the manufacturing industries. We do not propose to quibble with the names in this book, but we feel it is necessary to widen them to represent the move towards the retail and service-based economy. The three types of stock are:

- raw materials – this is probably most appropriate for manufacturing organizations. In manufactured products these are the components, parts, etc. that you use as part of your manufacturing process;

- work in progress – this will be applicable to manufacturing industries and for many service industries. It is the incomplete work. In manufacturing it is semi-finished products. In service businesses it is semi-finished projects that you have invested time and labour into but have not yet been able to recharge to your client;

- finished goods – this could be applicable to manufacturing, service and retail businesses. In manufacturing it is the finished product that you have not yet found a customer for. In service it is the finished projects that you have not yet invoiced. In retail it is the goods that you have bought for resale.

These can be summarized below:

	Raw materials	Work in progress	Finished goods
Manufacturing	✔	✔	✔
Service	✗	✔	✔
Retail	✗	✗	✔

The target in your organization will therefore be dependent on which industry you are in. If you are a service industry, simply fast forward to the target for work in progress; if retail, only the finished goods will apply. As manufacturing is the most complex, we will assume for an example that is the business you are in.

Let us look at how a standard product might be put together:

	Value	%
Selling price	10	100
Cost of raw material content	2	20
Cost of labour content	4	40
Total dynamic costs	6	60
Gross contribution	4	40
Static costs	3	30
Dynamic net contribution	1	10

Once you know this about your product or service you can start to calculate your targets.

Raw material target

There are two questions you need to ask yourself:

1   What percentage of my income are my raw materials (RM%)?

2   How long do I need to keep my raw materials in stock?

The answer to question 1 is straight from the table above, i.e. 20 per cent. The answer to question 2 will come from your knowledge of your business – your sales patterns and the ability and speed with which you can restock as required. Once you know these two things you can calculate the target using the following equation:

$$\textbf{Raw Material Target} = \frac{\textbf{Days Stock Holding}}{\textbf{Time Period}} \times \textbf{RM\%}$$

In the above example if we needed 30 days worth of stock this would give:

$$\textbf{Raw Material Target} = \frac{30}{30} \times \textbf{RM\%}$$

$$\textbf{Raw Material Target} = 1 \times \textbf{RM\%}$$

This suggests you hold one month's stock of raw materials. To convert this to a percentage of income we simply use the RM% as follows:

$$\textbf{Raw Material Target} = 1 \times 20\%$$

$$\textbf{Raw Material Target} = 20\%$$

i.e. your raw materials should represent 20 per cent of your monthly income.

Work in progress

In order to calculate the target for work in progress you again need to start with two questions:

1 What percentage of my income is my work in progress (WIP%)?

2 How long does it take me to produce my product or provide my service?

To answer the first question, a good rule of thumb for work in progress is to calculate it by including the total value of the raw materials and the total value of the labour and then assume on average that WIP is half complete. Using this method in the earlier example, WIP as a percentage of sales value will be raw materials at 20 per cent plus labour at 40 per cent = WIP 60 per cent of income. Finally, if jobs take two weeks to complete, the work in progress holding would be on average seven days old (one week). This would give a WIP target of:

$$\text{WIP Target} = \frac{\text{Days WIP Holding}}{\text{Time Period}} \times \text{WIP\%}$$

In the above example, if work in progress is typically seven days old, this would give:

$$\text{WIP Target} = \frac{7}{30} \times \text{WIP\%}$$

$$\text{WIP Target} = 0.233 \times \text{WIP\%}$$

To convert this to a percentage of income, we use the WIP% as follows:

$$\text{WIP Target} = 0.233 \times 60\%$$

$$\text{WIP Target} = 14\%$$

i.e. your work in progress should represent 14 per cent of your monthly income.

Finished goods

Finished goods have been fully worked. So again you can ask yourself two simple questions:

1 What percentage of my income is tied up in my finished goods (FG%)?

2 How long do I need to keep my finished goods in stock?

The value of our finished goods in the earlier example is 60 per cent of the selling price, i.e. all the raw materials at 20 per cent plus all the labour at 40 per cent. We know it takes two weeks to produce a job, so let's say we hold twice that amount as finished goods stock. Essentially a job already in progress could be finished within a week. We can go on to calculate the target using the following equation:

$$\text{Finished Goods Target} = \frac{\text{Days Stock Holding}}{\text{Time Period}} \times \text{FG\%}$$

In the above example, if we needed 30 days worth of stock this would give:

$$\text{Finished Goods Target} = \frac{30}{30} \times \text{FG\%}$$

$$\text{Finished Goods Target} = 1.0 \times \text{FG\%}$$

This suggests you hold one month's stock of finished goods, i.e. enough finished goods to supply your customers for one month without producing any more, and so perhaps four weeks is generous. To convert this to a percentage of income, we use the FG% as follows:

$$\text{Finished Goods Target} = 1.0 \times 60\%$$

$$\text{Finished Goods Target} = 60\%$$

i.e. your finished goods should represent 60 per cent of your monthly income.

Stock target

To calculate the final figure for Stock% to go into the radar chart, we add together these components as follows:

Summary	%
Raw materials	20
Work in progress	14
Finished goods	60
Total	**94**

If we are monitoring our stock on a month by month basis, the target should be 94 per cent of this month's income, i.e. stock represents nearly four weeks of income imprisoned in the time warp of your SNA figure.

Creditors%

The target for trade creditors is obviously going to depend on what you buy on credit. Again, using the 'rule of thumb' method we will assume all your raw materials (found within your dynamic costs) plus, say, half of your static costs are bought on credit.

In the example above, 'what you buy on credit' as a percentage of sales would give raw materials of 20 per cent plus half of static costs (half of 30 per cent), giving a total of 35 per cent. You can use the following formula to calculate the target based on how long your agreed credit terms are with your suppliers and what time period you are looking at:

$$\text{Cr\% Target} = \frac{\text{Days Credit Taken}}{\text{Time Period}} \times \text{CR Purchases\%}$$

In this example, if we generally take 60 days to pay our creditors and we are looking at the target for one month and using the credit purchases % we have just estimated of 35 per cent, the Cr% target would be:

$$\text{Cr\% Target} = \frac{60}{30} \times \text{CR Purchases\%}$$

$$\text{C\% Target} = 2.0 \times 35\%$$

$$\text{Cr\% Target} = 70\%$$

Your Cr% target on your monthly radar chart will be 70 per cent.

An example

Let us return to our Australian distribution company and make a few assumptions from which it can develop targets for the strands of its SNA. A distribution business is likely to have debtors and creditors but very little stock. If the business anticipates:

- debtors of 60 days
- a goods and service tax of 10 per cent
- stock relating to fuel. Fuel costs represent 10 per cent of the income
- an average stock holding of 30 days
- credit purchases of 50 per cent
- they intend to pay our creditors within 60 days

the Dr% target would be:

$$\text{Dr\% Target} = \frac{60}{30} \times (100 + 10\%\text{GST})$$

$$\text{Dr\% Target} = 220\%$$

The Stock% target would be:

$$\text{Stock\% Target} = \frac{30}{30} \times 10\%$$

$$\text{Stock Target} = 10\%$$

And the Cr% target would be:

$$\text{Cr\% Target} = \frac{60}{30} \times 50\%$$

$$\text{Cr\% Target} = 100\%$$

We can summarize the dynamic indicators so far for this company as follows:

W.A. Special Distribution Services

	Month 1	Month 2	Month 3	Month 4	Month 5	Month 6
Sales	$450,000	$460,000	$470,000	$480,000	$490,000	$500,000
GC%	60%	60%	59%	59%	58%	58%
DNC%	10%	11.09%	11.13%	12.13%	12.08%	13%
BeGap%	16.67%	18.48%	18.86%	20.56%	20.83%	22.41%
Stock%	10%	10%	10%	10%	10%	10%
Dr%	220%	220%	220%	220%	220%	220%
Cr%	100%	100%	100%	100%	100%	100%

Dynamic targets relating to cash

The final targets you will need to calculate are the ones relating to cash – DNA% and DCM%. Both of these are calculated from the other indicators but it is worth remembering where they come from:

Dynamic net assets% (DNA%)

Dynamic net assets are a result in the movement in the value of your static net assets:

Value of DNA = Value of This Period's SNA – Value of Last Period's SNA

We therefore need to backtrack a little so that we can calculate the value of the SNA. Your SNA comes from the strands of stock plus debtors less creditors. We have already established targets for these as a percentage of income and we have also set a target for income for our dynamic breakeven. So, for every period under consideration we can calculate the value of SNA by taking the following three steps.

Step one: calculate the SNA%

SNA% = Stock% + Dr% – Cr%

If a business had the following targets:

- Stock%   180%
- Dr%   176.25%
- Cr%   60%

this would give an SNA% of:

SNA% = 180% + 176.25% – 60%

SNA% = 296.25%

Step two: calculate the value of SNA

Value of SNA = Income × SNA%

If the month's income was forecast at a value of £500,000, the value of SNA would be:

Value of SNA = £500,000 × 296.25%

Value of SNA = £1,481,250

Step three: calculate the value of DNA

If we had calculated the value of SNA for the previous period to be £1,250,000, the dynamic net assets would be:

Value of DNA = £1,481,250 – £1,250,000

Value of DNA = £231,250

And the target for DNA% would be:

$$\text{DNA\% Target} = \frac{\text{DNA}}{\text{Income}} \times 100$$

$$\text{DNA\% Target} = \frac{£231,250}{£500,000} \times 100$$

$$\text{DNA\% Target} = 46.25\%$$

Using the example of the Australian distribution company we would calculate the DNA% target as follows:

W.A. Special Distribution Services

	Month 1	Month 2	Month 3	Month 4	Month 5	Month 6
Sales	$450,000	$460,000	$470,000	$480,000	$490,000	$500,000
Stock%	10%	10%	10%	10%	10%	10%
Dr%	220%	220%	220%	220%	220%	220%
Cr%	100%	100%	100%	100%	100%	100%
SNA%	130%	130%	130%	130%	130%	130%
SNA	$585,000	$598,000	$611,000	$624,000	$637,000	$650,000
DNA	$13,000	$13,000	$13,000	$13,000	$13,000	$13,000
DNA%	2.89%	2.83%	2.77%	2.71%	2.65%	2.60%

We can now go on to calculate the final target for the business, the DCM%.

Dynamic cash movement% (DCM%)

The formula for DCM% is:

$$\text{DCM\%} = \text{DNC\%} - \text{DNA\%}$$

So for the distribution business the final list for all eight targets would be:

W.A. Special Distribution Services

	Month 1	Month 2	Month 3	Month 4	Month 5	Month 6
GC%	60%	60%	59%	59%	58%	58%
DNC%	10%	11.09%	11.13%	12.13%	12.08%	13%
BeGap%	16.67%	18.48%	18.86%	20.56%	20.83%	22.41%
Stock%	10%	10%	10%	10%	10%	10%
Dr%	220%	220%	220%	220%	220%	220%
Cr%	100%	100%	100%	100%	100%	100%
DNA%	2.89%	2.83%	2.77%	2.71%	2.65%	2.60%
DCM%	7.11%	8.26%	8.36%	9.42%	9.43%	10.40%

This business is growing by introducing a new type of business to a new client. Monitoring the behaviour of this venture will be vital to its success. These very specific targets the business has developed will help it keep its finger on the pulse of the business and take management action as, if and when it is needed.

Question 4

How do I monitor my business against these dynamic targets?

Given the appropriate targets for your business, everyday operations can be monitored against these values to assess performance. This can be done either by comparing the results of your dynamic indicators or by using the visual representations of these already discussed: the radar chart, the dynamic breakeven graph and the dynamic cash graph. From these dynamic indicators, seeing where the gaps are can focus attention on the right area of the business, and it can do it very simply.

The radar chart

The radar chart offers a picture of the shape of your business and matches its current performance against a target performance. By using the dynamic targets as one line and the actual results (expressed as percentages of income) as the other line, the chart shows a shape of your business at any time and how 'fit' it is. Differences between actual and target values are easily seen and act as the pointer to where to focus attention in the business.

So how do we focus on these gaps? We ask ourselves several business-related questions. For example:

- Have sales gone up or down?
- Have credit terms changed?
- Have we given a discount on a large order?
- Is this a 'blip'?
- Is it the time warp?
- Is it a seasonal effect?
- Have we just been paid by a large customer?
- Have we had a stage payment on a big project?

When we have the answers to these questions we can decide on the appropriate management action. Of course there may be none. The deviation may be perfectly well explained, but at least we were warned in time, we investigated and reacted well.

There are alternative courses of corrective action that you could take as a manager. What you expect to see as a result is that at the next reporting period, the business is 'back in shape', i.e. the radar chart shows no gaps. You may, occasionally, react inappropriately – we all make mistakes. However, the speed of reaction that dynamic financial management facilitates allows for a second chance. You need not, therefore, overreact, which is often the case dealing with the old static information.

In the example of the Western Australian distribution company, it has drawn its own version of the radar chart to help it compare its actual performance with the target we helped it establish earlier in this chapter (*see* Fig 3.1).

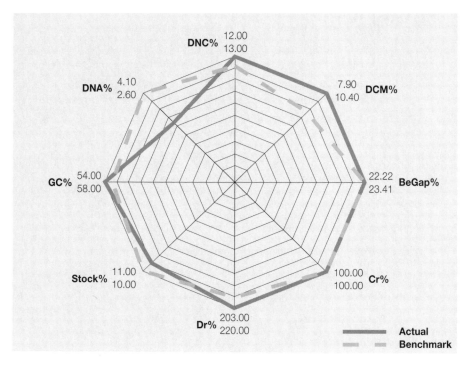

Fig 3.1 ● Distribution company radar – month 6

N.A. Special Distribution Services table of dynamic indicators against targets

	Actual	Target	Gap%	Performance against target
GC%	54.00%	58.00%	−4.00%	Bad
DNC%	12.00%	13.00%	−1.00%	Bad
BeGap%	22.22%	23.41%	−1.19%	Bad
Stock%	11.00%	10.00%	1.00%	Bad
Dr%	203.00%	220.00%	−17.00%	Good
Cr%	100.00%	100.00%	0.00%	No Difference
DNA%	4.10%	2.60%	1.50%	Bad
DCM%	7.90%	10.40%	−2.50%	Bad

The company can now examine the gaps and see where management action may be needed. It had anticipated a decline in the GC% but this has been worse than expected. The managers need to know why – have prices been decreasing or have dynamic costs been increasing, or is it because of the demands of this new contract? The DNA% is smaller than anticipated which suggests that less

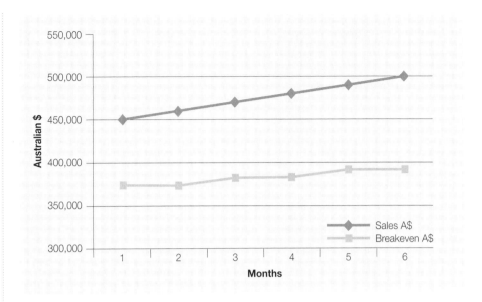

Fig 3.2 ● Distribution company forecast dynamic breakeven graph

cash has been imprisoned in the time warp – a positive indication which seems to be reflected in better control of the Dr%.

Some of these questions might be answered by examining trends over the period and this is the role of the other two graphs.

The dynamic breakeven graph

By using the dynamic breakeven graph, we can analyze the actual income, the breakeven income and the breakeven gap over a period in time.

Again looking at the forecast for the W.A. Special Distribution Services, the company was forecasting a steady increase in sales while keeping a fairly tight control over the breakeven (*see* Fig 3.2). Comparing this forecast with the month by month trends in both the actual income and the breakeven income will help identify whether the bad gaps in the radar for GC% are due to income value or high DC%.

The final trends you should examine are those that give you the vital signs of your business combined on one graph – the dynamic cash graph.

The dynamic cash graph

The dynamic cash graph gives trend information with regard to the three key dynamic indicators – DNC% indicating contribution, DNA% indicating the movement in the SNA, and DCM% showing the impact of the two on cash movement (*see* Fig 3.3). The lines represent the DNC% and the DNA% and the gap is the DCM%. For the distribution company the forecast was for the DCM% to be continuously positive – indeed, growing. DNC% is increasing as the business becomes more effective and, with good management of the SNA, the result is cash being released from the time warp.

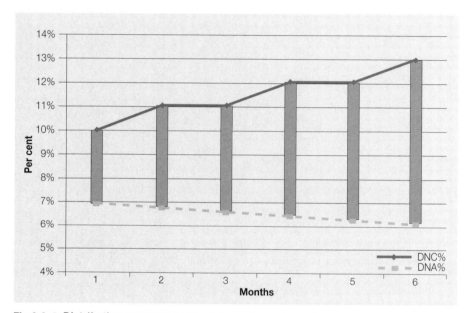

Fig 3.3 ● **Distribution company forecast dynamic cash graph**

The radar chart suggests that not all indicators are as sound as they should be at the end of the six months. The trends and management of the DCM% will be a good indication of whether this could cause the business any cash problems in the future.

Already, by using the eight dynamic indicators and setting dynamic targets against these, we have been able to comment in depth on the performance of a business we know little about. Even more excitingly, we can now go on to suggest dynamic decisions as options for the management of W.A. Distribution to consider.

So we know the shape of the business, we know the shape we think the business should be in. All we need to know is how to get back into shape, and that is the thrust of the next chapter, *Dynamic decisions*.

chapter 4

Dynamic decisions

In dynamic financial management we have a simple approach to decision making. Your dynamic indicators will change as a result of any decisions you make. The mathematical result of those decisions can easily be predicted. For example, if you reduce your price by 10 per cent, the result on all eight dynamic indicators can be predicted. But we can take you even further than that – we can help you look at the actions that you can take to dynamically manage the initial impact of these decisions. By increasing your knowledge of the situation you reduce the risk and perhaps magnify the rewards of your decisions.

In the previous chapters we were concerned with identifying our dynamic indicators, establishing appropriate targets, and comparing the performance against those targets. We have achieved this using the three visual representations of the dynamics of the business: the radar chart, the dynamic breakeven graph and the dynamic cash graph.

But there is another way you can use the radar chart and the gaps it can reveal. Instead of looking at the gap between the actual performance and the target, you can use it to compare the shape of the business before and after management decisions.

Decision making is about making a difference to your business. There are many decisions you may face every day to which you wish you had a better answer. Do you ever feel as if you are guessing the impact of a vital decision? Do you wish you could look into the future and see what was going to happen to the rest of the business based upon one decision today?

When does a manager make decisions? It may be that, now you are using dynamic indicators, you discover your business is out of shape. It is not performing in line with the targets that you believe the business is capable of achieving. If you want to improve your dynamic indicators, i.e. improve the shape you are in, there are a number of areas you may address:

- changing your prices;
- changing your dynamic costs;
- changing your static costs;
- changing your product mix;
- changing your cost structure, i.e. the ratio of dynamic to static costs;
- changing the structure of your SNA.

Most readers will agree that cost changes are relevant to their activities. But some may think prices are not. You may think 'I'm a cost centre manager' or 'I work in the public sector', so price changes do not affect me. We will try to turn that thinking on its head. How do you know what the budget you have been allocated is meant to cover? How could you make a proposal for a bigger budget? Your budget is allocated in relation to activity in some way, shape or form. So what price do you put on your discrete activities?

There are often changes imposed on your business. The competitive environment in which you operate may force you to reduce your price. Or it may be that your costs are increasing due to external impositions. You need to know the impact of these changes on your business. You may also need to know the decisions you need to take in order to manage these changes effectively.

Some decisions appear simple – there is a direct cause and a single, observable effect. However, with what you have learnt so far, this may now seem naïve. Some causes are relatively clear. For example, you may have just negotiated the annual pay increase, so your dynamic costs will obviously increase. But this will have a wider impact on your business than simply affecting the dynamic costs. You need to know the effect of this on the shape of your business – the radar.

Decisions may be taken in the hope of starting a chain reaction, e.g. you may decrease your prices hoping to increase the number of things you will sell, apparently a simple cause and effect decision. However, the information you need here is far more complex than it may seem. First, what is the initial impact of the pricing decision on the shape of your business? Ask yourself, given that, what do I need to do to get my radar chart back to the shape it was before I made this decision, e.g. by how much do I now need to increase my volume simply to get back to where I was before the price decrease?

Put simply, in the contribution statement there are only four things that can happen that can affect your eight dynamic indicators:

1 Prices can change.

2   Volume can change.

3   Dynamic costs can change.

4   Static costs can change.

Any change can be related to one of these four categories. But before going on to discuss these in any detail, we will try to answer some common management questions.

Common management questions

There are some questions in business that have a surprisingly easy answer. Consider the following.

- Question 1: What is the maximum possible discount I could give?
- Question 2: Will my cost structure affect my decision making?
- Question 3: When my costs go up, how much would I need to pass on to the customer to maintain my DNC%?
- Question 4: How much cash do I need to grow the business?
- Question 5: By how much would I need to grow to double my money?
- Question 6: If I lower my price, how much more do I need to sell to make the same money?

With dynamic financial management, we can show the answers to these questions very quickly.

Question 1

What is the maximum possible discount I could give?

Now that is an easy one and yet, ask most managers this question and they will give the wrong answer. The maximum discount you can give without that sale making a loss (i.e. to take the sale to breakeven) is the same percentage as your current DNC%.

Maximum Discount% = DNC%

Simple! If you know your DNC% you know any discount must be less than that figure. Try it. Now that is a piece of knowledge with which to impress your colleagues at meetings.

Consider the following businesses:

Business	A	B	C	D	E	F	G	H
Income	100	100	100	100	100	100	100	100
DC	80	70	60	50	40	30	20	10
GC	20	30	40	50	60	70	80	90
SC	10	20	30	40	50	60	70	80
DNC	10	10	10	10	10	10	10	10

All these businesses, although they have very different cost structures, have a DNC% of 10 per cent. If the theory is right, a 10 per cent decrease in price will take all these businesses down to breakeven:

Business	A	B	C	D	E	F	G	H
Income	90	90	90	90	90	90	90	90
DC	80	70	60	50	40	30	20	10
GC	10	20	30	40	50	60	70	80
SC	10	20	30	40	50	60	70	80
DNC	0	0	0	0	0	0	0	0

It is so obvious when you see this that you wonder why you never thought of it before. The fact that managers often forget is, if you *reduce your price*, the dynamic costs actually *stay the same*.

Question 2

Will my cost structure affect my decision making?

Yes, it will. Cost structure is the relationship between your dynamic and your static costs. Consider the following businesses:

Business	A	B	C	D	E	F	G	H
Income	100	100	100	100	100	100	100	100
DC	80	70	60	50	40	30	20	10
GC	20	30	40	50	60	70	80	90
SC	10	20	30	40	50	60	70	80
DNC	10	10	10	10	10	10	10	10

All these have the same DNC% yet different DC/SC relationships. Let us look at one situation. Each business is going to decrease its price and is looking for an increase in volume to compensate and return its DNC% back to 10 per cent. We will assume the discount they are going to give is 10 per cent. From the answer to question 1 we know this would mean they all reduced the DNC% to 0 per cent, they are at breakeven. Let's double check:

Business	A	B	C	D	E	F	G	H
Income	90	90	90	90	90	90	90	90
DC	80	70	60	50	40	30	20	10
GC	10	20	30	40	50	60	70	80
SC	10	20	30	40	50	60	70	80
DNC	0	0	0	0	0	0	0	0

What new volume of sales would be needed to get them back to DNC% of 10 per cent? Tables 8.5–8.7 (pp. 202–4) will show you how to calculate this quickly but for now we will just give you the answer:

	Additional volume needed to compensate for 10% price decrease							
	900%	82%	43%	29%	22%	18%	15%	13%
Business	A	B	C	D	E	F	G	H
Income	900	164	129	116	110	106	103	101
DC	800	128	86	65	49	35	23	11
GC	100	36	43	41	61	71	80	90
SC	10	20	30	40	50	60	70	80
DNC	90	16	13	11	11	11	10	10
DNC%	10%	10%	10%	10%	10%	10%	10%	10%

Before the price reduction, Business A has a GC% of 20 per cent. Business A would need to grow by 900 per cent! How many people could grow by 900 per cent to get the new income value of 900? And what about the static costs here? They would be unlikely to remain at their original level given such an increase in volume.

Even in Business D, where the GC% was as high as 50 per cent you would still need to increase volume by 29 per cent to compensate for a 10 per cent price discount. And this would merely get your DNC% back up to 10 per cent.

In summary, the lower the GC%, the less able you are to cope with a decrease in price, or a downturn in the market, so keep DC under control – be efficient.

Question 3

When my costs go up, how much would I need to pass on to the customer to maintain my DNC%?

Less than you might think you have to is the answer. Managers often make the mistake of passing on too much of an increase to their customer. Most of your competitors are probably in the same position as you are, facing greater costs and having to consider a price increase. If you pass on too much, you lose the market; if you can pass on less than your competitors, you may win the price war. So, getting the right figure to pass on could be crucial to your success. But identifying the right amount relies on understanding your cost structure. Again, let us look at the following businesses:

Business	A	B	C	D	E	F	G	H
Income	100	100	100	100	100	100	100	100
DC	80	70	60	50	40	30	20	10
GC	20	30	40	50	60	70	80	90
SC	10	20	30	40	50	60	70	80
DNC	10	10	10	10	10	10	10	10

What happens if their dynamic costs go up by 10 per cent?

Business	A	B	C	D	E	F	G	H
Income	100	100	100	100	100	100	100	100
DC	88	77	66	55	44	33	22	11
GC	12	23	34	45	56	67	78	89
SC	10	20	30	40	50	60	70	80
DNC	2	3	4	5	6	7	8	9

The lower your current GC%, the harder you are going to be hit by the 10 per cent increase. Also, the lower your GC%, the more of an increase you will need to pass on to your customer. What new price would be needed to get each of these businesses back to a DNC% of 10 per cent? Table 9.6 (p. 231) will show you how to quickly calculate this, but again we will just give you the answer:

| | Price increase needed to compensate for 10% DC increase | | | | | | | |
| | 8.89% | 7.78% | 6.67% | 5.56% | 4.44% | 3.33% | 2.22% | 1.11% |
Business	A	B	C	D	E	F	G	H
Income	109	108	107	106	104	103	102	101
DC	88	77	66	55	44	33	22	11
GC	21	31	41	51	60	70	80	90
SC	10	20	30	40	50	60	70	80
DNC	11	11	11	11	10	10	10	10
DNC%	10%	10%	10%	10%	10%	10%	10%	10%

In Business D, the GC% is currently 50 per cent and so it needs to pass on only a 5.56 per cent price increase rather than the full 10 per cent.

What would be the impact if the increase was in your static costs rather than your dynamic costs? Again, we will stick with a 10 per cent increase:

Business	A	B	C	D	E	F	G	H
Income	100	100	100	100	100	100	100	100
DC	80	70	60	50	40	30	20	10
GC	20	30	40	50	60	70	80	90
SC	11	22	33	44	55	66	77	88
DNC	9	8	7	6	5	4	3	2

What new price would be needed to get each of these businesses back to DNC% of 10 per cent? We have again used the tables in *Part Two* to provide the answer (*see* Table 11.2, p. 273):

| | Price rise needed to compensate for 10% SC increase | | | | | | | |
| | 1.11% | 2.22% | 3.33% | 4.44% | 5.56% | 6.67% | 7.78% | 8.89% |
Business	A	B	C	D	E	F	G	H
Income	101	102	103	104	106	107	108	109
DC	80	70	60	50	40	30	20	10
GC	21	32	43	54	66	77	88	99
SC	11	22	33	44	55	66	77	88
DNC	10	10	10	10	11	11	11	11
DNC%	10%	10%	10%	10%	10%	10%	10%	10%

The situation is exactly reversed. If your SC% is higher than your DC%, as in Company H, then an increase in your static costs, not surprisingly, hits you harder. This time it is Company H that needs to pass on the largest increase, of 8.89 per cent. But this is still lower than the 10 per cent that some managers might have thought they needed to pass on and consequently damage their market.

Question 4

How much cash do I need to grow the business?

The answer to this relates to something we introduced in *Chapter 2: What are dynamic indicators?* looking at maximum growth for a zero DCM%. We used the summary table:

Relationship			Effect on DCM%
DNC%	Equals	DNA%	Neutral
	Greater than		Positive
	Less than		Negative

Whether or not you have money in the bank is irrelevant. If DNC% is greater than DNA%, you can fund growth out of your DNC%. What we are interested in is what happens when DNC% is less than DNA%. How much cash will you need to fund this level of growth and how long will it take you to pay back that cash?

We have a simple relationship that calculates this:

$$\text{Dynamic Payback} = \frac{\text{DNA\%}}{\text{DNC\%}}$$

This relationship gives you a number which, if less than one, indicates you are growing within your means – at less than your maximum growth percentage. If the number is greater than one, you have a funding gap because money needed to buy new stock or additional credit given to new customers is imprisoned in the SNA time warp.

The dynamic payback indicates how long it will take to release this money from your time warp. For example, a business has the following budget:

	This year £	Next year £
Income	100,000	200,000
DNC	10,000	20,000
Stock	50,000	100,000
Debtors	100,000	200,000
Creditors	80,000	160,000
Static Net Assets	70,000	140,000

The business has put together a plan for growth and its DNA% would be:

DNA = New SNA – Old SNA

DNA = £140,000 – £70,000

DNA = £70,000

$$DNA\% = \frac{£70,000}{£200,000} \times 100 = 35\%$$

$$DNC\% = \frac{£20,000}{£200,000} \times 100 = 10\%$$

$$\text{Dynamic Payback} = \frac{DNA\%}{DNC\%} = \frac{35\%}{10\%} = 3.5$$

The dynamic payback is 3.5, but 3.5 what? Well, the business is looking at growing over a one-year period. The dynamic payback tells you how many periods it will take for you to generate enough DNC% to pay back the investment you have made, the cash you have imprisoned, in the SNA time warp. In this business it will take 3.5 years to pay back the investment in the SNA needed for this ambitious level of growth.

Question 5

By how much would I need to grow to double my money?

What do we mean by 'double my money'? We mean doubling the value of your DNC. The answer to this question could not be easier – a simple relationship gives you the answer immediately:

Volume% Increase Needed = BeGap%

Again let us look at a number of businesses:

Business	A	B	C	D	E	F	G	H
Income	100	100	100	100	100	100	100	100
DC	80	70	60	50	40	30	20	10
GC	20	30	40	50	60	70	80	90
SC	10	20	30	40	50	60	70	80
DNC	10	10	10	10	10	10	10	10
BeGap%	50%	33%	25%	20%	17%	14%	13%	11%

Does it work?

	Volume % increase needed to double your DNC value							
	50%	33%	25%	20%	17%	14%	12.5%	11%
Business	A	B	C	D	E	F	G	H
Income	150	133	125	120	117	114	113	111
DC	120	93	75	60	47	34	23	11
GC	30	40	50	60	70	80	90	100
SC	10	20	30	40	50	60	70	80
DNC	20	20	20	20	20	20	20	20
DNC%	13%	15%	16%	17%	17%	18%	18%	18%

For every business here, the DNC has doubled from 10 to 20, and they have also improved their DNC% as an additional benefit. However, you will double your money only if you can keep your static costs the same.

Question 6

If I lower my price, how much more do I need to sell to make the same money?

Again a dynamic calculation provides the answer straight away. By 'making the same money' we mean getting the same value of DNC.

$$\text{Volume\% Increase Needed} = \frac{\% \text{ Price Decrease}}{\text{Current GC\%} - \% \text{ Price Decrease}} \times 100$$

Note: this works only if the percentage price decrease is less than GC%. Surely you would not be giving this size of discount anyway! Let us look at a number of businesses:

Business	A	B	C	D	E	F	G	H
Income	100	100	100	100	100	100	100	100
DC	80	70	60	50	40	30	20	10
GC	20	30	40	50	60	70	80	90
SC	10	20	30	40	50	60	70	80
DNC	10	10	10	10	10	10	10	10

Let us look at the 10 per cent decrease we have used already:

Business	A	B	C	D	E	F	G	H
Income	90	90	90	90	90	90	90	90
DC	80	70	60	50	40	30	20	10
GC	10	20	30	40	50	60	70	80
SC	10	20	30	40	50	60	70	80
DNC	0	0	0	0	0	0	0	0

What volume percentage increase would be needed to get each of these businesses back to a DNC value of £10? The dynamic calculation above will allow you to quickly calculate this and the table below shows you the answer:

	Volume% increase needed to compensate for 10% price decrease							
	100%	50%	33%	25%	20%	17%	14%	13%
Business	A	B	C	D	E	F	G	H
New Price	0.90	0.90	0.90	0.90	0.90	0.90	0.90	0.90
Income	180	135	120	113	108	105	103	102
DC	160	105	80	63	48	35	23	12
GC	20	30	40	50	60	70	80	90
SC	10	20	30	40	50	60	70	80
DNC	10	10	10	10	10	10	10	10
DNC%	5.6%	7.4%	8.3%	8.8%	9.3%	9.5%	9.7%	9.8%

So you have managed to regain the value of your DNC. But this has had a detrimental effect on your DNC% – you are doing more work for relatively less money. In *Part Two* we will concentrate on regaining your DNC%, not the value of the DNC (*see* Table 13.1, p. 300).

The decision-making process

At its most sophisticated level dynamic financial management techniques can also be used to calculate the impact of changes on all your dynamic indicators. These may be due to changes in income, changes in dynamic costs or changes in static costs. The techniques are sophisticated and require some effort to learn how to use them. Once mastered, their use becomes second nature.

The detail behind the techniques forms *Part Two: Managing tomorrow*. It is structured in a way that reflects the types of decisions you may be faced with, analyzes the initial impact of those changes and gives you the alternative ways of getting the business back into shape, i.e. returning the DNC% to its current level.

The types of decisions you may be faced with fall into a number of categories.

● changes in income;

● changes in dynamic costs;

● changes in static costs;

● improving your DNC%.

The detailed explanation is included in the *Introduction to Part Two* but to whet your appetite, Tables 4.1 and 4.2 give an outline of the types of changes you will be faced with and how you could proactively manage these changes. They are split into two broad categories, first, changes in income, dynamic costs or static costs, and second, improving the DNC%.

Table 4.1 ● Changes in income, dynamic costs or static costs

Managing changes in	Type of change	Stage
Income	*Increases in income*	Initial impact
		Possible benefits
	Decreases in income	Initial impact
		Management action
DC	*Increases in DC*	Initial impact
		Management action
	Decreases in DC	Initial impact
		Possible benefits
SC	*Increases in SC*	Initial impact
		Management action
	Decreases in SC	Initial impact
		Possible benefits

Table 4.2 ● **Improving the DNC%**

Managing an increase in	Choice	Type of change
DNC%	*One*	Increase activity levels
	Two	Increase price
	Three	Decrease dynamic costs
	Four	Decrease static costs

We will use a number of case studies to show how these work in practice:

● For a decrease in price we are going to consider a small US-based consultancy in the petrochemical industry faced with a highly competitive market and looking at the impact of reducing its price.

● We will then examine a small manufacturing company in South Wales, UK, faced with an increase in its dynamic costs due to exchange rate fluctuations.

● To look at a decrease in static costs we will examine a charity based in Germany considering an option to reduce its static costs by relocating to a suburban business park.

● And finally, we will look at Elchip, a subsidiary of a larger organization, faced with a target increase in its DNC% demanded from head office from its current level of 20 per cent to a demanding target of 25 per cent.

Case study

Subject Price decrease
Industry sector Consultancy
Company name Petro Consultants

(This is based on Chapter 8: Decreases in your income)

We need to know the existing contribution statement, DNA statement and eight dynamic indicators for the business called Petro Consultants Inc.

Contribution statement	$	DNA statement	$
Income	537,983	Income	537,983
Dynamic Costs	242,092	Stock	268,992
Gross Contribution	295,891	Debtors	941,470
Static Costs	188,294	Creditors	403,487
DNC	107,597	Static Net Assets	806,975

Eight dynamic indicators

	%
GC%	55.00
DNC%	20.00
BeGap%	36.36
Stock%	50.00
Dr%	175.00
Cr%	75.00
DNA%	0.00
DCM%	20.00

The company has been stable for the past few months. As a result, the SNA has not changed between the periods. The DNA% is therefore 0 per cent and the DCM% the same as the DNC%, 20 per cent.

We can now add a bit of instability into the business and see the impact on the performance before and after the changes. All the calculations for this case study have been based on the process explored in *Chapter 8: Decreases in your income* and the appropriate tables will be referenced as we move through the case study.

Prices can go up or down. Any price movement will have an effect on all the dynamic indicators, with the exception of the Dr%. You need to know why this is. Dynamic financial management will not only help you understand this but will also tell you the size of the effect on the dynamic indicators, whether the change is favourable or unfavourable.

Let's look at Petro Consultants. There has been a downturn in the petrochemical industry and work is becoming more difficult to get. The managers are considering reducing their price by 10 per cent. This will make their price lower than most of their competitors' and should result in additional business being won. If an increased level of business cannot be found there is also the possibility of decreasing the consultants' rate of pay or moving to cheaper premises across the state border. The business needs to understand and predict the impact of each of these decisions, and the decision-making part of dynamic financial management is the way to do it.

First, Petro Consultants needs to know the initial impact of the price reduction on the radar chart – the shape of the business – assuming that nothing else happens (*see* Fig 4.1). This radar chart shows that Dr% will not change, DNC%, GC% and BeGap% will decrease, and Stock% and Cr% will increase. The impact on DNA% and DCM% will depend on the relationship of all the indicators within Petro Consultants.

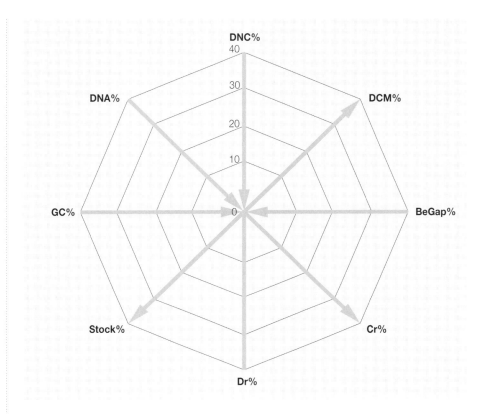

Fig 4.1 ● Radar chart of Petro Consultants' dynamic indicators

However, dynamic financial management can tell you more than this. It can tell you the actual magnitude of *all* the changes.

So, what will happen to Petro Consultants if it implements its 10 per cent price reduction? The eight dynamic indicators before and after the decrease in prices are shown in Table 4.3. And once we know the new dynamic indicators we can quickly recalculate the value of the contribution and DNA statements:

Table 4.3 ● Petro Consultants' eight dynamic indicators

	Before	After	Dynamic decision maker
GC%	55.00%	50.00%	Dynamic look-up table
DNC%	20.00%	11.11%	Dynamic look-up table
BeGap%	36.36%	22.22%	Calculation
Stock%	50.00%	55.56%	Dynamic look-up table
Dr%	175.00%	175.00%	No change in %
Cr%	75.00%	83.33%	Dynamic look-up table
DNA%	0.00%	(19.44)%	Calculation
DCM%	20.00%	30.55%	Calculation

Contribution statement

	Before	After
Income	537,983	484,185
Dynamic Costs	242,092	242,092
Gross Contribution	295,891	242,093
Static Costs	188,294	188,833
Dynamic Net Contribution	107,597	53,260

A 10 per cent cut in price has reduced the DNC% from 20 per cent down to 11.11 per cent, an actual reduction in value of 44 per cent from $107,597 to $53,260. And the safety of the business expressed through the BeGap% has decreased from 36.36 per cent to 22.22 per cent.

DNA statement

	Before	After
Income	537,983	484,185
Stock	268,992	268,992
Debtors	941,470	847,323
Creditors	403,487	403,487
Static Net Assets	806,975	712,828

The DNA statement makes interesting reading. The stock and creditors values have remained the same. Just because Petro Consultants has made a decision to reduce its price, its employees have not reduced their labour cost, and this forms the basis of the work in progress calculation for the stock. The suppliers have not reduced their prices, so the value of creditors has stayed the same at $403,487. But the shape of the business has changed, the figures as a percentage of income have changed. This business will now respond differently when decisions are made (*see* Fig 4.2).

With a decision to reduce price, the DNA% and DCM% are also interesting. In this case there is a positive impact on DNA% as the debtors value falls from $941,470 to $847,323. Normally, reducing the SNA would suggest that cash has been released from the time warp and, therefore, good management. In the case of a price decrease it is almost the reverse: the sales value is less so some cash from these sales has not even got as far as the time warp. The debtors value is not lower because of good cash collection, it is lower because a lower sales price results in less cash coming into the business.

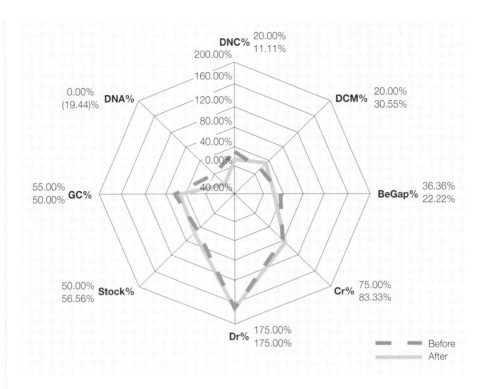

Fig 4.2 ● **Petro Consultants Inc.**

But this is only half the story. The price reduction for Petro Consultants is supposed to have a knock-on effect, either a positive impact on the volume of business, or the management will have to make compensating cost reductions to reduce costs. But what size of change is needed to return the DNC% to the same level as before this pricing decision?

In summary, Petro Consultants has three alternatives:

Change		Appropriate action to regain DNC%
Decrease in income	⮕	Increase volume
	⮕	Decrease dynamic costs
	⮕	Decrease static costs

With dynamic financial management techniques we can predict very accurately the size of the decision needed to get a successful result, i.e. to regain the original DNC%.

Increase volume

Petro Consultants needs to regain its original DNC% of 20 per cent and one way to achieve this is to increase volume. But by how much? In *Part Two* you will find that you simply need to look up two figures in three tables in order to find the answer (*see* Tables 8.5–8.7, pp. 202–4). Petro Consultants needs to increase its volume by 30 per cent to return its DNC% to 20 per cent. Is this right?

	Before	After initial impact	Volume up by 30%
Income	537,983	484,185	629,441
Dynamic Costs	242,092	242,092	314,720
Gross Contribution	295,891	242,093	314,721
Static Costs	188,294	188,833	188,833
Dynamic Net Contribution	107,597	53,260	125,888

A volume increase of 30 per cent gives a new income of $629,441 and a new DNC of $125,888 that is a DNC% of 20 per cent. Does this seem a possible option for Petro Consultants? The market would have to be extremely price sensitive to achieve a volume increase of 30 per cent. The company has already indicated that things are difficult in this market at the moment.

But this is not the only problem for Petro Consultants with this particular option. A growth of 30 per cent has other impacts on the eight dynamic indicators. But first we need to look at the DNA statement.

	Before	After initial impact	Volume up by 30%
Income	537,983	484,185	629,441
Stock	268,992	268,992	349,717
Debtors	941,470	847,323	1,101,522
Creditors	403,487	403,487	524,513
Static Net Assets	806,975	712,828	926,726

The SNA has had to grow from $806,975 to $926,726, a growth of $119,751; in other words a DNA% of 19 per cent. This will need to be funded somehow. There is of course money in the DNC%, but only just enough. The investment has virtually wiped out all this month's DNC, and that assumes the volume increase was indeed achieved.

	Before	After initial impact	Increase volume by 30%	Dynamic decision maker
GC%	55.00%	50.00%	50.00%	Calculation
DNC%	20.00%	11.11%	20.00%	Dynamic look-up tables
BeGap%	36.36%	22.22%	40.00%	Calculation
Stock%	50.00%	55.56%	55.56%	No change in %
Dr%	175.00%	175.00%	175.00%	No change in %
Cr%	75.00%	83.33%	83.33%	No change in %
DNA%	0.00%	(19.44)%	19.02%	Calculation
DCM%	20.00%	30.55%	0.98%	Calculation

These figures came straight from the processes discussed in *Part Two* (*see* Table 8.8, p. 207).

So what about the other options open to Petro Consultants?

Reduce dynamic costs

Petro Consultants believes that, as the market is so competitive, it should be able to persuade its consultants to take a reduction in salaries. This will decrease the dynamic costs. But how much of a reduction does the company need to regain its original DNC%? Again *Part Two* will take you through the process of calculating the answer. In summary, it needs to reduce dynamic costs by 17.8 per cent. Let's look at the new contribution statement to see if this works:

	Before	After initial impact	Dynamic costs down 17.8%
Income	537,983	484,185	484,185
Dynamic Costs	242,092	242,092	198,999
Gross Contribution	295,891	242,093	285,185
Static Costs	188,294	188,833	188,833
Dynamic Net Contribution	107,597	53,260	96,352

The DNC of $96,352 is close enough to the required DNC% of 20 per cent.

What about the impact on the eight dynamic indicators and DNA statement?

	Before	After initial impact	Dynamic costs down 17.8%	Dynamic decision maker
GC%	55.00	50.00	58.90	Calculation
DNC%	20.00	11.11	20.00	Dynamic look-up table
BeGap%	36.36	22.22	33.96	Calculation
Stock%	50.00	55.56	41.00	Dynamic look-up table
Dr%	175.00	175.00	175.00	No change in %
Cr%	75.00	83.33	68.25	Dynamic look-up table
DNA%	0.00	(19.44)	(18.92)	Calculation
DCM%	20.00	30.55	38.92	Calculation

This looks a fabulous option. This time the DNA% shows the company has truly released cash from the time warp. Look at the DNA statement below:

	Before	After initial impact	Dynamic costs down 17.8%
Income	537,983	484,185	484,185
Stock	268,992	268,992	198,515
Debtors	941,470	847,323	847,323
Creditors	403,487	403,487	330,456
Static Net Assets	806,975	712,828	715,382

The reduction in DC has had a beneficial impact on the value of stock. And we have maintained our DNC% at 20 per cent so the DCM% is positively bursting with cash. But let's not get carried away. This is the financial result of a decision which is probably not possible for Petro Consultants to implement. Would you accept a cut in salary of 17.8 per cent to help your business through this difficult time? Probably not!

The final option could be to reduce the static costs.

Reduce static costs

Petro Consultants believes that cheaper premises are available across the state border. But how much of a reduction does the company need to regain its original DNC%? It needs a huge cut in static costs of 22.9 per cent. To look at the new contribution statement:

	Before	After initial impact	Static costs down 22.9%
Income	537,983	484,185	484,185
Dynamic Costs	242,092	242,092	242,092
Gross Contribution	295,891	242,093	242,093
Static Costs	188,294	188,833	145,590
Dynamic Net Contribution	107,597	53,260	96,503

We probably do not need to carry on here. A 22.9 per cent decrease in static costs seems unlikely. Rent accounts for a small portion of the static costs and the business needs to reduce the value by $43,243. The SC% was only 35 per cent of income before the change; this would mean reducing the SC% to 30 per cent.

Let us look at the other indicators anyway:

	Before	After initial impact	Static costs down 22.9%	
GC%	55.00	50.00	50.00	No change in %
DNC%	20.00	11.11	20.00	Dynamic look-up table
BeGap%	36.36	22.22	40.00	Calculation
Stock%	50.00	55.56	55.56	No change in %
Dr%	175.00	175.00	175.00	No change in %
Cr%	75.00	83.33	83.33	No change in %
DNA%	0.00	(19.44)	(19.44)	No change in %
DCM%	20.00	30.55	39.44	Calculation

As static costs do not affect the SNA strands of this business, the DNA statement will not change (except of course as a result of the initial impact). Therefore the DNA% is the same. The DCM% will increase because the company has increased the DNC%.

Again, numerically this looks great, but what can Petro Consultants do now?

Price decrease – a summary

You do not need to know all of the detail we have shown you in the process of this case study in order to manage your business dynamically. We have taken you through the detail for Petro Consultants to prove that our techniques work. All *you* will want to know is the answer – your new dynamic indicators and thus the new shape of your business. What you do need to do is to trust the answer – what we have presented is the 'process and the proof' so that you *can* trust the answer that you get when looking at your own business.

The answers for Petro Consultants faced with a 10 per cent price decrease were:

	Before	After
GC%	55.00	50.00
DNC%	20.00	11.11
BeGap%	36.36	22.22
Stock%	50.00	55.56
Dr%	175.00	175.00
Cr%	75.00	83.33
DNA%	0.00	(19.44)
DCM%	20.00	30.55

Plus the possible actions the managers of Petro Consultants could take to regain DNC%:

Change		Appropriate action to regain DNC%	Amount
10% decrease	⇒	Increase volume	By 30.00%
in price	⇒	Decrease dynamic costs	By 17.80%
	⇒	Decrease static costs	By 22.90%

What should they do? They can now calculate the impact of increasing volume by less than 30 per cent, or reducing costs by less than the required amount. They will be suffering unmanaged growth. But in the short term, maybe that is what the market dictates. Maybe they could afford to give a smaller price decrease? They could now do a quick dynamic analysis to see how this would affect the possible actions they could take.

Or perhaps they could think radically. Is there a niche part of the market for which they could charge a premium price? They may be able to put up their prices and, as a consequence, scale down the level of activities. Dynamic financial management could tell them how much they could allow the volume to drop and still make the required DNC%.

This is the point of dynamic decision making. We have taken you through the process step by step. Once you are familiar with the processes in *Part Two*, you can quickly test a number of options and see the impact on the eight dynamic indicators. No need for a detailed budget of profit, balance sheet and cash flow. Here you get a 'back of an envelope' calculation that really is value added.

Case study

Subject DC increase
Industry sector Manufacturing
Company name Speciality Steels

(This is based on Chapter 9: Increases in your dynamic costs)

We need to know the existing contribution statement, DNA statement and eight dynamic indicators for the business called Speciality Steels Ltd.

Contribution statement		DNA statement	
	£		£
Income	791,543	Income	791,543
Dynamic Costs	633,234	Stock	1,187,315
Gross Contribution	158,309	Debtors	1,978,857
Static Costs	79,299	Creditors	1,385,200
DNC	79,010	Static Net Assets	1,780,972

Eight dynamic indicators

	%
GC%	20.00
DNC%	9.98
BeGap%	53.90
Stock%	150.00
Dr%	250.00
Cr%	175.00
DNA%	0.00
DCM%	9.98

The dynamics of this business are very different to the dynamics of the consultancy business in the previous case study. GC% is very low. In the past the business environment has been volatile. The company has pushed many of its costs into dynamic costs so that, if the economy takes another downturn, there will be less risk. In addition, the manufacturing process uses lots of materials and is labour intensive. The company's control over its SNA also leaves a lot to be desired. The Stock% is high because much of the material comes from overseas and deliveries are unreliable. The Dr% is high as many of the sales are export. Also, like many smaller businesses, the credit control procedures are inadequate. As a consequence, cash is usually tight and Speciality Steels delays paying its creditors for as long as it can.

For the past few years the pound has been strong. However, a rapid decrease is predicted. As Speciality Steels buys most of its materials from overseas, it estimates this could result in an increase in dynamic costs of more than 5 per cent. The company knows that, with the DC% already so high, it can ill afford this rise and it needs to know what it can do.

But first it needs to know the exact impact this change will have on the business. It needs to know the magnitude of the problem it is dealing with.

Figure 4.3 shows the direction of the impact on each of the eight dynamic indicators. An increase in DC% will decrease GC%, DNC% and, as a result, BeGap%. Dr% will stay the same. Stock% will increase as much of the value of stock comes from the dynamic costs. Cr% will increase as we will have to pay more to our suppliers for the materials. DNA% will increase as the increase in Stock% is anticipated to be higher than the increase in Cr%. Finally, DCM% could go up or down depending on the relationship of all the figures involved. In Speciality Steels, it should go down. There will be a negative effect on cash.

So, what will happen to Speciality Steels if it cannot overcome the 5 per cent increase in dynamic costs? The eight dynamic indicators before and after the decrease in prices can be calculated using techniques from *Chapter 9: Increases in your dynamic costs* but for now we will give you the answers:

	Before	**After**	
GC%	20.00%	16.00%	Dynamic adjuster
DNC%	9.98%	5.98%	Dynamic adjuster
BeGap%	53.90%	42.38%	Calculation
Stock%	150.00%	157.50%	Dynamic look-up table
Dr%	250.00%	250.00%	No change in %
Cr%	175.00%	179.38%	Dynamic look-up table
DNA%	0.00%	3.12%	Calculation
DCM%	9.98%	2.86%	Calculation

Fig 4.3 ● **Radar chart of Speciality Steels' dynamic indicators**

Once we know the new dynamic indicators we can quickly recalculate the value
of the contribution and DNA statements:

Contribution statement

	Before	After
Income	791,543	791,543
Dynamic Costs	633,234	664,896
Gross Contribution	158,309	126,647
Static Costs	79,299	79,299
Dynamic Net Contribution	79,010	47,348

A 5 per cent increase in the dynamic costs has reduced the DNC% from 9.98
per cent to 5.98 per cent, from £79,010 to £47,348, an actual reduction of 40
per cent. And the safety of the business expressed through the breakeven gap
has decreased from 53.9 per cent to 42.38 per cent.

DNA statement

	Before	After
Income	791,543	791,543
Stock	1,187,315	1,246,680
Debtors	1,978,857	1,978,857
Creditors	1,385,200	1,419,870
Static Net Assets	1,780,972	1,805,667

The DNA statement shows that more cash is now imprisoned in the time warp. The Stock% has increased from 150 per cent to 157.5 per cent tying up £59,365 more in the time warp. There has been a compensating decrease in the SNA from the Cr%. But the Cr% is now approaching 180 per cent which is increasing the pressures on the cash. How long can we continue with such long creditor terms? For Speciality Steels, this equates to three months.

The radar chart in Fig 4.4 shows the shape of the business before and after the anticipated increase in dynamic costs. The indicators for contribution and cash are showing the strain of this change – they are shrinking fast – while the SNA strands are growing and so is the DNA%. The business is being stretched to its limits. Again this is apparent from the overall impact on the DCM%.

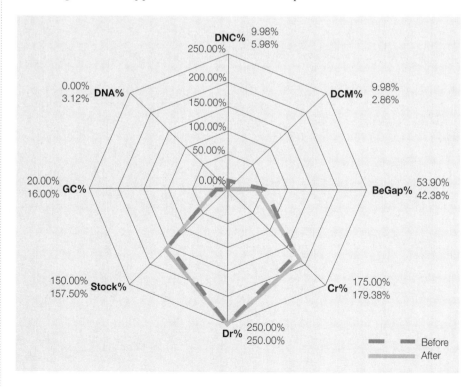

Fig 4.4 ● Speciality Steels

Speciality Steels cannot afford to cope with this increase. It must take management action. But what actions are open to it? Obviously it can look for new suppliers so that this increase is avoided. But what if this is not possible? What must the company do to get back into shape? It has three options:

Change		Appropriate action to regain DNC%
Increase in	⇒	Increase volume
dynamic	⇒	Increase price
costs	⇒	Decrease static costs

What dynamic financial management can do is to tell you the exact magnitude of these actions that is needed to get the DNC% back to its original level of 9.98 per cent.

Increase volume

The new volume required can be read from Table 9.5 (p. 228) and Speciality Steels would need to increase volume by 67 per cent. Can this be true? Let's check with the contribution statement:

	Before	After initial impact	Volume up by 67%
Income	791,543	791,543	1,331,897
Dynamic Costs	633,234	664,896	1,118,794
Gross Contribution	158,309	126,647	213,103
Static Costs	79,299	79,299	79,299
Dynamic Net Contribution	79,010	47,348	133,804

This is a huge increase in volume just to get us back to the DNC% we had before. And this is going to have an additional, and probably adverse, effect on our already challenged DCM%. Let's carry on the analysis through to the DNA statement.

	Before	After initial impact	Volume up by 67%
Income	791,543	791,543	1,331,897
Stock	1,187,315	1,246,680	2,097,738
Debtors	1,978,857	1,978,857	3,329,743
Creditors	1,385,200	1,419,870	2,389,157
Static Net Assets	1,780,972	1,805,667	3,038,325

The percentage of these indicators will not change but the value will change dramatically. This will have a knock-on effect on the DNA% and then the DCM%. So how will their indicators look if they take this option (assuming so huge an increase is possible)?

	Before	After initial impact	Increase volume by 67%	Dynamic decision maker
GC%	20.00	16.00	16.00	No change in %
DNC%	9.98	5.98	10.04	Dynamic look-up tables
BeGap%	53.90	42.38	62.75	Calculation
Stock%	150.00	157.50	157.50	No change in %
Dr%	250.00	250.00	250.00	No change in %
Cr%	175.00	179.38	179.38	No change in %
DNA%	0.00	3.12	94.40	Calculation
DCM%	9.98	2.86	(84.36)	Calculation

There are some massive assumptions the business would need to take:

- the market can support this volume increase;
- it has the capacity to supply this increase;
- it can keep the static costs at the current level;
- it can get the funding needed for this growth.

These are unlikely in the foreseeable future. It may be a long-term strategic option but it will not help the company out of its current crisis.

Increase price

This is often an unpopular option. Managers believe the customer will never accept a price increase. But think about it. This is exactly what Speciality Steels is doing. It is accepting a price increase from its suppliers. Why shouldn't its customers accept a price increase? Having accepted that a price increase to the customer may actually be possible, the problem is often determining a level of increase. Managers often pass on too high a price increase. The assumption is often simply, my costs have gone up 5 per cent therefore I need to increase my sales price by 5 per cent. This is not true. You do need to increase your sales price. Dynamic financial management can tell you by exactly how much.

With the shape of Speciality Steels, an increase in dynamic costs of 5 per cent needs only a price increase of about 4.45 per cent to regain the DNC% (*see* Table 9.6, p. 231). Again, let's see the figures:

	Before	After initial impact	Price up 40%
Income	791,543	791,543	826,767
Dynamic Costs	633,234	664,896	664,896
Gross Contribution	158,309	126,647	161,871
Static Costs	79,299	79,299	79,299
Dynamic Net Contribution	79,010	47,348	82,572

Remember, with a price increase the value of the dynamic costs will stay the same. So we have improved the GC% and the DNC% as a result of this increase.

Also remember, the lower your GC%, the higher the price increase will need to be to cope with an increase in DC%. For Speciality Steels the GC% is only 20 per cent, a very low figure, but it still only needs to pass on an increase of 4.45 per cent, not the full 5 per cent. It may not sound much, but this could make all the difference in a competitive market.

	Before	After initial impact	Price up 40%
Income	791,543	791,543	826,767
Stock	1,187,315	1,246,680	1,246,680
Debtors	1,978,857	1,978,857	2,066,918
Creditors	1,385,200	1,419,870	1,419,870
Static Net Assets	1,780,972	1,805,667	1,893,728

If the only change is price then as a value, stock and creditors will stay the same. However, this means that the Stock% and Cr% go down as a percentage of the new income value. The Dr% will stay at the same percentage of income. This means the value has gone up. As the combined result of these changes, the SNA value and therefore the DNA% will also change.

	Before	After initial impact	Price up 4.45%	Dynamic decision maker
GC%	20.00	16.00	19.58	Calculation
DNC%	9.98	5.98	9.99	Dynamic look-up tables
BeGap%	53.90	42.38	50.97	Calculation
Stock%	150.00	157.50	150.79	Calculation
Dr%	250.00	250.00	250.00	No change in %
Cr%	175.00	179.38	171.74	No change in %
DNA%	0.00	3.12	13.64	Calculation
DCM%	9.98	2.86	(3.65)	Calculation

So, an increase in price of 4.45 per cent will get the DNC% back to the original 10 per cent, but the GC% and therefore the BeGap% will still be slightly lower than before the increase in DC. Stock% and Cr% look slightly lower; the higher price should give Speciality Steels a better ability to pay. The DNA% suggests an overall increase in money tied up in the stands of the DNA but this is due to the extra potential cash coming from the Dr% due to the price increase. The DCM% is negative but this is a temporary blip as the additional money from debtors works its way through the system.

This option, therefore, looks possible. Speciality Steels needs to pass on an increase of 4.45 per cent to customers. If the price is not too sensitive in this market, and all the competitors are in the same shape, this could be feasible. But let's consider the last option, reducing the static costs.

Decrease static costs

For many businesses this is often the only option and some static costs make easy targets. The marketing or training budgets are slashed. This may help in the short term but is often disastrous in the long term. However, this option may not be possible for Speciality Steels. The static costs are already relatively low due to its earlier decision to reduce risk and keep most of the costs as dynamic costs. How much would it need to reduce these already minimal costs? The full details of how to calculate this for this, or any other business, can be found in *Part Two* (*see* Table 9.7, p. 235).

With dynamic costs at 80 per cent and static costs at about 10 per cent of income, a 5 per cent increase in DC would need a compensating decrease in SC of 40 per cent. This seems an unexpectedly large decrease so we need to see if it works:

	Before	After initial impact	SC down 40%
Income	791,543	791,543	791,543
Dynamic Costs	633,234	664,896	664,896
Gross Contribution	158,309	126,647	126,647
Static Costs	79,299	79,299	47,579
Dynamic Net Contribution	79,010	47,348	79,068

With a change in static costs, the values stay the same, down to the level of gross contribution. The subsequent decrease in static costs of 40 per cent has done the trick. The DNC% is about back to where it was before.

Speciality Steels also needs to check if there is an impact on its DNA% by looking at the strands of the DNA:

	Before	After initial impact	SC down 40%
Income	791,543	791,543	791,543
Stock	1,187,315	1,246,680	1,246,680
Debtors	1,978,857	1,978,857	1,978,857
Creditors	1,385,200	1,419,870	1,419,870
Static Net Assets	1,780,972	1,805,667	1,805,667

The strands of the DNA are not affected by changes in the static costs. So there will be no additional change in DNA% as a result of this possible action.

	Before	After initial impact	Static costs down 40%	Dynamic decision maker
GC%	20.00	16.00	16.00	Calculation
DNC%	9.98	5.98	9.98	Dynamic look-up tables
BeGap%	53.90	42.38	62.44	Calculation
Stock%	150.00	157.50	157.50	Calculation
Dr%	250.00	250.00	250.00	No change in %
Cr%	175.00	179.38	179.38	No change in %
DNA%	0.00	3.12	3.12	Calculation
DCM%	9.98	2.86	6.86	Calculation

So, an increase in DC of 5 per cent for Speciality Steels needs a compensating decrease of 40 per cent in SC – an unlikely option.

Increase in dynamic costs – a summary

We have taken you through the detail for Speciality Steels, again to prove that our techniques work. But remember, in practice you do not need to know all this detail in order to manage your business dynamically. What you do need to know is the answer – the new shape of your business – rather than the process and the proof that we have presented here.

What the managers of Speciality Steels need to know is the result of the 5 per cent increase in dynamic costs from 80 per cent to 84 per cent. This is shown clearly below:

	Before	After initial impact
GC%	20.00	16.00
DNC%	9.98	5.98
BeGap%	53.90	42.38
Stock%	150.00	157.50
Dr%	250.00	250.00
Cr%	175.00	179.38
DNA%	0.00	3.12
DCM%	9.98	2.86

Plus their possible actions to regain DNC%.

Change		Appropriate action to regain DNC%	Amount
5% increase	⮕	Increase volume	By 67.00%
in DC	⮕	Increase price	By 4.45%
	⮕	Decrease static costs	By 40.00%

What should they do? At first glance the only options for this business, given the nature of its cost structure, are to pass on the price increase to the customer or seek a new supplier at the existing cost. The managers could now calculate the impact of increasing volume by less than 67 per cent, or reducing static costs by less than the 40 per cent. But these are such large variations that it seems likely they would be spending a lot of effort for relatively little reward.

Of course, this will not be the case for all businesses. The amounts will change, depending on the shape of your business, by the size of your dynamic indicators.

It is worth repeating that this is the point of dynamic decisions. We have taken you through the process step by step. Once you are familiar with the process in *Chapter 9: Increases in your dynamic costs* you can quickly test a number of options and see the impact on the eight dynamic indicators. No need for a detailed budget of profit, balance sheet and cash flow.

Let us move on to the next case study, this time looking at an organization faced with a positive choice – the freedom it will have if it can reduce the percentage of its static costs.

Case study

Subject SC decrease
Industry sector Charitable
Company name KinderAid

(This is based on Chapter 12: Decreases in your static costs)

We need to know the existing contribution statement, DNA statement and eight dynamic indicators for the business called KinderAid.

Contribution statement

	€
Income	26,986
Dynamic Costs	8,096
Gross Contribution	18,890
Static Costs	17,541
DNC	1,349

DNA statement

	€
Income	26,986
Stock	0
Debtors	26,986
Creditors	13,493
Static Net Assets	13,493

Eight dynamic indicators

	%
GC%	70.00
DNC%	5.00
BeGap%	7.14
Stock%	0.00
Dr%	100.00
Cr%	50.00
DNA%	0.00
DCM%	5.00

The charity, based in Germany, has traditionally kept its headquarters in the city centre. This gave it a prestigious address and kept it near to the places where fund-raising events were held. But the world of the charitable institution has changed. Fund raising tends to be by direct appeal, either through the post or by telephone. The prestigious headquarters no longer serve their purpose. The charity is therefore considering a move to the suburbs, to a small business park. The savings are substantial and are anticipated to reduce the static costs by 15 per cent.

There is still some resistance to this option. Many of the workers for the charity like the image of a city centre address and many live in the city. The charity needs to put forward a case for the move. Additional DNC% will not be a motivator. Indeed, you may wonder why there is any DNC% if this is a charity.

History has shown that the organization needs to keep some funds in the business for two reasons: first, in case fund raising in the next year is less successful, this will give it a buffer, and second, even a charity needs to invest in new equipment. The change in charitable donations has already resulted in the investment in a new telephone system. The charity needs to ensure it has the systems in place to retain its effectiveness in raising money.

However, a DNC% of 5 per cent is considered adequate for these purposes. If reducing the static costs increases this figure, the management need to say what they are going to do with this additional money. Dynamic financial management will give them the information they need to produce this report.

First KinderAid needs to know the initial impact of the static cost reduction on the radar chart – the shape of the business – assuming that nothing else happens (*see* Fig 4.5). This radar chart shows that the strands of the DNA will not change as static cost does not usually impact on these. GC% will not change as the dynamic costs are unaffected at the moment, but DNC% and BeGap% will increase. As a result the DCM% should also increase – real cash to spend on new projects.

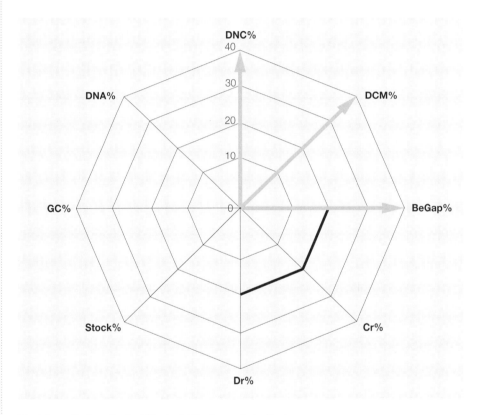

Fig 4.5 ● **Radar chart of KinderAid's dynamic indicators**

Again, dynamic financial management can tell you more than this. It can tell you the actual magnitude of *all* these changes.

What will happen to KinderAid if it achieves its 15 per cent reduction in static costs? The eight dynamic indicators before and after the decrease in static costs are:

	Before	After	Dynamic decision maker
GC%	70.00%	70.00%	No change in %
DNC%	5.00%	14.75%	Dynamic look-up table
BeGap%	7.14%	21.07%	Calculation
Stock%	0.00%	0.00%	No change in %
Dr%	100.00%	100.00%	No change in %
Cr%	50.00%	50.00%	No change in %
DNA%	0.00%	0.00%	No change in %
DCM%	5.00%	14.75%	Calculation

Once we know the new dynamic indicators we can quickly recalculate the value of the contribution and DNA statements.

Contribution statement

	Before	After
Income	26,986	26,986
Dynamic Costs	8,096	8,096
Gross Contribution	18,890	18,890
Static Costs	17,541	14,910
Dynamic Net Contribution	1,349	3,980

A 15 per cent decrease in the static costs has increased the DNC% to 14.75 per cent from the targeted 5 per cent. This increase is not acceptable in this charity, so the managers need to say what they are going to do with the extra funds. However, one benefit is the safety factor in this business expressed through its BeGap%, which has increased substantially.

Before going on to look at what the managers can do, it would normally be appropriate to look at the DNA statement as well.

DNA statement

	Before	After
Income	26,986	26,986
Stock	0	0
Debtors	26,986	26,986
Creditors	13,493	13,493
Static Net Assets	13,493	13,493

The nature of this change has no impact (so far) on the DNA statement. This can be shown in the radar chart looking at the shape of the business before and after the anticipated decrease in static costs (*see* Fig 4.6). This is not a very exciting radar as the only changes are in DNC%, BeGap% and DCM%. However, these are very important indicators for this type of business.

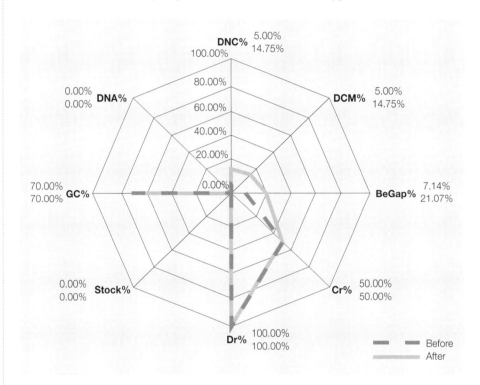

Fig 4.6 ● KinderAid

What can KinderAid propose to support its move to the suburbs? Again it has three options:

Change		Appropriate action to retain DNC%
Decrease in	⏩	Decrease volume
static costs	⏩	Decrease price
	⏩	Increase dynamic costs

What do each of these mean in a charity? A decrease in volume suggests a decrease in the level of activity of the charity. That means it could now do less and still make the same DNC% – not a sound argument for a charity. What about a reduction in price? For a charity this means the average donation has decreased. This is not a strategy for the charity, but using it as part of the report would allow it to show how the business could continue with the same level of activity even if the level of donations decreased.

The final option, increasing dynamic costs, could be the thrust of the report. The charity could employ more active charity workers and therefore provide more of a service out of the savings made in the static costs. But how much more? A dynamic financial management analysis of the charity will provide the answer. For this charity we will discard the decrease in volume and concentrate on the decrease in price or the increase in dynamic costs.

Decrease price

Charities are dependent on their level of charitable donations. When the economy is less buoyant, the average value of donations may fall. If KinderAid has a lower level of static costs it may be more able to cope with any downturn. The static cost change it is predicting is a decrease of 15 per cent. Does this mean KinderAid could cope with a decrease in donations of 15 per cent? No!

With static costs currently at 65 per cent and a proposed decrease of 15 per cent, the actual price decrease it can cope with is 10.26 per cent. This can be checked following the information in *Chapter 12: Decreases in your static costs* (*see* Table 12.2, p. 291). Let's see if it works:

	Before	After initial impact	Price down 10.26%
Income	26,986	26,986	24,226
Dynamic Costs	8,096	8,096	8,096
Gross Contribution	18,890	18,890	16,130
Static Costs	17,541	14,910	14,910
Dynamic Net Contribution	1,349	3,980	1,220

So the charity could now experience a 10.26 per cent downturn in donations and still provide the full level of service while retaining a DNC% of 5 per cent towards future investment. There will also be a marginal impact on the DNA. There is no stock, and the creditor value will not be affected. However, as the income, the anchor of our dynamic indicators, has fallen, the Cr% will change. On the other hand, the Dr% will remain the same, but because the income has changed, the value of this figure will change accordingly:

	Before	After initial impact	Price down 10.26%
Income	26,986	26,986	24,226
Stock	0	0	0
Debtors	26,986	26,986	24,226
Creditors	13,493	13,493	13,493
Static Net Assets	13,493	13,493	10,733

As a result the SNA has actually fallen and there will be an impact on the DNA% and the DCM%. So what do the dynamic indicators for KinderAid look like now?

	Before	After initial impact	Price down 10.26%	
GC%	70.00	70.00	66.58	Calculation
DNC%	5.00	14.75	5.04	Dynamic look-up tables
BeGap%	7.14	21.07	7.57	Calculation
Stock%	0.00	0.00	0.00	Calculation
Dr%	100.00	100.00	100.00	No change in %
Cr%	50.00	50.00	55.70	Calculation
DNA%	0	0	(11.40)	Calculation
DCM%	5.00	14.75	16.44	Calculation

One positive impact of lower donations is lower debtors and this shows its impact on the DNA%. But, as with all changes in price, treat this figure with caution. It reflects the fact that there is now money that the charity will never receive. However, this does seem to give the charity a safety factor. It can cope with a decrease in donations of more than 10 per cent and still fulfil its obligations.

But let us consider the other option, increasing the level of service, i.e. the dynamic costs.

Increase dynamic costs

If one set of costs go down, it is often the case that you can move the costs into another category. We often know the value of the increase in our dynamic costs but we also need to know what percentage this represents so that we can again start to examine the changed shape of our business.

KinderAid, with a current SC% of 65 per cent and a proposed decrease of 15 per cent, would be able to increase its investment in dynamic costs. The new DC% could be increased by about 33 per cent from its current DC% of 30 per cent to around 40 per cent.

	Before	After initial impact	DC up 33%
Income	26,986	26,986	26,986
Dynamic Costs	8,096	8,096	10,794
Gross Contribution	18,890	18,890	16,192
Static Costs	17,541	14,910	14,910
Dynamic Net Contribution	1,349	3,980	1,282

This is an estimate from Table 12.3 (p. 294) but for dynamic financial management it is close enough. KinderAid now really does have a proposal to put forward. It would now be able to spend 40 per cent of all its funds raised on direct provision of aid, as opposed to 30 per cent if it stays in its premises. A worthwhile and ethical goal for any charity!

Let us just look at the new shape of the business, first looking at the DNA statement and then the eight dynamic indicators:

	Before	After initial impact	DC up 33%
Income	26,986	26,986	26,986
Stock	0	0	0
Debtors	26,986	26,986	26,986
Creditors	13,493	13,493	15,719
Static Net Assets	13,493	13,493	11,267

It is possible that Cr% may rise as a result of the change in DC%, although in reality KinderAid will probably spend the money on wages. But we will stick with the full analysis.

	Before	After initial impact	DC up 33%	
GC%	70.00	70.00	60.00	Calculation
DNC%	5.00	14.75	4.75	Dynamic look-up tables
BeGap%	7.14	21.07	7.92	Calculation
Stock%	0.00	0.00	0.00	Calculation
Dr%	100.00	100.00	100.00	No change in %
Cr%	50.00	50.00	58.25	Dynamic look-up tables
DNA%	0	0	(8.25)	Calculation
DCM%	5.00	14.75	13.00	Calculation

It would seem that the report should emphasize the benefit of the move to the new premises in terms of the increased level of direct provision in the first instance, and also the ability to cope with future downturns in the economy and the average value of donations.

Or maybe the charity can think creatively. May be a smaller city centre presence can be maintained with an associated overall decrease in static costs. The issue is open to negotiation. Each option can be evaluated in terms of the financial results and the softer issues of presence and the needs of the benefactors of the charity.

Case study

Subject Increase in DNC%
Industry sector Manufacturing subsidiary
Company name Elchip

The final case to consider is, perhaps, another familiar situation. Business is becoming even more competitive. Many businesses find they cannot survive unless they continue to improve their performance. And for many, rightly or wrongly, improved performance usually means more contribution – in dynamic financial management terms, improving your DNC%. But how can businesses achieve this? There are, in fact, only four options:

Change		Appropriate action to retain DNC%
Increase in	➠	Increase volume
DNC%	➠	Increase price
	➠	Decrease dynamic costs
	➠	Decrease static costs

In *Part Two*, dynamic financial management will tell you by exactly how much each of these will need to change in your business to meet a new DNC% target. It will also show you the impact of these changes on all the eight dynamic indicators in your business. The full method will be explored in *Chapter 13: Meeting more demanding DNC% targets* and these techniques have been used to look at the following case study.

Elchip Ltd is a division of Northern Circuits which manufactures circuits in the north-east of England. The division is a profit centre within the group and sells both within the group and to other worldwide customers. Group sales account for 60 per cent of the annual sales figure and the existing annual contribution statement, DNA statement and eight dynamic indicators for the business are shown below.

Contribution statement

	£000s
Income	23,876
Dynamic Costs	11,938
Gross Contribution	11,938
Static Costs	7,163
DNC	4,775

DNA statement

	£000s
Income	23,876
Stock	4,775
Debtors	3,581
Creditors	4,178
Static Net Assets	4,178

Eight dynamic indicators

	%
GC%	50.00
DNC%	20.00
BeGap%	40.00
Stock%	20.00
Dr%	15.00
Cr%	17.50
DNA%	0.00
DCM%	20.00

The DNC% for Elchip is its contribution to the head office. Many of its administration services are provided centrally. In order to improve the provision of those central services Northern Circuits needs to increase the contribution it receives from its subsidiary companies from the current 20 per cent to a new target of 25 per cent. For Elchip this means increasing its DNC by 25 per cent.

Elchip has been asked to provide a plan for the next financial year to show how it will achieve this new target and it needs to consider the best of the four options listed above. We will look at each of these in turn.

Increase price

As Elchip is a profit centre and has a product to sell, there is always the option of increasing the selling price. The market is not too price sensitive but the biggest restriction for Elchip is the internal price it can charge. Head office will not get any real benefit if the increased income for this division is simply an increased cost for another division.

Nevertheless, Elchip needs to know its alternatives. What price increase would be needed to reach the new target DNC% of 25 per cent? For this alternative all you need to know is the two figures mentioned – your current DNC% and the new, targeted DNC%. These figures are 20 per cent and 25 per cent respectively for Elchip. In *Chapter 13: Meeting ever more demanding DNC% targets* a simple dynamic formula will show that the price increase needed is 6.67 per cent (*see* Table 13.2, pp. 305–6). Let's see if it works:

	Before	Price up 6.67%
Income	23,876	25,469
Dynamic Costs	11,938	11,938
Gross Contribution	11,938	13,531
Static Costs	7,163	7,163
Dynamic Net Contribution	4,775	6,368
DNC%	20.00%	25.00%

Although Elchip has had an increase in this targeted DNC% of 25 per cent (5 per cent increase divided by the original DNC% of 20 per cent), the price increase needed to reach the target is only 6.67 per cent. But this may still be too much for the business to bear.

There will also be an impact on the DNA as the Debtor value will increase; the Dr% will not change but every customer now owes more due to the price increase. There will be no change in the value of the stock or the creditors as there is no change in the costs. However, as the income, the anchor of our dynamic indicators, has increased, the Stock% and the Cr% will decrease.

	Before	Price up 6.67%
Income	23,876	25,469
Stock	4,775	4,775
Debtors	3,581	3,820
Creditors	4,178	4,178
Static Net Assets	4,178	4,417

As a result the SNA has increased and there will, therefore, be an impact on the DNA% and the DCM%. So what do the dynamic indicators for Elchip look like now?

	Before	Price up 6.67%	
GC%	50.00%	53.13%	Calculation
DNC%	20.00%	25.00%	Targeted
BeGap%	40.00%	47.05%	Calculation
Stock%	20.00%	18.75%	Calculation
Dr%	15.00%	15.00%	No change in %
Cr%	17.50%	16.40%	Calculation
DNA%	0.00%	0.94%	Calculation
DCM%	20.00%	24.06%	Calculation

The price increase is attractive to the managers of Elchip but may not be acceptable to head office or, indeed, may price the company out of the wider market. Looking at this through the radar chart we can see the changes are all positive and the business has stretched as a result (*see* Fig 4.7). It is not surprising it would find this attractive. But as head office is unlikely to accept this alternative, Elchip needs to examine the feasibility of the other three options – volume up, DC down or SC down.

Increase volume

As with any increase in volume, the division will benefit from becoming more effective – as long as it can keep its static costs static. This would probably be the preferred option from head office as its division would now be larger and more effective. However, there are again the constraints of the plans of the other businesses in the group. As they account for 60 per cent of the sales, an increase

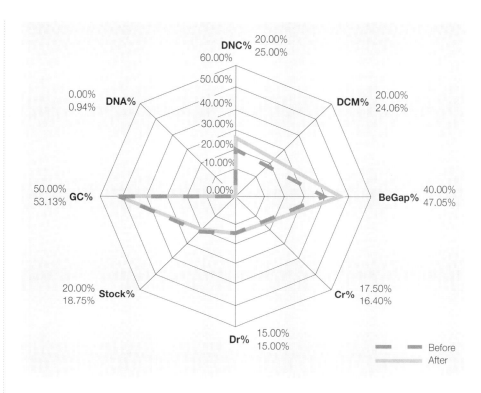

Fig 4.7 ● Elchip – price increase for new DNC%

in volume would seem to require the sister companies to grow as well. But by how much? Again, Table 13.1 (p. 300) will take you through the detail of the process for working out your own volume increase needed, and we have used this information to produce the summarized information for Elchip. For Elchip the BeGap% is 40 per cent and the percentage increase required in DNC% is 25 per cent, an increase from 20 per cent to 25 per cent. Table 13.1 shows Elchip would require a volume increase of 20 per cent. Let's see if it works:

	Before	Volume up 20%
Income	23,876	28,651
Dynamic Costs	11,938	14,326
Gross Contribution	11,938	14,325
Static Costs	7,163	7,163
Dynamic Net Contribution	4,775	7,162
DNC%	20.00%	25.00%

A volume increase of 20 per cent would seem to be very challenging, especially when many of the sales are within the group. It would also demand a fairly large investment in the strands of the DNA. All the percentages should stay the same but the value would need to increase to cope with the rise:

	Before	Volume up 20%
Income	23,876	28,651
Stock	4,775	5,730
Debtors	3,581	4,298
Creditors	4,178	5,014
Static Net Assets	4,178	5,014

As a result the SNA has increased significantly and there will, therefore, be an impact on the DNA% and the DCM%. So what do the dynamic indicators for Elchip look like now?

	Before	Volume up 20%	
GC%	50.00%	50.00%	No change in %
DNC%	20.00%	25.00%	Targeted
BeGap%	40.00%	50.00%	Calculation
Stock%	20.00%	20.00%	Calculation
Dr%	15.00%	15.00%	No change in %
Cr%	17.50%	17.50%	Calculation
DNA%	0.00%	2.92%	Calculation
DCM%	20.00%	22.08%	Calculation

This growth will require an investment in the strands of the DNA to a tune of 2.92 per cent of the annual income of Elchip. The DCM% over the whole year is still positive but has been dented. The effects can be seen more visually on the radar chart in Fig 4.8. The bottom half of the radar has not moved, but the three main dynamic indicators, DNC%, DNA% and DCM%, have all been affected.

The BeGap% has perhaps shown the greatest movement and makes us think about the realism of this alternative. Not only would a 20 per cent increase in volume be difficult to achieve but it would seem to be an almost impossible target to achieve and still maintain the static costs at their current level. It would suggest there is a lot of slack in the system at the moment if a business could do this.

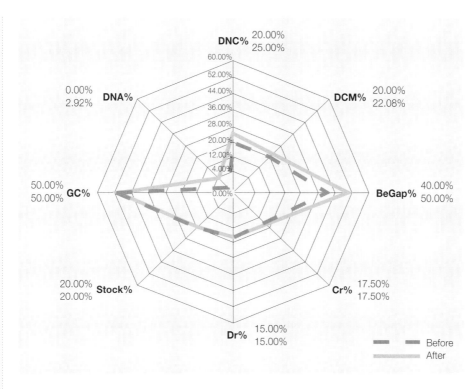

Fig 4.8 ● **Elchip – volume increase for new DNC%**

Decrease dynamic costs

For this option the managers of Elchip need to know one simple relationship. The percentage point increase in the DNC% needs to be matched by the same percentage point decrease in the DC%. What do we mean by a percentage point increase or decrease? You need to use the following formula:

New Percentage = Current Percentage – Percentage Point Increase or Decrease

So for Elchip the percentage point increase in DNC% is:

   25% – 20% = 5% point increase

This means the DC% needs to decrease by 5 percentage points:

   New DC% = 50% – 5% = 45%

i.e. we need to reduce our DC% to 45 per cent. Let's see if this works:

	Before	**DC down 10%**
Income	23,876	23,876
Dynamic Costs	11,938	10,744
Gross Contribution	11,938	13,132
Static Costs	7,163	7,163
Dynamic Net Contribution	4,775	5,969
DNC%	20.00%	25.00%

If we reduce our DC% by 5 percentage points to 45 per cent this represents a decrease in DC of:

DC reduction =   5%/50%

DC reduction =   10%

Our dynamic costs need to be 10 per cent less than the current level. If we can achieve this we should also see significant benefits in our DNC% and DCM%. Using *Chapter 10: Decreases in your dynamic costs*, we would be able to see the impact of this change on Stock% and Cr%. The Dr% and value in this option should remain the same.

	Before	**DC down 10%**
Income	23,876	23,876
Stock	4,775	4,298
Debtors	3,581	3,581
Creditors	4,178	4,011
Static Net Assets	4,178	3,868

There has been a significant decrease in the value of the SNA and this will shine through in the DNA% and DCM% in the eight dynamic indicators below:

	Before	DC down 10%	
GC%	50.00%	55.00%	Table and adjuster
DNC%	20.00%	25.00%	Targeted
BeGap%	40.00%	45.45%	Calculation
Stock%	20.00%	18.00%	Calculation
Dr%	15.00%	15.00%	No change in %
Cr%	17.50%	16.80%	Calculation
DNA%	0.00%	(1.30)%	Calculation
DCM%	20.00%	26.30%	Calculation

Remember, Elchip is looking at an annual budget. A 1.3 per cent movement in DNA% may seem small as a percentage of annual sales but the value this represents in real cash is significant.

Figure 4.9 emphasizes the possibilities of this option. The business is growing in its indicators of contribution but shrinking in its indicators of DNA. Head office will certainly be favouring this proposal. But can it be achieved? Can Elchip's production process be more efficient – 10 per cent more efficient?

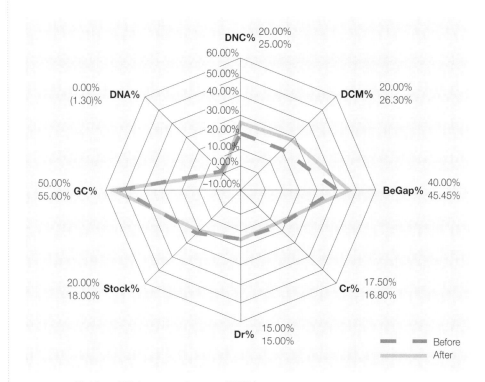

Fig 4.9 ● Elchip – DC decrease for new DNC%

The final choice looks at how effective it can be, and with some of the administrative resources provided by head office maybe this is an area where Elchip can begin to negotiate.

Decrease static costs

For this option the managers of Elchip again need to use the one simple relationship. The percentage point increase in the DNC% needs to be matched by the same percentage point decrease in the SC%. What do we mean by a percentage point increase or decrease? You need to use the following formula:

New Percentage = Current Percentage – Percentage Point Increase or Decrease

So for Elchip the percentage point increase in DNC% is:

New SC% = 30% – 5% = 25%

This means the SC% needs to decrease by 5 percentage points:

New Percentage – 30% = (5%)

i.e. we need to reduce our SC% to 25 per cent. Let's see if this works:

	Before	SC% down to 20%
Income	23,876	23,876
Dynamic Costs	11,938	11,938
Gross Contribution	11,938	11,938
Static Costs	7,163	5,969
Dynamic Net Contribution	4,775	5,969
DNC%	20.00%	25.00%

This is a 20 per cent decrease in Elchip's static costs.

For this type of change in static costs, for most businesses the normal assumption is that it has no impact on the strands of the DNA. And that is the case for Elchip. Therefore there will be no change in the DNA%. However, the DCM% will still show the benefit of the improvement in the DNC%. The eight dynamic indicators will be:

	Before	SC down 20%	
GC%	50.00%	50.00%	Table and adjuster
DNC%	20.00%	25.00%	Targeted
BeGap%	40.00%	50.00%	Calculation
Stock%	20.00%	20.00%	Calculation
Dr%	15.00%	15.00%	No change in %
Cr%	17.50%	17.50%	Calculation
DNA%	0.00%	0.00%	Calculation
DCM%	20.00%	25.00%	Calculation

Look at the BeGap% for this option. It increases to 50 per cent, better than reducing the DC%. But the negative comparison here is in the DCM%. The DC% option releases cash from the time warp as well as increasing DNC%. The SC% option reduces risk as well as increasing DNC%.

Figure 4.10 shows how this would look on the radar chart. Again everything is very positive. But this option gives the managers of Elchip the ability to negotiate with head office. Reducing DC% means that a change imposed by head office has to be managed internally. But head office says it needs the increase in DNC% to provide a better service – to make the group more effective. Maybe some services Elchip has had to provide for itself can now be provided by head office, coming out of its budget. As with a customer/supplier arrangement, Elchip should negotiate with head office for an improved service level to cover its effective 'price increase' for the provision of these services.

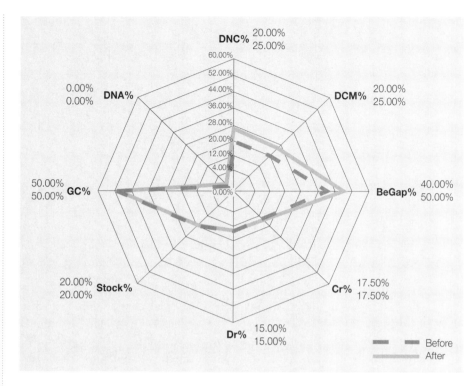

Fig 4.10 ● Elchip – SC decrease for new DNC%

Summary

Dynamic decisions are the key to managing tomorrow today. In this chapter, we have approached dynamic decisions in two ways. First, we have given you some quick and effective answers to commonly asked questions which dynamic managers carry around in their heads. Second, we have introduced a sophisticated approach to understanding the financial consequences of decisions and shown that dynamic financial management has the knowledge to predict the magnitude of the response you need to make to keep your business in shape.

chapter 5

You are not alone

Introduction

You are certainly not alone when it comes to evaluating your business. Banks, accountants, shareholders, family – there are many views taken of what shape your business is in.

This chapter will review the various stakeholders in your business and take their point of view for a while. What do they look for, what is important to them, and if it is so important shouldn't you maintain these indicators anyway?

Who is 'out there'?

It is very rare, in any type of organization, that you can always take the decisions you want to take. Business is a fine balancing act – keeping the business running the way you want it and keeping other stakeholders in your business happy. But who are these stakeholders and why should they be looking at your business in a different way to you? Surely if you are managing dynamically, producing good results, they should be happy as well! Unfortunately not. Different stakeholders measure you by different criteria. As Fig 5.1 shows, a manager can be seen as being at the hub of the wheel. Each of the stakeholders will have different views about you and your business, as outlined in Table 5.1.

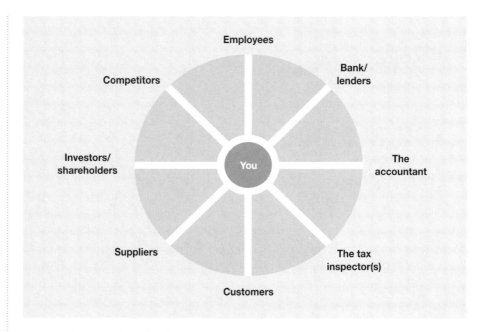

Fig 5.1 ● Interested parties in a business

So which stakeholder(s) does dynamic financial management aim at? It can aim at them all, but we have so far concentrated on the dynamic indicators for *you*. You may be the owner/manager of a very small firm, part of the management team of a medium-sized firm, or an operational manager in a larger firm. You may work in the public sector or in a charitable organization. You may be in manufacturing, the service industry or in retail. Wherever you are, dynamic financial management will help you keep your finger on the pulse of the business and manage tomorrow today.

We are helping people who make and implement the day-to-day decisions inside an organization. But we realize that operational decisions are going to impact on the contentment of the other stakeholders. Using dynamic financial management should lead a business towards sustained and manageable growth – dynamic growth – if that is what the strategic vision desires.

Some of these stakeholders can be very important to your business. In this chapter we shall look at some of the more influential ones and consider what dynamic financial management tells them, what dynamic financial management techniques could tell them, and what information should come from other sources.

Table 5.1 ● What your business means to different people

The stakeholder	Why they are interested in your business	
The bank/lenders	● hold your account ● overdraft ● factoring ● loans ● credit facilities	● reputation ● personal career ● future of the company ● payment of loans ● interest payments
The accountant	● an adviser ● keeps the books ● the auditor	● his/her reputation ● personal career ● can give recommendations
The tax inspector(s)	● accuracy of information ● payment of taxes	● taxable profits
Customers/debtors	● price of the product ● quality of the product ● life of the product ● future of the company	● guarantees ● repeat purchases ● credit terms ● image/delivery
Suppliers/creditors	● your ability to pay ● quantity of orders ● frequency of orders	● payment terms ● rejections ● future of the company
Investors/ shareholders	● return on investment ● profits ● balance sheet	● future of the company ● dividends paid ● control
Competitors	● price of product ● quality of product ● life of product ● future of company	● guarantees ● repeat purchases ● credit terms
Other employees	● price of product ● quality of product ● life of product ● future of company ● performance of their part of the business	● guarantees ● repeat purchases ● credit terms ● working conditions
YOU!	Your dynamic indicators: ● the radar chart ● the dynamic breakeven graph ● the dynamic cash graph	Long-term decisions: ● investment ● funding ● accounting policies ● tax minimization

We will consider using 'spin-off' radar charts as a technique for communicating performance to other stakeholders. You have identified the dynamic indicators that are appropriate to you; there will be different stakeholder indicators that can be added or substituted on the spin-off radar chart. The tools of dynamic financial management are universal, only the specific dynamic indicators may change. So let us look at some of these stakeholders.

You

This may seem a strange place to start. We have just said that dynamic financial management is aimed at you. However, we do not claim that it covers every aspect of your business. It deals with the dynamic bit, the bits that change on a day-to-day basis, the bits you are required to keep continuously under your control, the operational bits of your business.

But there are other things you need to consider if you also want to develop the business on a more strategic basis:

● cash flow forecasting

● funding requirements

● investment decisions

● tax minimization

● impact of strategic, long-term decisions.

Many of the dynamic techniques, and certainly the philosophy we adopt to financial management, can be used to answer some of these issues. But these will be the subject of a later book. For now you simply need to be aware of what is *not* covered.

Perhaps the most important of these is the cash flow forecast. We have restricted ourselves to dynamic indicators, and the dynamic indicator of cash is DCM%. We do not claim that this will be the total cash flow movement in your business. It is only the cash movement that results from your DNC% and the DNA%. We have purposefully excluded some things as they are typically static payments and so are not part of a dynamic analysis. For example, we have excluded payments to 'other creditors'. In the UK this would include the VAT payments, the tax payments and payments of dividends. To complete your cash flow forecast you must consider how you will record and manage these.

The bank manager

The bank manager has specific information requirements from your business. However, he is interested in many of the indicators from your dynamic analysis. In Table 5.1 we said the bank manager was interested in your business because:

- hold your account
- overdraft
- factoring
- loans
- credit facilities
- reputation
- personal career
- future of the company
- payment of loans
- interest payments

This may point to the real area of concern – whether you can repay the bank. The bank measures this in two main ways:

1 Liquidity – your ability to pay your creditors on time.
2 Gearing – the way your business is funded, by loans or money from your shareholders.

We will delve into neither of these in this book. This is one stakeholder who might benefit from a modified radar. We suggest you modify it in two ways. First, we feel this radar chart should be produced historically after the management accounts have been prepared. This is because the banks need a higher level of accountancy accuracy than you need to run the business on a day-to-day basis. Indeed, some bank managers only want to see information that has come from the audited annual accounts – not the most dynamic and up-to-date piece of information, but they can feel assured that the figures have been checked by an independent third party.

Second, the bank may prefer you to substitute DNA% and DCM%, with OtherCr% and net working assets % (Stock% + Dr% – Cr% – OtherCr%). These indicators would help in its analysis of short-term liquidity and will fit within its own internal system of measurement and monitoring of your performance.

DNA% and DCM% are phenomena unique to dynamic financial management. Bank managers, with a more traditional approach to finance, may not immediately appreciate the relevance of these for the decisions they may make about your business. Most bank managers are also taught the relevance and significance of the breakeven calculation. Some may even be familiar with the dynamic breakeven graph. We would suggest that this be included in any information you need to supply to the bank. However, yet again, there may be a different emphasis with regard to time. Banks often like to see the historic performance over a number of years. Quarterly results for the past two or three years with forecasts for the next two or three years may be a more appropriate format for the dynamic breakeven graph you present to the bank.

The dynamic cash graph is another phenomenon unique to dynamic financial management. It is designed to help you manage the cash inside your business. The bank manager may need a traditional cash flow forecast to help him appreciate your understanding of your longer term funding requirements and your gearing.

The accountant

Accountants come in a number of shapes and forms – the accountant employed by your company (the internal accountant), an accountant used by the business to produce financial information for the business, and the auditors. In this section we are not concerned with the auditors. They have an annual and specialized job and need to ensure their work and accounts presentations conform to the audit and accounting standards of the country in which you operate.

We are concerned with accountants – internal or external – who are paid to produce financial information to help you manage your business. In larger companies the influential stakeholders for financial information are often the internal accountants. In some organizations this can often feel like a case of the tail wagging the dog. Information is traditionally produced in a way that lets the accountants interpret how the business is performing financially. It is often slow to prepare and your meetings with the accountants are concerned with a detailed analysis of the history – usually focusing on the bad parts.

The external accountant – often the only source of financial expertise available to smaller business – is geared towards producing annual, statutory accounts. Even those producing monthly or quarterly information for their clients often continue to produce it in a form more suitable for the shareholders – the stakeholder for whom the annual audited accounts are produced.

You now have a strong financial view of your business that the accountant has to appreciate. He needs to appreciate your dynamic view of the business but you also need to understand his point of view. In Table 5.1 we said why the accountants were interested in your business:

- an adviser
- keeps the books
- the auditor
- his/her reputation
- personal career
- can give recommendations

Accountancy training is long and arduous. It focuses on precision and has developed complex systems of checks and balances. An accountant's reputation is often developed from the accuracy of the information they produce. Dynamic financial management goes against the grain – we are talking about 80:20 financial information, information good enough and quick enough to keep your finger on the pulse of the business.

Dynamic financial management excludes the following static measures of your business:

- full balance sheet analysis;
- other creditors or special provisions;
- depreciation is assumed to be constant;
- stock valuation is not audited;
- other operating income, extraordinary and exceptional items are excluded;
- deferred tax;
- directors' loans (to or from the business).

Some of these static measures may need to be included in information for other stakeholders.

Working with your accountant is vital. We have talked about targets, gaps and decision making and avoiding overreaction, not responding to temporary blips. What dynamic financial management needs is good financial systems in place to provide timely information – good systems and a good book-keeper are the prerequisites. More of this in the next chapter.

But you can probably see the worries your accountant is going to have. Indeed, the language and techniques of dynamic financial management will be unfamiliar to most accountants. They may feel their expertise is being challenged. That is not the case. Dynamic financial management does not replace traditional financial statements, it simply changes the emphasis on when and how financial information is produced. In fact, an accountant may be delighted to be told there is less panic for the monthly or quarterly accounts because you have today's dynamic indicators from which to manage tomorrow.

Working together, you can interpret the changing shape of the business. Your accountant can then drill down into the financial detail to find out where the management actions and possible business benefits could be taken most effectively.

If, up to now, you have relied solely on reports from external accountants you may feel it would be better to simply employ a good book-keeper and produce your own dynamic indicators. These would then be available on a more frequent basis than you currently receive detailed information from the external accountant. This will allow you to recognize the need to call on your external accountant for specialist advice when you need it. You can now use your accountant in a much more dynamic way, that really adds value to your business.

Other employees

The dynamic indicators we have looked at so far reflect the business as a whole, or for larger companies, a department as a whole. Within that business or department there may be a number of managers who manage specific parts of the business and may need more detailed information on their part of the business. The deeper you get inside the organization, the closer you are to where decisions are made that really impact on your dynamic indicators. What you really need are spin-off radar charts.

This is easier to explain looking at a number of examples. Let us consider a production manager. Despite being in production and not sales, income is still the anchor point for the radar. After all, the level of production activity should correspond to the level of income-generating activity. If not, the business is out of balance. But the production manager may not be interested in all the dynamic indicators used by the business. For example, they may have no control over the Dr%, so showing this on their radar would be seen as superfluous. However, they may be passionately interested in Stock%. In order to better manage the figure for the business as a whole they may need this broken down into more detail, e.g. split between raw material, work in progress, and finished goods. The thing that you must ensure is that these are not produced from a totally different system to the one used to produce the business Stock% – the spin-off radar chart and the business radar chart need to be synchronized. Again, more of this in the next chapter. The result here may be that the radar chart for the production manager has ten arms rather than the eight we have used for the business as a whole.

Another example might be the sales manager. They are interested in breaking down that income figure into its component parts, for example by sales by region. They are interested only in the dynamic indicators of contribution plus the Dr% – their impact on the DNA% and the DCM%. They may be interested in the movement in the Dr% so they can see exactly what impact they have had on the DCM%. Sales might, therefore, end up with a number of radar charts but with only five dynamic indicators on each. Again, these must spin off from the business radar chart.

Both these managers will also be interested in the company radar chart as they will be able to see what impact their decisions have had on the overall shape of the business.

So the strength of dynamic financial management – its speed, its unique terminology and its visual impact – can be maintained throughout the organization.

The tax inspector

Another, often over-influential stakeholder in many smaller businesses has been the tax inspector, especially the one concerned with corporation tax. Many business owners become obsessed with making decisions simply to reduce their tax burden. These may or may not be the right decisions; however the logic behind them is often flawed. Information is often prepared with the annual tax return in mind, which may not be the best format for management decisions. We are not advocating you ignore the tax implications of running a business, simply that decisions that are annual, or at best irregular, be treated as such. Remember, you've got to earn it to pay it and dynamic financial management could mean you earn even more of it.

Investors and shareholders

In large businesses these stakeholders – who are not normally actively involved in or reliant on income from the business – are well catered for by the annual, audited accounts. These are prepared for them and it is the role of the auditor to protect the interests of the shareholders.

In smaller businesses, investors and shareholders may need to be managed more actively. They may have representation on the board of directors or may carry influential voting rights. In not-for-profit organizations the investor can be a benefactor who needs to feel comfortable about how their donations are being used. For this discussion we will assume these investors and shareholders are influential but not part of the management of the business.

It would not seem appropriate to bombard these people with the day-to-day detail of dynamic financial management. You may even want to keep some of this to yourself. Information should be provided at board meetings and one thing to remember is that many investors may not be trained in finance. Using the visual imagery of dynamic financial management, you could give a story about the business performance since your last meeting. Investors are said to be most impressed by the quality of management and this should give them the confidence they need in your ability to manage the business successfully.

However, investors are also likely to require more information about what you have used your DNC for. How much do you propose to pay to them as a dividend? How much cash have you released from the time warp for the internal funding of growth? How much new cash do you need in the business to meet your plans for the future? More traditional financial information will be needed to support your dynamic indicators.

Other dynamic indicators

As we have said, the eight dynamic indicators are a core to the success of most businesses. There are clearly more potential dynamic indicators specific to your business or other stakeholder views. What could these be? We cannot possibly give you the complete list of dynamic indicators that will describe the shape of your business. However, we can offer suggestions on what may be appropriate:

- orders
- loans
- interest
- average income per project
- 'key costs', e.g. salaries in a service business
- average income per customer
- average income per order
- fixed asset value
- retained profit
- production
- service provision.

Remember, to make these dynamic you must be able to express them as a percentage of the income.

How do you decide which ones are right for you?

To some extent you may have to rely on trial and error: every journey begins with the first step. However, there are a number of things that you need to consider on this journey. To measure something you must be able to collect that information and most importantly, within the time frames demanded by a dynamic analysis of your business. Conversely, if you firmly believe something to be a dynamic indicator in your business and you cannot currently collect that information, you must put systems in place to enable you to capture that information.

chapter 6

Making it happen

Introduction

All of the hard work learning the tools and techniques of dynamic financial management is over, all that's left for you to do is to make it happen! To achieve this, we will briefly walk through five steps that will guide you through an implementation plan to introduce dynamic financial management into your business.

- Step 1: Identifying your dynamic indicators
  - choosing and creating appropriate dynamic indicators
  - the relevance of our eight dynamic indicators
  - the information systems required to record and report dynamically
  - the information systems required to record and report graphically
  - how to allocate your costs as dynamic or static
  - deciding on the frequency of recording and reporting necessary to reflect the activities of your business.

- Step 2: Monitoring your performance against targets
  - exploring the best ways to choose and set your dynamic targets
  - when should you take account of history?
  - when should you start to compare internal to external values?

In this step we also suggest that you just start the process and let your experience (your learning) increase the accuracy of your dynamic targets.

- Step 3: Making dynamic decisions
  - looking at how you can interpret the trends portrayed by your dynamic indicators

– considering dynamic action rather than reaction to these trends
– following the seven dynamic routes to success – to dynamic growth.

● Step 4: Communicating the DFM message
– considering the stakeholder views of your business
– how to record the information they value as a measure of your performance.

But remember, dynamic financial management is about managing *your* business for *you*!

● Step 5: Help

Contact us if you have any problems or suggestions about implementing dynamic financial management in your business – we are out there and want to hear from you. The web site address is given in the *Preface*.

Step 1: Identifying your dynamic indicators

Choosing your dynamic indicators

The first step to using dynamic financial management has to be choosing your own dynamic indicators. These may well be the standard eight that we have introduced and used throughout the book, but only you will know their relevance to your own business activities.

Whatever you choose, the dynamic system we work within requires all indicators to be expressed as a percentage of income. Remember the reason for this anchorage to income is to provide an indication of the level of activity of your business. This then allows you to monitor the proportionate effects of any changes to your business as a result of your decisions or external forces. Therefore always choose your indicators so that this representation makes sense. Remember, dynamic indicators are those that change dynamically with the operational activities of your business.

Dynamic indicators are used to allow you to keep your finger on the pulse of the business. As such, we would strongly advocate that the indicators

● GC%
● DNC%
● BeGap%
● DNA%
● DCM%

are relevant to every business as they monitor the vital signs of health.

With DNA, perhaps it is the strands of DNA that will be more or less relevant to a particular business. We will take each of the strands of DNA in more detail.

Stock%

In dynamic targets we widened the discussion about stock, away from the traditional manufacturing organization approach to one of thinking of stock as any holding of work done and not yet invoiced for. If you have now considered the alternative thoughts on stock and decided that it is not an appropriate dynamic indicator for your business, then fine, do not use it. Equally, you may indeed hold stock, but it is inconsequential in value as a percentage of your income, so again you may decide it is inappropriate.

Dr%

With the exception of retail businesses, every business will have a debtor value. Again it is up to you whether this is important to you. If you are a departmental manager, perhaps it is not, but if you are the managing director then it must be.

Cr%

Most businesses buy on credit. However, the same argument applies here about Dr%; if you are a departmental manager you may not have to monitor this value. For business owners this indicator is very important.

Other indicators

As we discussed in *Chapter 5: You are not alone*, different stakeholders will have varying views of your business. These views are very important when choosing your dynamic indicators. If by keeping stakeholder indicators you are able to convey the right message at the right time to those important to your future, all will be well. It is no use having indicators that only tell *you* everything is fine if, say, the bank is getting worried because it does not get the right information or signals from you. Certainly, choose your primary indicators for your own use and keep these on a primary radar, but also keep a secondary radar to portray stakeholder indicators so that you can quickly illustrate the company performance in their language and so project yourself as someone who has their finger on the pulse. Confidence is essential in business.

Frequency of monitoring

This issue can be answered only with knowledge of your business. Is there a cycle of time that is relevant to your activities, say a day, a week, a month or a quarter? Whatever the cycle time chosen, it has to be feasible to collect and collate the relevant information in time to facilitate analysis. If you can get the information daily, and this is relevant to you, then do it. If you think it should be relevant but the figures turn out to be too volatile to make any sense, try another period. The quicker and more often you can gather this information, the more you will be able to manage the business dynamically.

Information systems

If information is vital to a business, then its information systems are the vehicle that collects and collates the data and so provides such information. The nature of information systems can be as simple as a few numbers recorded on a sheet of paper to a full-blown enterprise resource planning system. Use whatever is suitable for your needs.

However, for your dynamic indicators, whatever systems you may already have, you may still need to provide special recording and reporting procedures to enable the rapid analysis that dynamic financial management can easily provide. For example, you may receive monthly reports of financial information, but you may want a weekly dynamic analysis of your business. This will therefore require special procedures to be put in place – can your department, organization or company provide such information at an acceptable level of accuracy and in a timely fashion?

Most importantly, dynamic financial management relies on visual representation of the performance of your business. Again, this can be as simple as drawing your own three dynamic graphs. Ideally, your computer package will produce these types of graphs automatically. If you do not know how to do this, look in the tutorial for your system or get help. In the long term it may be worth the effort. However, many of the companies we work with prefer to produce their graphs by hand. It is quicker than waiting for a specialist to come along. After all, it is you who should be the dynamic manager.

Levels of accuracy

We are often asked how accurate this dynamic financial information needs to be. That is best explained using the 80:20 rule. For most business needs, 20 per cent of the effort will give you 80 per cent of the result, e.g. 20 per cent of your customers will bring in 80 per cent of your income or 20 per cent of your employees will need 80 per cent of your time. For most people reading this book the 80:20 rule will hold true when gathering information for dynamic indicators.

Dynamic financial management does not need the accuracy of a set of statutory accounts because you are getting the information quickly and regularly. You are taking dynamic actions, not reacting and certainly not overreacting. Gaps will occur, as discussed in Chapters 2 and 3, but as your experience develops, you should understand your business well enough to know the reason behind the gaps, or even to start to predict those gaps.

However, the beauty of dynamic financial management is that, as your experience of the techniques increases, your level of accuracy will too. You will start to focus on those parts of the information system that produce the information for your dynamic indicators and work on improving these.

Perhaps the most frequently asked question in this area is how do you identify dynamic and static costs. There are obvious targets for dynamic costs – materials, wages, sales commissions – so use these and as your experience improves you will fine-tune them in a way that reflects your business. Again follow the 80:20 rule. But don't get bogged down in 'paralysis by analysis': the speed of information is equally as important – you need to make a decision *now*.

Becoming an expert user

Expert users of dynamic financial management have their finger on the pulse of their business. At a glance they will be able to interpret the shape their business is in and know what to do to get it back into shape. They will also recognize when more detail is needed and when to call on specialists for help.

Step 2: Monitoring your performance against targets

Dynamic targets are an important part of dynamic financial management. Without these there will be nothing to compare yourself against. If a figure is important enough to be a dynamic indicator, it is important enough to have a target.

So how do you set good targets for your business? In *Chapter 3: What are dynamic targets?* we went through this in detail for our eight dynamic indicators. History may be important to you, and if you can get the historical information for your dynamic indicators this will give you some idea of how your business has been performing – good place to start.

You may already use a budgeting system. Another good starting place is to convert your existing budgets into dynamic indicators. When should you take account of history? When should you start to compare internal to external values? In this step we also suggest that you just start the process and let your experience (your learning) increase the accuracy of your dynamic targets.

As dynamic managers you will avoid the political game play that often occurs around the budgeting process. You need to move on to develop targets that truly reflect what your business could do. A good way to look at the potential of your business is to look outside the business. Do not be restricted by what *you* have done and what *you* can see as the future. Look at how others see the potential for your business, your industry, your future.

As mentioned in *Chapter 1: The dynamic landscape*, dynamic financial management is oriented in all three phases of time: the past, the present and the future. Good targets will be built from an understanding of all these orientations. As with the dynamic indicators, the accuracy and challenge of your dynamic targets will improve as your experience increases. The sooner you start setting and assessing targets, the quicker you will gain this experience.

Step 3: Making dynamic decisions

In *Chapter 2: What are dynamic indicators?* we introduced the dynamic breakeven matrix which shows the nine possible trends that may be happening in your business (*see* Fig 6.1).

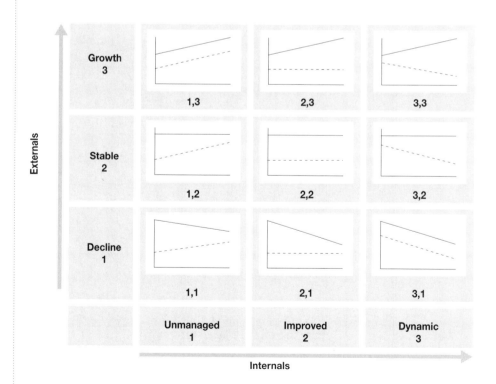

Fig 6.1 ● **The dynamic breakeven matrix**

From wherever you may currently be in this matrix, 'making it happen' involves taking action to improve the performance of your business. These actions are encompassed in seven dynamic routes to success and, in order to explain all of these, we will start every journey from Box (1,1), 'unmanaged decline – a disaster scenario', although you are probably ahead of this step already.

We need to look at each of the seven dynamic routes in turn. But first let us review the major options we introduced in *Chapter 2* – the three main choices in management:

● trying to manage the internal factors – costs;

● trying to manage the external factors – price and volume;

● trying to manage both at the same time – the internals and externals.

The seven dynamic routes give a different priority to each of these factors. The path taken by each of the routes is shown by the shaded squares in the mini matrix.

Route One is the route of strong internal management – getting the internal costs under control before moving on to take advantage of external factors and opportunities.

Internal management goes through all its stages – unmanaged to improved – until you eventually achieve the status of a dynamic manager of the internal aspects of your business. Only then, from a position of maximum fitness, do you take your business from a decline in activity through to stable and finally to achieve growth in activity. This could be through growing sales in your current products or services, or may involve diversifying into new product lines.

To achieve maximum fitness you will need to focus on reducing dynamic and/or static costs. As a pointer to which you attack first, go for whichever is the greater percentage, DC% or SC%. *Chapter 10: Decreases in your dynamic costs* and *Chapter 12: Decreases in your static costs* will clearly illustrate the magnitude of the changes you should be introducing based on the current shape of your business.

The dynamic breakeven graph for Route One is shown in Fig 6.2. The steps from (1,1) to (3,1) lower your breakeven income by lowering your internal costs. The steps from (3,1) to (3,3) are when your activity and thus your income starts to increase as you take advantage of the externals while retaining your internal level of fitness. No overindulgence here!

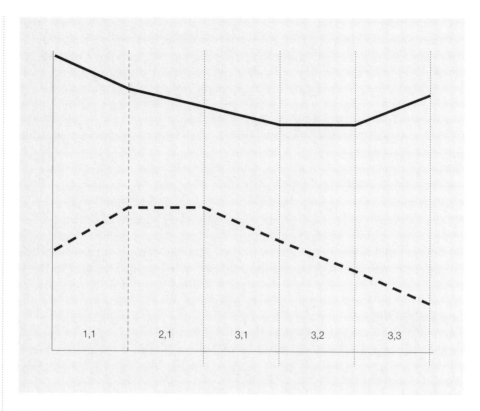

Fig 6.2 ● **The dynamic breakeven graph for Route One**

Route Two takes a very different approach. It is an adventure into the opportunities of the external environment – maximizing your activity level according to demand and only then focusing on the internal cost structure you need to support this.

The dynamic breakeven graph in Fig 6.3 shows a very different trend to that for Route One. The steps from (1,1) to (1,3) increase your activity and so your income but have no effect on breakeven income. Steps (1,3) to (3,3) start to refocus on your fitness, reducing the breakeven by reducing costs – the internals.

Is this a good strategy? How appropriate do you feel it is to your current business situation? What are the risks involved? This graph assumes your internals can be kept stable. Many businesses think they are on this route when in reality the internals are out of control. The breakeven line follows the route of your income line – more work for less money! But with dynamic financial management you should be able to spot these trends and change to a safer route if necessary.

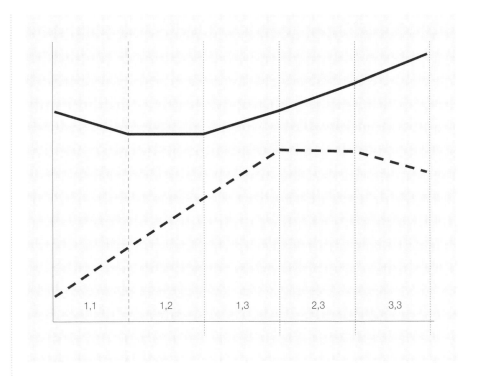

Fig 6.3 ● **The dynamic breakeven graph for Route Two**

Route Three is the 'express way', but as ever, travelling at high speed is fraught with danger, so you need to remain alert. You are trying to do everything at once – improve the internals while taking opportunities from the external environment. This gives a three-step route to dynamic growth.

In Fig 6.4, from (1,1) to (2,2) you move from unmanaged decline to improved stability. When you have achieved this you probably need to take time out to consolidate your efforts. From (2,2) to (3,3) you carry on in the same manner to achieve dynamic growth.

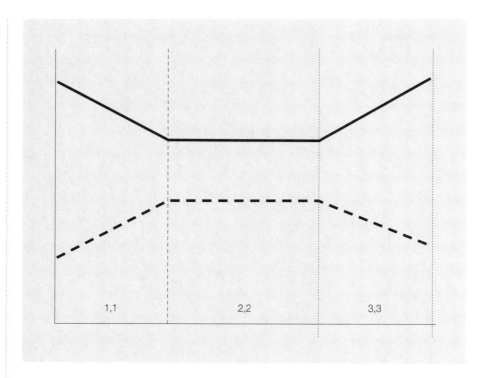

Fig 6.4 ● The dynamic breakeven graph for Route Three

Routes Four to Seven are all back to a five-step route and will result in a dynamic breakeven graph that is a combination of Route One, Route Two and Route Three. Each of these may help you decide the best combination of risk and reward for your business.

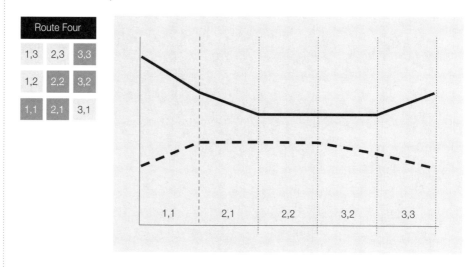

Fig 6.5 ● The dynamic breakeven graph for Route Four

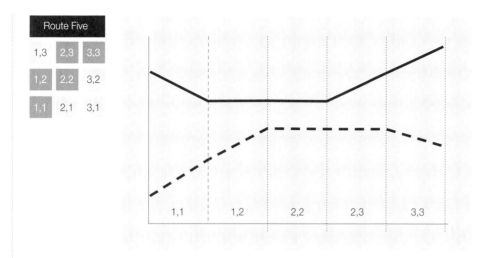

Fig 6.6 ● The dynamic breakeven graph for Route Five

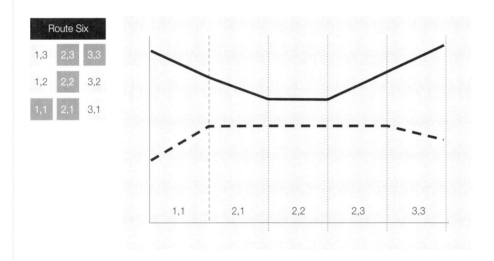

Fig 6.7 ● The dynamic breakeven graph for Route Six

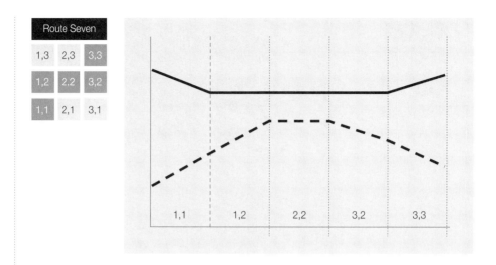

Fig 6.8 ● The dynamic breakeven graph for Route Seven

You now know the alternative routes to success – to dynamic growth – but you still need to *make it happen!* Whether the first step of your route is managing internals or managing externals, part of the answer will come from *Part Two*, but the rest of the answer will come from your knowledge of the environment – what is happening in your market place.

When a decision for your business is needed, referring to the processes in *Part Two* will direct you to the *financial* answer to your problem, the financial results of business decisions, i.e. the dynamic relationship between your indicators. This is a huge leap forward in knowledge about your business, but it is only one piece of the jigsaw – you need to combine this with your knowledge of the external factors to come up with the *business* answer to your problem.

Step 4: Communicating the DFM message

Dynamic financial management is about helping you to get the optimum performance from your business. Businesses are about people. People make decisions that affect the performance of your business. Our experience of companies using dynamic financial management is that the visual representations of the business can do more than just help them interpret, understand and improve the business.

The visual representations of the business can be an invaluable tool in communicating the importance of dynamic financial management throughout the organization. Managers are no longer faced with streams of historic figures that are supposed to tell them about tomorrow's performance of their business. They can see the changing shape of the business, they can identify and interpret gaps, and they can see the trends in dynamic breakeven and dynamic cash, all in three pictures. This is not finance as a function within your business – it *is* the business.

You can start moving them up their own learning curve of dynamic financial management, developing their own dynamic indicators that help them improve the overall dynamic indicators.

External stakeholders can also benefit from your knowledge of dynamic financial management. Banks and venture capitalists say their belief in the ability of the management team is one of the key factors in deciding whether to support a business in a new venture. These stakeholders may not be familiar with dynamic financial management but they will be amazed at your ability to produce these visual images of your business and dazzled by the way you are able to interpret what is happening in your business from these images. It may not stop them asking for more information for their own purposes – again, you may need periodic help from specialists to produce this additional information – but the external stakeholders will believe this information when they receive it and they will also believe that you will be a professional custodian of their investment.

They may even suggest you change some of your dynamic indicators to provide them with periodic information. But be careful. You know why you chose your dynamic indicators. Is there a good reason to change? Dynamic financial management is about managing inside your business, although there is no problem in developing stakeholder radar reflecting the dynamic indicators of these external stakeholders if you feel this will be beneficial.

Step 5: Help

We have every confidence in dynamic financial management providing you with a desirable future. However, no route to success, not even a dynamic route, is entirely smooth. You may need help (see the *Preface*).

The beginning

Making it happen is not the end, it is the beginning of your journey towards DFM.

Whichever of the seven routes to success you choose and for whatever reasons, the end result is dynamic growth. Your business performance has improved and the future is bright. If you have followed the step-by-step guide in this chapter, you will already have started to make it happen.

We are confident that you will continue your success and enjoy the fruits of dynamic financial management, both today and tomorrow.

You can now manage today. *Part Two* continues the journey into managing tomorrow.

Managing tomorrow

Introduction to part two

Having begun to adopt dynamic financial management tools and techniques you will quickly become adept at seeing the trends in your business and knowing when to act. Entrepreneurial action will allow you to create a desirable future rather than reacting to yesterday.

There are options available to you as benefits to the business or as necessary actions to recapture a situation. The whole of *Part Two*, therefore, offers an easy-to-use reference to these benefits and actions, taking you step by step through how to calculate the future. You may read all of *Part Two* to acquaint yourself with the methods, or once you are familiar with the pattern evolving you may reference relevant chapters when required.

In summary, *Part Two* describes in detail how to use the dynamic financial management tools and techniques to calculate the new shape of your business as a response to either internal changes or external factors. It also tells you the actions you need to take to get your business back into shape. These are the mathematical answers. But of course it is up to you as a manager to decide whether the calculated course of action is possible or even appropriate for your business and compromise.

The changes in question are:

- increase in price
- decrease in price
- increase in DC
- decrease in DC
- increase in SC

- decrease in SC
- meeting ever increasing targets on DNC%.

The model business

Throughout *Part Two* we will be demonstrating how, by using the dynamic look-up tables and calculations, you can predict the impact of these changes on the performance of the model business. The key things you need to know about the model business are the current contribution and DNA statements. These are:

Contribution statement		DNA statement	
	£		£
Income	100.00	Income	100.00
Dynamic Costs	60.00	Stock	50.00
Gross Contribution	40.00	Debtors	100.00
Static Costs	30.00	Creditors	80.00
Dynamic Net Contribution	10.00	Static Net Assets	70.00

We have purposely kept the figures in the model business reasonably simple so that it is easier to see how they move as a result of the changes affecting the business. The contribution statement represents a month's activity in the model business.

The eight dynamic indicators can be calculated from this as follows:

	%
GC%	40.00
DNC%	10.00
BeGap%	25.00
Stock%	50.00
Dr%	100.00
Cr%	80.00
DNA%	0.00
DCM%	10.00

The DNA% is 0 per cent assuming the value of the SNA is not expected to change.

Approach

For each change affecting the business we look at the impact on the model business in two stages:

- Stage One – the initial impact;
- Stage Two – possible management actions or possible business benefits.

Stage One – the initial impact

Every time a change happens within the contribution statement there is going to be a potential impact on each of the eight dynamic indicators. Before considering how to manage such changes you need to understand the magnitude of these initial impacts. How do you know how best to respond if you do not know the result of the initial impact?

We show this initial impact in a structured manner when considering any possible changes – changes in income, changes in DC and changes in SC. We start by using an arrowed radar to show two things:

- which dynamic indicators will be affected by the change;
- the direction of that change.

Figure 2A shows an example. The arrows show whether the individual dynamic indicators will increase or decrease as a result of the decision. An arrowhead pointing to the centre of the radar means that indicator is decreasing. An arrowhead pointing outwards means the indicator is increasing. A double-headed arrow means the impact could go either way depending on the magnitude of change in the other indicators. Remember, our eight dynamic indicators are linked and changes in one will result in changes in others.

We also show a table of the tools that will be used to calculate the new value for each of these dynamic indicators (*see* Table 2A). This table of tools shows the method of deriving the new value of your dynamic indicators after the initial impact. They will be discussed later in this section.

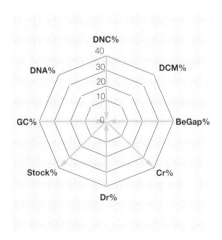

Fig 2A ● **Radar chart of dynamic indicators**

Stage Two – possible management actions or possible business benefits

Table 2A ● **Table of tools**

The eight dynamic indicators	Increase in DC	
		Tool
GC%	Look-up	
DNC%	Look-up	
BeGap%	Calculation	
Stock%	Look-up	
Dr%		
Cr%	Look-up	
DNA%	Calculation	
DCM%	Calculation	

As this is a book on dynamic financial management we assume you are going to work dynamically to manage changes in your business. After you know the initial impact of any change you need to know how you could respond to that change. If the initial change is bad for the business, you need to take management action; if the initial change is good, you need to be aware of the possible benefits you can now take advantage of for your business. Let us think about each of these separately.

If the initial impact is bad for your business, e.g. your dynamic costs have increased, what are your management actions seeking to achieve? You want to get your business back into shape. To do this you must take actions for dynamic management of the change. In dynamic financial management we have a specific definition of getting back into shape:

'To return the DNC% to the same level as it was before the change.'

That is, to keep the 'bottom line' in the same proportions to your activities. You will see this again and again in this part of the book. In addition to looking at the alternative ways of getting your business back into shape, dynamic financial management will show the impact on all your other dynamic indicators. Once you can see the final shape of your business – see tomorrow today – you can choose between the alternative courses of action that are open to you – real dynamic management of changes in your business.

The approach – a summary

For the first three changes under consideration there is a very visible and hierarchical structure:

Managing change in	Type of change	Stage
Income	*Increases in income*	Initial impact
		Possible benefits
	Decreases in income	Initial impact
		Management action
DC	*Increases in DC*	Initial impact
		Management action
	Decreases in DC	Initial impact
		Possible benefits
SC	*Increases in SC*	Initial impact
		Management action
	Decreases in SC	Initial impact
		Possible benefits

For the final change, meeting ever increasing demands on your DNC%, the approach is much more simple. There is no initial impact, and ever increasing demands tells you that the target has gone one way – up. So the only thing left to you is how to achieve this target and we believe this is limited to four choices:

Managing an increase in	Choice	Type of change
DNC%	*One*	Increase activity levels
	Two	Increase price
	Three	Decrease dynamic costs
	Four	Decrease static costs

Signposts

You will quickly become familiar with the structure of the sections within each chapter of *Part Two*. We feel this is useful as it provides familiarity and comfort, and to help you further we have planted signposts such as:

Cause Price down
Effect on GC%
Method Table

This is an example of a signpost resulting from Stage One – the initial impact. This tells you the key information you need to know to check that you are at the decision point that you intended to be:

- the cause is the cause of the change in the business; in the above signpost it is a price decrease;
- the effect is the dynamic indicator we are currently calculating the effect on; in this signpost it is the GC%;
- the method is the tool or technique used to calculate the new dynamic indicator; in this signpost it is a dynamic look-up table.

There are similar signposts planted within the analysis of Stage Two, possible management actions or possible business benefits:

Cause Price down
Possible action Increase volume
Method Calculation/look-up

- the cause is again the cause of the change; in this signpost it would be a price decrease;
- possible action is the management action you could take to compensate for the detrimental effect on your DNC% of the initial impact; in this signpost it is to increase your volume or activity level;
- the method is the tool or technique used to calculate the new value of the dynamic indicator; in this signpost it is using both a calculation and then a dynamic look-up table to find the new figure.

Tools and techniques

The tools and techniques for calculating the new percentage for all your dynamic indicators fall into two categories. The appropriate method is shown in the table at the start of each section.

Dynamic look-up tables

If this method is shown, then calculating the new percentage for your dynamic indicator could not be easier. You simply look it up in a table. Look at the following example:

New Stock% after a dynamic cost increase

Existing Stock%	Percentage increase in DC%				
	3	4	5	6	7
90	92.70	93.60	94.50	95.40	96.75
100	103.00	104.00	105.00	106.00	107.50
110	113.30	114.40	115.50	116.60	118.25

In this example we are looking at calculating the new Stock% that would result if your business had to cope with a 5 per cent increase in your dynamic costs. All you need to know is:

● your current Stock% – in this example let's assume it is 100 per cent;

● the percentage increase in your dynamic costs – in this example let's assume it is 5 per cent.

You can read from the dynamic look-up table that your new Stock% should be 105 per cent as a result of the initial impact of this change in dynamic costs. It could not be easier.

Dynamic adjuster

Sometimes calculating the new percentage is a two-step process. A dynamic adjuster is needed before you can use the dynamic look-up table or the dynamic look-up table provides the dynamic adjuster for use in a subsequent calculation.

An example is:

New GC% = Existing GC% – 'Dynamic Adjuster'

This calculation tells you that a dynamic adjuster needs to be subtracted for the existing GC% to calculate the new GC%. The value of the dynamic adjuster is read from a standard dynamic look-up table:

Dynamic adjuster for new GC% after a dynamic cost increase

Existing DC%	Percentage increase in DC%				
	3	4	5	6	7
50	1.50	2.00	2.50	3.00	3.50
60	1.80	2.40	3.00	3.60	4.20
70	2.10	2.80	3.50	4.20	4.90

In this example, if you have an increase in your dynamic costs of 5 per cent and your existing DC% is 60 per cent the dynamic adjuster will be 3.00. This figure can then be slotted into the earlier equation.

Calculations

Sometimes a simple calculation is all that is needed. Often these simple calculations are obvious once you see them, but when in the thick of decision making we do not always see the obvious.

Using Part Two

Part Two: Managing tomorrow offers solutions to common management situations. The choice for you will always be which of the options offered is most appropriate to your business and to what extent. To fully appreciate the power of dynamic financial management you may want to work your way through *Part Two*. Alternatively you may want to dip into this part as and when you need it – when you are in one of these situations. We have developed the dynamic tool kit for you to use in any way you want. The choice is yours.

chapter 7

Increases in your income

Why does income increase?

Your income may increase due to an increase in levels of activity (volume) of your business or it may be due to an increase in 'price' (value) – increased selling price, increased budget allocation, etc. This chapter looks solely at managing increases in the value of your income driven by some sort of price increase.

Even increases to the income need to be managed, and two stages will help in understanding the impact on your business:

- the initial impact of the increase;
- the alternative actions you could take to dynamically benefit from this increase.

With most increases in income the initial impact can be visualized using the eight dynamic indicators on the radar chart. The trends you will be monitoring using the dynamic breakeven graph and the dynamic cash graph will put these increases into context – the freedom this has given you to develop your business.

Increases in income caused by an effective 'price' increase have a positive effect on your business, but more importantly they give you some management options to choose from to maximize this benefit. Many managers are afraid to increase price because they assume they will lose customers. But how many customers could you lose without detriment to your overall income? Dynamic financial management will predict this outcome. We cannot claim to be able to predict exactly what is going to happen to the volume of activity in your business, but we can tell you what needs to happen.

After a price increase, we would like to see our radar in at least the same shape that it was before the increase. As a result of this management decision, the shape of your business *stretches*. We believe that a meaningful definition of successfully implementing a price increase is to at least retain the same DNC% as before the management decision.

For example, let us look at the model business. If its price goes up by 5 per cent, the initial impact on the contribution statement would show that the DNC% has been increased to 15 per cent. We need to know the possibilities and benefits you could exploit and retain your DNC% at its original level of 10 per cent. For example, the additional income may allow you to invest in a new resource, e.g. a quality manager for the long-term benefit of the business.

What we will present in this chapter are the effects of an increase in your income. We will do this in the two stages mentioned earlier, i.e. look at the simple impact of the increase and then the measures available to us to manage these dynamically and regain our level of fitness, i.e. regain our original DNC%.

Increases in your income

Let us begin with a summary of what could happen if your business achieved an increase in its income. For the model business, if prices increase by 5 per cent, the possible areas of freedom for the business are:

Change		Appropriate action to regain DNC%	Amount
Increase	⮕	Decrease volume	To 86.97%
in price	⮕	Increase dynamic costs	By 7.50%
of 5%	⮕	Increase static costs	By 15.00%

What will be the shape of your business after these changes?

	Before any change	After initial impact Price increase 5%	After volume decrease 86.97%	After DC increase 7.5%	After SC increase 15%
GC%	40.00%	42.86%	42.86%	38.57%	42.86%
DNC%	10.00%	14.29%	10.00%	10.00%	10.00%
BeGap%	25.00%	33.34%	23.33%	25.93%	23.33%
Stock%	50.00%	47.62%	47.62%	51.19%	47.62%
Dr%	100.00%	100.00%	100.00%	100.00%	100.00%
Cr%	80.00%	76.19%	76.19%	79.05%	76.19%
DNA%	0.00%	4.76%	(5.22)%	5.48%	4.76%
DCM%	10.00%	9.53%	15.22%	4.52%	5.24%

The decision is now yours:

● work strategically towards one of the above;

● accept the new shape of your business and change your targets accordingly;

● somewhere in between.

Whatever your decision, you can predict its impact before you are committed to any changes – managing tomorrow today.

So, how did we get to these results? First, we need to find out the result of the initial impact, then we need to look at all the possible benefits that could be accrued as a result of this increase in income.

The initial impact

Sometimes you may want to put up your price. 'What do you mean *sometimes*?', you may say. 'Wouldn't I always like to put up my price!' Well yes, but sometimes it is a strategic decision to do so. In this chapter we are excluding the times when you *have* to put up your price to pass on increasing costs. They are dealt with under the respective sections in *Chapter 9: Increases in your dynamic costs* and *Chapter 11: Increases in your static costs*. Here we are interested in the benefit you can get if you can achieve a marginal increase in price at no extra cost. We will later go on to consider what may happen as a consequence of this, e.g. you may lose volume, and consider the overall impact of such things on your business.

When your income increases due to an increase in value – an increase in price or an increase in your budget allocation – there are going to be a number of impacts on your eight dynamic indicators. These can be shown in Fig 7.1.

The eight dynamic indicators	Increase in prices
	Tool
GC%	Look-up
DNC%	Look-up
BeGap%	Calculation
Stock%	Look-up
Debtor%	
Cr%	Look-up
DNA%	Calculation
DCM%	Calculation

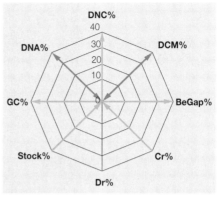

Fig 7.1 ●
Radar chart of dynamic indicators

With a decision to increase prices, all but one of the eight dynamic indicators are affected. Permanent effects will be an increase in GC%, DNC% and BeGap% and a decrease in Stock% and Cr%. However, DNA% and DCM% could either go up or go down depending on the structure of your SNA. And a word of caution is needed here about the Dr%. This is not affected in the long term, but there will be an impact as the pricing decision works its way through the time warp.

Throughout this chapter we will assume that the effective price has increased by 5 per cent, i.e. the amount of income has gone up to 105 per cent of its previous level without any change in the level of activity.

So now let us take both of these effects individually in the order presented above, the first being change to GC%.

Cause Price up
Effect on GC%
Method Look-up

Not surprisingly, if you increase your selling price, and nothing else happens, your GC% must go up. But by how much? Table 7.1 allows you to simply read the new GC% straight from this.

Table 7.1 ● New GC% after a price increase

Current GC%	% Increase in price										
	1	3	5	7	9	10	12	14	16	18	20
10	10.89	12.62	14.29	15.89	17.43	18.18	19.64	21.05	22.41	23.73	25.00
15	15.84	17.48	19.05	20.56	22.02	22.73	24.11	25.44	26.72	27.97	29.17
20	20.79	22.33	23.81	25.23	26.61	27.27	28.57	29.82	31.03	32.20	33.33
25	25.74	27.18	28.57	29.91	31.19	31.82	33.04	34.21	35.34	36.44	37.50
30	30.69	32.04	33.33	34.58	35.78	36.36	37.50	38.60	39.66	40.68	41.67
35	35.64	36.89	38.10	39.25	40.37	40.91	41.96	42.98	43.97	44.92	45.83
40	40.59	41.75	**42.86**	43.93	44.95	45.45	46.43	47.37	48.28	49.15	50.00
45	45.54	46.60	47.62	48.60	49.54	50.00	50.89	51.75	52.59	53.39	54.17
50	50.50	51.46	52.38	53.27	54.13	54.55	55.36	56.14	56.90	57.63	58.33
55	55.45	56.31	57.14	57.94	58.72	59.09	59.82	60.53	61.21	61.86	62.50
60	60.40	61.17	61.90	62.62	63.30	63.64	64.29	64.91	65.52	66.10	66.67
65	65.35	66.02	66.67	67.29	67.89	68.18	68.75	69.30	69.83	70.34	70.83
70	70.30	70.87	71.43	71.96	72.48	72.73	73.21	73.68	74.14	74.58	75.00
75	75.25	75.73	76.19	76.64	77.06	77.27	77.68	78.07	78.45	78.81	79.17
80	80.20	80.58	80.95	81.31	81.65	81.82	82.14	82.46	82.76	83.05	83.33
85	85.15	85.44	85.71	85.98	86.24	86.36	86.61	86.84	87.07	87.29	87.50
90	90.10	90.29	90.48	90.65	90.83	90.91	91.07	91.23	91.38	91.53	91.67

We have an immediate positive benefit on our GC%. It has risen to 42.86 per cent (not to 45 per cent as many managers may expect). What this means in reality is that for everything we sell we now make an extra 2.86 per cent, so if we sell an extra $1,000 we make an extra $286 gross contribution – and for no more work. Looking at how this would impact on the model business:

	Before	After
Income	$100.00	$105.00
Dynamic Costs	$60.00	$60.00
Gross Contribution	$40.00	$45.00
GC%	40.00%	42.86%

Why not pay yourself a bonus!

But my customers would never accept a 5 per cent increase, you might say? That is why, on p. 176, we will consider the potential consequences of these decisions. But first we need to look at the initial impact of the changes on the other dynamic indicators.

Cause Price up

Effect on DNC%

Method Look-up

In the model business the existing DNC% is 10 per cent. How much do you think it could increase the DNC% by for a small increase in price? Again, a dynamic look-up table can give you the answer at a glance. Table 7.2 allows us to look up the impact of the 5 per cent increase in price.

Table 7.2 ● New DNC% after a price increase

Current	% Increase in price										
DNC%	1	3	5	7	9	10	12	14	16	18	20
1	1.98	3.88	5.71	7.48	9.17	10.00	11.61	13.16	14.66	16.10	17.50
2	2.97	4.85	6.67	8.41	10.09	10.91	12.50	14.04	15.52	16.95	18.33
3	3.96	5.83	7.62	9.35	11.01	11.82	13.39	14.91	16.38	17.80	19.17
4	4.95	6.80	8.57	10.28	11.93	12.73	14.29	15.79	17.24	18.64	20.00
5	5.94	7.77	9.52	11.21	12.84	13.64	15.18	16.67	18.10	19.49	20.83
6	6.93	8.74	10.48	12.15	13.76	14.55	16.07	17.54	18.97	20.34	21.67
7	7.92	9.71	11.43	13.08	14.68	15.45	16.96	18.42	19.83	21.19	22.50
8	8.91	10.68	12.38	14.02	15.60	16.36	17.86	19.30	20.69	22.03	23.33
9	9.90	11.65	13.33	14.95	16.51	17.27	18.75	20.18	21.55	22.88	24.17
10	10.89	12.62	**14.29**	15.89	17.43	18.18	19.64	21.05	22.41	23.73	25.00
12	12.87	14.56	16.19	17.76	19.27	20.00	21.43	22.81	24.14	25.42	26.67
14	14.85	16.50	18.10	19.63	21.10	21.82	23.21	24.56	25.86	27.12	28.33
16	16.83	18.45	20.00	21.50	22.94	23.64	25.00	26.32	27.59	28.81	30.00
18	18.81	20.39	21.90	23.36	24.77	25.45	26.79	28.07	29.31	30.51	31.67
20	20.79	22.33	23.81	25.23	26.61	27.27	28.57	29.82	31.03	32.20	33.33
25	25.74	27.18	28.57	29.91	31.19	31.82	33.04	34.21	35.34	36.44	37.50
30	30.69	32.04	33.33	34.58	35.78	36.36	37.50	38.60	39.66	40.68	41.67
35	35.64	36.89	38.10	39.25	40.37	40.91	41.96	42.98	43.97	44.92	45.83
40	40.59	41.75	42.86	43.93	44.95	45.45	46.43	47.37	48.28	49.15	50.00
50	50.50	51.46	52.38	53.27	54.13	54.55	55.36	56.14	56.90	57.63	58.33

In the model business the existing DNC% is 10 per cent and we are, effectively, going to increase our price by 5 per cent. Taking these figures and looking them up in the table we see the new DNC% is 14.29 per cent – an increase of nearly 50 per cent. In fact, the smaller your existing DNC%, the more dramatic the improvement with every small increase in price.

This is more contribution to reinvest in the business – a virtuous circle – and, as we shall see in the BeGap%, a much safer business. So let us look at the new contribution statement for the model business:

	Before		After	
Income	$100.00	100.00%	$105.00	100.00%
Dynamic Costs	$60.00	60.00%	$60.00	57.14%
Gross Contribution	$40.00	40.00%	$45.00	42.86%
Static Costs	$30.00	30.00%	$30.00	28.57%
Dynamic Net Contribution	$10.00	10.00%	$15.00	14.29%

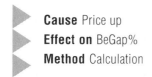

Cause Price up
Effect on BeGap%
Method Calculation

The basic calculation for the new BeGap% value is simple and is based upon the two previous results:

$$\text{New BeGap\%} = \frac{\text{New DNC\%}}{\text{New GC\%}}$$

$$\text{New BeGap\%} = \frac{14.29\%}{42.86\%}$$

$$\text{New BeGap\%} = 33.34\%$$

This is an increase from the original level of 25 per cent to a new high of 33.34 per cent – a huge increase in the safety factor in your business from only a 5 per cent increase in price.

We can summarize the dynamic indicators of contribution as:

GC%	was	40.00%	is now	42.86%
DNC%	was	10.00%	is now	14.29%
BeGap%	was	25.00%	is now	33.34%

Remember, for dynamic management, income is the anchor. Although we have increased the price, it is still the point from which all other figures are calculated.

Cause Price up
Effect on Stock%
Method Look-up

We now need to know the magnitude of the effect of the price increase on stock so that we can predict the impact on the radar chart. This is where the dynamic look-up table comes in (*see* Table 7.3).

Table 7.3 ● **New Stock% after a price increase**

Current Stock%	% Increase in price										
	1	3	5	7	9	10	12	14	16	18	20
10	9.90	9.71	9.52	9.35	9.17	9.09	8.93	8.77	8.62	8.47	8.33
20	19.80	19.42	19.05	18.69	18.35	18.18	17.86	17.54	17.24	16.95	16.67
30	29.70	29.13	28.57	28.04	27.52	27.27	26.79	26.32	25.86	25.42	25.00
40	39.60	38.83	38.10	37.38	36.70	36.36	35.71	35.09	34.48	33.90	33.33
50	49.50	48.54	**47.62**	46.73	45.87	45.45	44.64	43.86	43.10	42.37	41.67
60	59.41	58.25	57.14	56.07	55.05	54.55	53.57	52.63	51.72	50.85	50.00
70	69.31	67.96	66.67	65.42	64.22	63.64	62.50	61.40	60.34	59.32	58.33
80	79.21	77.67	76.19	74.77	73.39	72.73	71.43	70.18	68.97	67.80	66.67
90	89.11	87.38	85.71	84.11	82.57	81.82	80.36	78.95	77.59	76.27	75.00
100	99.01	97.09	95.24	93.46	91.74	90.91	89.29	87.72	86.21	84.75	83.33
110	108.91	106.80	104.76	102.80	100.92	100.00	98.21	96.49	94.83	93.22	91.67
120	118.81	116.50	114.29	112.15	110.09	109.09	107.14	105.26	103.45	101.69	100.00
130	128.71	126.21	123.81	121.50	119.27	118.18	116.07	114.04	112.07	110.17	108.33
140	138.61	135.92	133.33	130.84	128.44	127.27	125.00	122.81	120.69	118.64	116.67
150	148.51	145.63	142.86	140.19	137.61	136.36	133.93	131.58	129.31	127.12	125.00

After a 5 per cent increase in price with an existing Stock% of 50 per cent, we can simply read from the table the new Stock% of 47.62 per cent. So we have relatively less stock tied up in our SNA. The value may not have changed but in relation to our anchor point – income – it has decreased. This has effectively released money from your time warp to invest in the success of your business.

Cause Price up
Effect on Cr%
Method Look-up

If you have increased your price, your first assumption might be that there would be no changes in your creditors. You might be selling for more, but your costs of buying are still the same. That means you have not been landed with any compensating differences in your dynamic costs and as a result no change in your creditors. However, it is true that your creditors value should remain the same but your Cr% should reduce. Income is up in value but creditors have remained the same so as a percentage Cr% should go down. But we still need to know by how much so that we can restate our targets.

Another dynamic look-up table is available to simply read the new figure (*see* Table 7.4). After a 5 per cent increase in price with an existing Cr% of 80 per cent, we can simply read from the table the new Cr% of 76.19 per cent. This is the figure we should now anticipate in the future targets for the business.

Table 7.4 ● New Cr% after a price increase

Current Cr%	% Increase in price										
	1	3	5	7	9	10	12	14	16	18	20
10	9.90	9.71	9.52	9.35	9.17	9.09	8.93	8.77	8.62	8.47	8.33
20	19.80	19.42	19.05	18.69	18.35	18.18	17.86	17.54	17.24	16.95	16.67
30	29.70	29.13	28.57	28.04	27.52	27.27	26.79	26.32	25.86	25.42	25.00
40	39.60	38.83	38.10	37.38	36.70	36.36	35.71	35.09	34.48	33.90	33.33
50	49.50	48.54	47.62	46.73	45.87	45.45	44.64	43.86	43.10	42.37	41.67
60	59.41	58.25	57.14	56.07	55.05	54.55	53.57	52.63	51.72	50.85	50.00
70	69.31	67.96	66.67	65.42	64.22	63.64	62.50	61.40	60.34	59.32	58.33
80	79.21	77.67	**76.19**	74.77	73.39	72.73	71.43	70.18	68.97	67.80	66.67
90	89.11	87.38	85.71	84.11	82.57	81.82	80.36	78.95	77.59	76.27	75.00
100	99.01	97.09	95.24	93.46	91.74	90.91	89.29	87.72	86.21	84.75	83.33
110	108.91	106.80	104.76	102.80	100.92	100.00	98.21	96.49	94.83	93.22	91.67
120	118.81	116.50	114.29	112.15	110.09	109.09	107.14	105.26	103.45	101.69	100.00
130	128.71	126.21	123.81	121.50	119.27	118.18	116.07	114.04	112.07	110.17	108.33
140	138.61	135.92	133.33	130.84	128.44	127.27	125.00	122.81	120.69	118.64	116.67
150	148.51	145.63	142.86	140.19	137.61	136.36	133.93	131.58	129.31	127.12	125.00

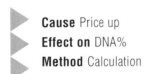

Cause Price up

Effect on DNA%

Method Calculation

In order to calculate the dynamic net assets as a result of this change we need to look at the strands of our static net assets imprisoned in the time warp before and after the anticipated change. This can be shown as:

DNA = SNA *after* Change − SNA *before* Change

And then DNA% will be:

$$DNA\% = \frac{DNA}{Income} \times 100$$

So, for the model business the strands of the SNA, both in terms of value and percentage, are shown below:

	Before	After
Income	$100.00	$105.00
Stock	$50.00	$50.00
Debtors	$100.00	$105.00
Creditors	$80.00	$80.00
SNA	$70.00	$75.00
Stock%	50.00%	47.62%
Dr%	100.00%	100.00%
Cr%	80.00%	76.19%
SNA%	70.00%	71.43%

The DNA can now be calculated as:

$$DNA = \$75.00 - \$70.00 = \$5.00$$

And the DNA% is

$$DNA\% = \frac{\$5.00}{\$105.00} \times 100 = 4.76\%$$

So real money has been tied up in the time warp and this is because we are now charging our customers more. They owe us the same percentage, but of a larger value.

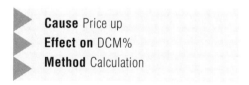

Cause Price up
Effect on DCM%
Method Calculation

The final dynamic indicator is now very easy to calculate:

$$DCM\% = DNC\% - DNA\%$$

$$DCM\% = 14.29\% - 4.76\% = 9.53\%$$

Your DCM% after the change is 9.53 per cent, compared with the 10 per cent you were forecasting before the change, which states you have released relatively less cash from the time warp than you might have. But when you are considering an increase in price this may not be a bad thing. This is new money coming into your time warp for the first time – money coming from the increase in price your customers are now prepared to pay (you hope).

And think what will happen next month when the business stabilizes: the DCM% will, like the DNC%, return to a stable level of 14.29 per cent, meaning more real cash available to the business.

The new shape of your business

The eight dynamic indicators before and after the decrease in prices are:

Contribution statement			DNA statement		
	Before	**After**		**Before**	**After**
Income	$100.00	$105.00	Income	$100.00	$105.00
Dynamic Costs	$60.00	$60.00	Stock	$50.00	$50.00
Gross Contribution	$40.00	$45.00	Debtors	$100.00	$105.00
Static Costs	$30.00	$30.00	Creditors	$80.00	$80.00
Dynamic Net Contribution	$10.00	$15.00	Static Net Assets	$70.00	$75.00

Eight dynamic indicators

	Before	**After**
GC%	40.00%	42.86%
DNC%	10.00%	14.29%
BeGap%	25.00%	33.34%
Stock%	50.00%	47.62%
Dr%	100.00%	100.00%
Cr%	80.00%	76.19%
DNA%	0.00%	4.76%
DCM%	10.00%	9.53%

This can be shown on the radar chart, as in Fig 7.2. As you can see – the contribution indicators for your business are stretching! Yet DCM% looks to be lagging behind. This is because the income figure has increased rather than cash being taken out of the business. However, money has not been imprisoned in the time warp; in fact this represents new money that you will be able to use in your future activities.

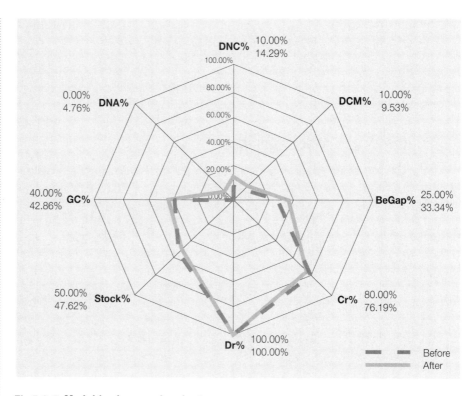

Fig 7.2 ● **Model business radar chart**

Actions for dynamic management of an increase in income

Again, this is only the initial step. As we mentioned at the start of this chapter there are a number of actions you could take to dynamically manage this change so that we maintain our DNC%. These can be summarized as follows:

Change		Appropriate action to regain DNC%
Increase	ⅲ➡	Decrease volume
in income	ⅲ➡	Increase dynamic costs
	ⅲ➡	Increase static costs

These may seem like strange concepts – increasing your dynamic costs: why would you want to do that? What this section does is give you an idea of the magnitude of the freedom that this change has given you. We most certainly do not advocate that you allow your dynamic costs to increase, not without some real value added.

A truer example might be if you were running a project and you could get a higher price than you thought, so you could perhaps hire one more person to work on that project, i.e. increase your dynamic costs. This person would still have to add value, perhaps an additional skill for the team. You could then afford to increase the knowledge base of your project and this might lead to future benefits.

We will need to revisit our model business and it makes sense to look at it after the initial impact of the change of price, i.e. an increase of 5 per cent from $100 to $105.

> **Cause** Price up
> **Possible benefit** Decrease volume
> **Method** Look-up/Look-up

The first possible action to anticipate is a decrease in the volume or level of activity. We could be moving into a higher value, lower volume type of business. However, to ensure you have got the right balance between price and volume you need to carefully monitor your DNC%. In the model business we are looking at an increase of 5 per cent in our price. What volume decrease could the model business allow yet maintain its original DNC% of 10 per cent?

There are several factors involved in calculating the volume benefit of a price increase, and these are best explained using a two-table approach, the first table to tell us the dynamic adjuster and the second to tell us the new Volume%. What do we need to know first? We have to work out our dynamic adjuster from Table 7.5.

Table 7.5 ● Dynamic adjuster

Current DNC%	% Increase in price									
	2	4	6	8	10	12	14	16	18	20
1	1.98	3.96	5.94	7.92	9.90	11.88	13.86	15.84	17.82	19.80
2	1.96	3.92	5.88	7.84	9.80	11.76	13.72	15.68	17.64	19.60
3	1.94	3.88	5.82	7.76	9.70	11.64	13.58	15.52	17.46	19.40
4	1.92	3.84	5.76	7.68	9.60	11.52	13.44	15.36	17.28	19.20
5	1.90	3.80	5.70	7.60	9.50	11.40	13.30	15.20	17.10	19.00
6	1.88	3.76	5.64	7.52	9.40	11.28	13.16	15.04	16.92	18.80
7	1.86	3.72	5.58	7.44	9.30	11.16	13.02	14.88	16.74	18.60
8	1.84	3.68	5.52	7.36	9.20	11.04	12.88	14.72	16.56	18.40
9	1.82	3.64	5.46	7.28	9.10	10.92	12.74	14.56	16.38	18.20
10	1.80	3.60	5.40	7.20	9.00	10.80	12.60	14.40	16.20	18.00
12	1.76	3.52	5.28	7.04	8.80	10.56	12.32	14.08	15.84	17.60
14	1.72	3.44	5.16	6.88	8.60	10.32	12.04	13.76	15.48	17.20
16	1.68	3.36	5.04	6.72	8.40	10.08	11.76	13.44	15.12	16.80
18	1.64	3.28	4.92	6.56	8.20	9.84	11.48	13.12	14.76	16.40
20	1.60	3.20	4.80	6.40	8.00	9.60	11.20	12.80	14.40	16.00
25	1.50	3.00	4.50	6.00	7.50	9.00	10.50	12.00	13.50	15.00
30	1.40	2.80	4.20	5.60	7.00	8.40	9.80	11.20	12.60	14.00
35	1.30	2.60	3.90	5.20	6.50	7.80	9.10	10.40	11.70	13.00
40	1.20	2.40	3.60	4.80	6.00	7.20	8.40	9.60	10.80	12.00
50	1.00	2.00	3.00	4.00	5.00	6.00	7.00	8.00	9.00	10.00

If our anticipated price increase is 5 per cent and our existing DNC% is 10 per cent, using the above table we can derive our dynamic adjuster of 4.50. We can then use this in Table 7.6 for which we need to know that, in the model business, our static costs are 30 per cent and our dynamic adjuster from the first table is 4.50 (to estimate 4.50 from Table 7.6 simply calculate the halfway point between 4 and 5). If your dynamic adjuster is between 1 and 10, use Table 7.6 and if your dynamic adjuster is between 11 and 20, use Table 7.7.

Table 7.6 ● New Volume% to maintain same DNC% with a price increase

Static cost%	Dynamic adjuster 1	2	3	4	5	6	7	8	9	10
10	90.91	83.33	76.92	71.43	66.67	62.50	58.82	55.56	52.63	50.00
15	93.75	88.24	83.33	78.95	75.00	71.43	68.18	65.22	62.50	60.00
20	95.24	90.91	86.96	83.33	80.00	76.92	74.07	71.43	68.97	66.67
25	96.15	92.59	89.29	86.21	83.33	80.65	78.13	75.76	73.53	71.43
30	96.77	93.75	90.91	88.24	85.71	83.33	81.08	78.95	76.92	75.00
35	97.22	94.59	92.11	89.74	87.50	85.37	83.33	81.40	79.55	77.78
40	97.56	95.24	93.02	90.91	88.89	86.96	85.11	83.33	81.63	80.00
45	97.83	95.74	93.75	91.84	90.00	88.24	86.54	84.91	83.33	81.82
50	98.04	96.15	94.34	92.59	90.91	89.29	87.72	86.21	84.75	83.33
55	98.21	96.49	94.83	93.22	91.67	90.16	88.71	87.30	85.94	84.62
60	98.36	96.77	95.24	93.75	92.31	90.91	89.55	88.24	86.96	85.71
65	98.48	97.01	95.59	94.20	92.86	91.55	90.28	89.04	87.84	86.67
70	98.59	97.22	95.89	94.59	93.33	92.11	90.91	89.74	88.61	87.50
75	98.68	97.40	96.15	94.94	93.75	92.59	91.46	90.36	89.29	88.24
80	98.77	97.56	96.39	95.24	94.12	93.02	91.95	90.91	89.89	88.89
85	98.84	97.70	96.59	95.51	94.44	93.41	92.39	91.40	90.43	89.47
90	98.90	97.83	96.77	95.74	94.74	93.75	92.78	91.84	90.91	90.00

Table 7.7 ● New Volume% to maintain same DNC% with a price increase

Static cost%	Dynamic adjuster 11	12	13	14	15	16	17	18	19	20
10	47.62	45.45	43.48	41.67	40.00	38.46	37.04	35.71	34.48	33.33
15	57.69	55.56	53.57	51.72	50.00	48.39	46.88	45.45	44.12	42.86
20	64.52	62.50	60.61	58.82	57.14	55.56	54.05	52.63	51.28	50.00
25	69.44	67.57	65.79	64.10	62.50	60.98	59.52	58.14	56.82	55.56
30	73.17	71.43	69.77	68.18	66.67	65.22	63.83	62.50	61.22	60.00
35	76.09	74.47	72.92	71.43	70.00	68.63	67.31	66.04	64.81	63.64
40	78.43	76.92	75.47	74.07	72.73	71.43	70.18	68.97	67.80	66.67
45	80.36	78.95	77.59	76.27	75.00	73.77	72.58	71.43	70.31	69.23
50	81.97	80.65	79.37	78.13	76.92	75.76	74.63	73.53	72.46	71.43
55	83.33	82.09	80.88	79.71	78.57	77.46	76.39	75.34	74.32	73.33
60	84.51	83.33	82.19	81.08	80.00	78.95	77.92	76.92	75.95	75.00
65	85.53	84.42	83.33	82.28	81.25	80.25	79.27	78.31	77.38	76.47
70	86.42	85.37	84.34	83.33	82.35	81.40	80.46	79.55	78.65	77.78
75	87.21	86.21	85.23	84.27	83.33	82.42	81.52	80.65	79.79	78.95
80	87.91	86.96	86.02	85.11	84.21	83.33	82.47	81.63	80.81	80.00
85	88.54	87.63	86.73	85.86	85.00	84.16	83.33	82.52	81.73	80.95
90	89.11	88.24	87.38	86.54	85.71	84.91	84.11	83.33	82.57	81.82

In the model business our static costs are 30 per cent and our dynamic adjuster from the first table is 4.50. This tells us that the sales volume could go down to a new level of 86.97 per cent of the current volume of sales.

	Before	After initial impact	After volume decrease	%
Income	$100.00	$105.00	$91.32	100.00
Dynamic Costs	$60.00	$60.00	$52.18	57.14
Gross Contribution	$40.00	$45.00	$39.13	42.86
Static Costs	$30.00	$30.00	$30.00	32.86
Dynamic Net Contribution	$10.00	$15.00	$9.13	10.00

Don't forget, if your volume has decreased so will your dynamic costs. In this example we have decreased volume to 86.97 per cent of its previous level, therefore our dynamic costs will also be 86.97 per cent of their previous level. The DC% decreased to 57.14 per cent after the price increase. Your GC% will also stay at the same level as it was after the initial impact of the price increase. A change in volume has no impact on GC%.

But what about the rest of the dynamic indicators?

> **New BeGap% = New DNC% / New GC%**
>
> **New BeGap% = 10.00% / 42.86% = 23.33%**

And the impact on DNA%? There are no additional changes to the underlying SNA strands as a result of this secondary action of reducing the volume. If the only change is one of volume then, as a percentage of sales, these indicators should stay the same, that is, at the levels after the impact of the change in price. We are still benefiting from the associated positive effect of the decreased costs tied up in our stock and the decreasing amount we will have to pay out to our suppliers for the reduced cost. In addition, the decrease in volume means we can decrease the SNA value, from the original value of $70 to $65.23, a decrease in actual SNA value.

The figures after the initial impact and the volume decrease will be:

	Before	After initial impact	After volume decrease
Income	$100.00	$105.00	$91.32
Stock	$50.00	$50.00	$43.49
Debtors	$100.00	$105.00	$91.32
Creditors	$80.00	$80.00	$69.58
SNA	$70.00	$75.00	$65.23
Stock%	50.00%	47.62%	47.62%
Dr%	100.00%	100.00%	100.00%
Cr%	80.00%	76.19%	76.19%
SNA%	70.00%	71.43%	71.43%

For the DNA% this means:

DNA = SNA *after* Decision – SNA *before* Initial Impact

DNA = $65.23 – $70.00 = $(4.77)

And then DNA% calculates as:

$$\text{DNA\%} = \frac{\$(4.77)}{91.32} \times 100 = (5.22)\%$$

We now know the decrease in volume that we would find acceptable, and it has also decreased the cash tied up in the time warp of your SNA. An increase in price can result in a decrease in volume, but what is wrong with this if you are making the same DNC% – more money for less work, you can't beat it! Or can you? The final impact we need to consider is the impact on DCM.

DCM% = DNC% – DNA%

DCM% = 10.00% – (5.22)% = 15.22%

The DCM% is an amazing 15.22 per cent. Not only have we increased price and reduced our level of activity but we have freed up cash to use in the further development of the business.

This option can be summarized as:

Eight dynamic indicators

	Before	After initial impact	After volume decrease
GC%	40.00%	42.86%	42.86%
DNC%	10.00%	14.29%	10.00%
BeGap%	25.00%	33.34%	23.33%
Stock%	50.00%	47.62%	47.62%
Dr%	100.00%	100.00%	100.00%
Cr%	80.00%	76.19%	76.19%
DNA%	0.00%	4.76%	(5.22)%
DCM%	10.00%	9.53%	15.22%

But a volume decrease may not be your best option. You still need to consider the other two options.

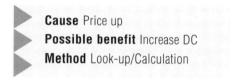

Cause Price up

Possible benefit Increase DC

Method Look-up/Calculation

If our price increases by 5 per cent, the compensating DC increase you could accept can be calculated. This may seem a strange concept – we manage to get an increase in price and then start to give it all away. But there could be good strategic reasons behind it. You may want to move into a higher value niche. You know the price that niche will stand, what you need to know is how much cost you can spend in adding the extra value perceived by the customer in order to earn that higher price. The cost increase may be a dynamic one (discussed here) or a static one (*see* p. 185).

To identify the allowable increase in dynamic costs requires two stages: a dynamic look-up table to find the dynamic adjuster (*see* Table 7.8) followed by a simple calculation.

Reading from Table 7.8, with our static costs before any change being 30 per cent and our dynamic costs being 60 per cent, this gives us a dynamic adjuster of 1.50. Slotting this into the calculation would give:

% Increase in DC = Price Increase × Dynamic Adjuster

% Increase in DC = 5.00 × 1.50 = 7.50%

Table 7.8 ● **Dynamic adjuster for new DC% with a price increase**

Current DC%	Existing SC%								
	10	20	30	40	50	60	70	80	90
10	2.00	3.00	4.00	5.00	6.00	7.00	8.00	9.00	10.00
15	1.67	2.33	3.00	3.67	4.33	5.00	5.67	6.33	7.00
20	1.50	2.00	2.50	3.00	3.50	4.00	4.50	5.00	5.50
25	1.40	1.80	2.20	2.60	3.00	3.40	3.80	4.20	4.60
30	1.33	1.67	2.00	2.33	2.67	3.00	3.33	3.67	4.00
35	1.29	1.57	1.86	2.14	2.43	2.71	3.00	3.29	3.57
40	1.25	1.50	1.75	2.00	2.25	2.50	2.75	3.00	3.25
45	1.22	1.44	1.67	1.89	2.11	2.33	2.56	2.78	3.00
50	1.20	1.40	1.60	1.80	2.00	2.20	2.40	2.60	2.80
55	1.18	1.36	1.55	1.73	1.91	2.09	2.27	2.45	2.64
60	1.17	1.33	**1.50**	1.67	1.83	2.00	2.17	2.33	2.50
65	1.15	1.31	1.46	1.62	1.77	1.92	2.08	2.23	2.38
70	1.14	1.29	1.43	1.57	1.71	1.86	2.00	2.14	2.29
75	1.13	1.27	1.40	1.53	1.67	1.80	1.93	2.07	2.20
80	1.13	1.25	1.38	1.50	1.63	1.75	1.88	2.00	2.13
85	1.12	1.24	1.35	1.47	1.59	1.71	1.82	1.94	2.06
90	1.11	1.22	1.33	1.44	1.56	1.67	1.78	1.89	2.00

This table has given you the actual increase you could allow in the value of your dynamic costs. The dynamic costs were $60 before any change was made, i.e. before the initial impact. $60 plus an increase of 7.50 per cent would give the new figure of $64.50, the figure we have used in the contribution statement.

	Before	After initial impact	After DC decrease	%
Income	$100.00	$105.00	$105.00	100.00%
Dynamic Costs	$60.00	$60.00	$64.50	61.43%
Gross Contribution	$40.00	$45.00	$40.50	38.57%
Static Costs	$30.00	$30.00	$30.00	28.57%
Dynamic Net Contribution	$10.00	$15.00	$10.50	10.00%

And $64.50 as a percentage of the new income level of $105 gives you a DC% figure of 61.43 per cent.

What does this do to the GC%? It is actually lower now than it was before any decision. It has, as a result of these two decisions, fallen from 40 per cent to 38.57 per cent which suggests that the DC increase allowable is actually higher than the price increase. And this is true. Your price went up by 5 per cent yet you can afford to spend 7.5 per cent on dynamic costs to support this new strategy.

But what about the other dynamic indicators?

New BeGap% = New DNC% / New GC%

New BeGap% = 10.00% / 38.57% = 25.93%

As a result of these changes the model business seems slightly less risky than before. It has shifted (relatively) more of its costs into dynamic costs. But remember, with a reduced risk comes the potential for less reward. All future sales will be generating slightly less GC for you. Was this your intention when moving into the higher value niche?

This action has resulted in an increase in our dynamic costs of 7.5 per cent. This should also result in an increase in Stock% and Cr%. This requires going through the initial impact tables for an increase in dynamic costs. With a Stock% of 47.62 per cent after the initial impact and a subsequent increase in DC% of 7.5 per cent, the new Stock% will be 51.19 per cent. Similarly, with a Cr% of 76.19 per cent after the initial impact the new Cr% will be 79.05 per cent. You can check these figures using the tables at your leisure. The strands of your SNA at each point in this process would look like:

	Before	After initial impact	After DC increase
Income	$100.00	$105.00	$105.00
Stock	$50.00	$50.00	$53.75
Debtors	$100.00	$105.00	$105.00
Creditors	$80.00	$80.00	$83.00
SNA	$70.00	$75.00	$75.75
Stock%	50.00%	47.62%	51.19%
Dr%	100.00%	100.00%	100.00%
Cr%	80.00%	76.19%	79.05%
SNA%	70.00%	71.43%	72.14%

The Dr% will stay the same as we are not changing the price or the volume. This means that the Dr value will have increased but will stay at the same level as after the initial impact.

For the DNA% this means:

$$\text{DNA} = \text{SNA } \textit{after} \text{ Decision} - \text{SNA } \textit{before} \text{ Initial Impact}$$

$$\text{DNA} = \$75.75 - \$70.00 = \$5.75$$

And then DNA% will be:

$$\text{DNA\%} = \frac{\$5.75}{\$105.00} \times 100 = 5.48\%$$

And the impact on the DCM% is:

$$\text{DCM\%} = \text{DNC\%} - \text{DNA\%}$$

$$\text{DCM\%} = 10.00\% - 5.48\% = 4.52\%$$

The DCM% has been considerably reduced because of the additional cost of stock with this option.

To summarize this option:

Eight dynamic indicators

	Before	After initial impact	After DC increase
GC%	40.00%	42.86%	38.57%
DNC%	10.00%	14.29%	10.00%
BeGap%	25.00%	33.34%	25.93%
Stock%	50.00%	47.62%	51.19%
Dr%	100.00%	100.00%	100.00%
Cr%	80.00%	76.19%	79.05%
DNA%	0.00%	4.76%	5.48%
DCM%	10.00%	9.53%	4.52%

Although we have, overall, reduced the GC%, we have maintained the original DNC%. The cost of this additional investment in dynamic costs shows up most strongly in the DCM%. Like any investment, the rewards should be reaped later.

Cause Price up
Possible benefit Increase SC
Method Look-up/Calculation

The alternative response to increasing your dynamic costs is, obviously, increasing your static costs. Again this will have a different impact on the cost structure and risk within the business. If our price increases by 5 per cent, the compensating SC increase allowed can be calculated. This requires two stages, a dynamic look-up table to find the dynamic adjuster (*see* Table 7.9) followed by a simple calculation.

Table 7.9 ● Dynamic adjuster for new SC% with a price increase

Current SC%	Existing DC%								
	10	20	30	40	50	60	70	80	90
10	2.00	3.00	4.00	5.00	6.00	7.00	8.00	9.00	10.00
15	1.67	2.33	3.00	3.67	4.33	5.00	5.67	6.33	7.00
20	1.50	2.00	2.50	3.00	3.50	4.00	4.50	5.00	5.50
25	1.40	1.80	2.20	2.60	3.00	3.40	3.80	4.20	4.60
30	1.33	1.67	2.00	2.33	2.67	**3.00**	3.33	3.67	4.00
35	1.29	1.57	1.86	2.14	2.43	2.71	3.00	3.29	3.57
40	1.25	1.50	1.75	2.00	2.25	2.50	2.75	3.00	3.25
45	1.22	1.44	1.67	1.89	2.11	2.33	2.56	2.78	3.00
50	1.20	1.40	1.60	1.80	2.00	2.20	2.40	2.60	2.80
55	1.18	1.36	1.55	1.73	1.91	2.09	2.27	2.45	2.64
60	1.17	1.33	1.50	1.67	1.83	2.00	2.17	2.33	2.50
65	1.15	1.31	1.46	1.62	1.77	1.92	2.08	2.23	2.38
70	1.14	1.29	1.43	1.57	1.71	1.86	2.00	2.14	2.29
75	1.13	1.27	1.40	1.53	1.67	1.80	1.93	2.07	2.20
80	1.13	1.25	1.38	1.50	1.63	1.75	1.88	2.00	2.13
85	1.12	1.24	1.35	1.47	1.59	1.71	1.82	1.94	2.06
90	1.11	1.22	1.33	1.44	1.56	1.67	1.78	1.89	2.00

The dynamic adjuster for this change, given SC% of 30 per cent and DC% of 60 per cent, is 3.00 and the calculation for a 5 per cent price increase is therefore:

% Increase in SC = Price Increase × Dynamic Adjuster

% Increase in SC = 5.00 × 3.00

% Increase in SC = 15.00%

This table has given you the actual increase you could handle in the value of your static costs. The static costs were $30 before any change was made, i.e. before the initial impact; 15 per cent of this figure is $4.50 and allowing an increase to $34.50, the figure we have used in the contribution statement.

	Before	After initial impact	After SC increase	%
Income	$100.00	$105.00	$105.00	100.00
Dynamic Costs	$60.00	$60.00	$60.00	57.14
Gross Contribution	$40.00	$45.00	$45.00	42.86
Static Costs	$30.00	$30.00	$34.50	32.86
Dynamic Net Contribution	$10.00	$15.00	$10.50	10.00

And $34.50 as a percentage of the new income level of $105 gives you a SC% figure of 32.86 per cent.

Changing the static costs leaves the GC% unchanged at its new level after the initial impact, i.e. at 42.86 per cent. With this higher level of GC% there is less pressure on you to become more effective in your use of your static costs. You can invest in additional resources if you feel this will benefit the business as a whole.

Let us see what happens with the rest of the dynamic indicators.

New BeGap% = New DNC% / New GC%

New BeGap% = 10.00% / 42.86% = 23.33%

There appears to be a slight increase in risk, which is what we would expect if we had allowed a relative increase in the static costs, i.e. you have effectively changed your cost structure. However, if we envisage the future as rosy – volumes will start to rise – we will be rewarded by a higher level of GC%.

We could now go through the analysis of changes in DNA%. However, in *Chapter 11: Increases in your static costs* we identify that the strands of our DNA are not affected by changes in the static costs. So there will be no change in DNA% as a result of this possible action. However, there is still the change in DNA as a result of the initial impact to consider.

	Before	After initial impact	After SC increase
Income	$100.00	$105.00	$105.00
Stock	$50.00	$50.00	$50.00
Debtors	$100.00	$105.00	$105.00
Creditors	$80.00	$80.00	$80.00
SNA	$70.00	$75.00	$75.00
Stock%	50.00%	47.62%	47.62%
Dr%	100.00%	100.00%	100.00%
Cr%	80.00%	76.19%	76.19%
SNA%	70.00%	71.43%	71.43%

For the DNA% this means:

DNA = SNA *after* Decision – SNA *before* Initial Impact

DNA = \$75.00 – \$70.00 = \$5.00

And then DNA% is:

$$\text{DNA\%} = \frac{\$5.00}{\$105.00} \times 100 = 4.76\%$$

And the impact on the DCM% is:

DCM% = DNC% – DNA%

DCM% = 10.00% – 4.76% = 5.24%

To summarize this option:

Eight dynamic indicators

	Before	After initial impact	After SC increase
GC%	40.00%	42.86%	42.86%
DNC%	10.00%	14.29%	10.00%
BeGap%	25.00%	33.34%	23.33%
Stock%	50.00%	47.62%	47.62%
Dr%	100.00%	100.00%	100.00%
Cr%	80.00%	76.19%	76.19%
DNA%	0.00%	4.76%	4.76%
DCM%	10.00%	9.53%	5.24%

Although contribution percentages have increased, the BeGap% has gone down, suggesting a slight increase in risk for the model business. In addition, there has been a decrease in DCM% that needs to be managed in the short term. Increasing static costs is a long-term decision – you need to be sure of long-term rewards.

chapter 8

Decreases in your income

Your income may decrease due to a fall in levels of activity (volume) of your business or it may be due to a drop in 'price' (value) – decreased selling price, decreased budget allocation, etc. This chapter looks solely at managing decreases in the value of your income driven by some sort of price decrease.

Decreases to the income need to be managed and two stages help in understanding the impact on your business:

1 The initial impact of the decrease.

2 The alternative actions you could take to dynamically manage this decrease.

With decreases in income the initial impact can be visualized using the eight dynamic indicators on the radar chart. The trends you will be monitoring using the dynamic breakeven graph and the dynamic cash graph will put these decreases into context – do you need to react or is it simply a momentary blip?

Decreases in income caused by an effective 'price' decrease are perhaps among the most common and the most difficult to deal with. How many managers have not been faced with such issues? It may be, as a department manager or a manager in the public sector, that your budget is currently being slashed and yet you have the same activity levels to maintain. Or as a retail manager you are involved in a highly competitive situation where the customer is looking for even lower prices. Yet this is the area where the relationships between effective price, level of activity and overall contribution are least understood. Dynamic financial management has some of the answers. We will consider not only the impact of having to reduce your income but also the steps you have to take to recover from these pressures.

We cannot claim to be able to predict exactly what is going to happen in your business, but we can tell you what needs to happen.

Decreases in price often have a different source to decreases in costs. The decrease can come from internally generated decisions – positive management action. Changing costs are often imposed on us from the outside, e.g. from a supplier. Management decisions to decrease price are often taken in order to make a secondary event happen – a chain reaction. The classic example of this is the attempt to increase volume by reducing price. You do not know what will happen, but with these dynamic financial management techniques we can predict very accurately what needs to be done to get a successful result.

What do we mean by a successful result? Ideally we would like our radar to be in at least the same shape that it was before the decrease. As a result of this management decision, the shape of your business shrinks, often in unexpected ways. But getting everything back into shape with a series of chain reactions is too ambitious. We believe that a meaningful definition of getting back to the status quo is returning the DNC% to the same level as it was before the initial management decision.

For example, let us look at the model business. If its price goes down by 5 per cent, the initial impact on the contribution statement would show that the DNC% has been reduced to 5 per cent. We need to know what the alternative ways are of getting your DNC% back up to its original level of 10 per cent.

What we will present here are the effects of a decrease in your income. We will do this in the two stages mentioned earlier, i.e. look at the simple impact of the decrease and then the measures available to us to manage these dynamically and regain our level of fitness, i.e. regain our original DNC%.

Decreases in your income

We will begin with a summary of what could happen if your business suffered from a decrease in its income. For the model business, if price fell by 5 per cent, the possible actions to compensate would be:

Decrease		Appropriate action to regain DNC%	Amount
Decrease	⇒	Increase volume	By 17.65%
in price	⇒	Decrease dynamic costs	By 7.50%
of 5%	⇒	Decrease static costs	By 15.00%

The shape of the model business after these decreases would be:

Eight dynamic indicators

	Before any decrease	After initial impact Price decrease 5%	After volume increase 17.65%	After DC decrease 7.50%	After SC decrease 15.00%
GC%	40.00%	36.84%	36.84%	41.58%	36.84%
DNC%	10.00%	5.26%	10.00%	10.00%	10.00%
BeGap%	25.00%	14.28%	27.14%	24.05%	27.14%
Stock%	50.00%	52.63%	52.63%	48.68%	52.63%
Dr%	100.00%	100.00%	100.00%	100.00%	100.00%
Cr%	80.00%	84.21%	84.21%	81.05%	84.21%
DNA%	0.00%	(5.26)%	5.79%	(6.05)%	(5.26)%
DCM%	10.00%	10.52%	4.21%	16.05%	15.26%

The decision will now be yours to either:

- accept the new shape of your business after the initial impact and decrease your targets accordingly;
- work dynamically towards one of the above possible actions;
- somewhere in between.

Whatever your decision, you can predict its impact before you are committed to any decreases – managing tomorrow today.

So, how did we get to these results? First we need to find out the result of the initial impact, then we need to look at all the possible actions that could be taken to compensate for this decrease in income.

The initial impact

When your income falls due to a decrease in value – a decrease in price or in your budget allocation – there are going to be a number of impacts on your eight dynamic indicators. These are shown in Fig 8.1.

The eight dynamic indicators	Decrease in price		DNC%	
	Tool			
GC%	Look-up			
DNC%	Look-up			
BeGap%	Calculation			
Stock%	Look-up			
Dr%				
Cr%	Look-up			
DNA%	Calculation			
DCM%	Calculation			

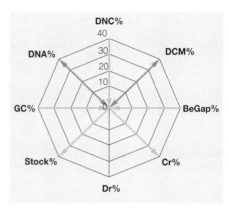

Fig 8.1 ●
Radar chart of dynamic indicators

With a decision to decrease prices, all but one of the eight dynamic indicators are affected. Permanent effects will be a decrease in GC%, DNC% and BeGap% and an increase in Stock% and Cr%. However, DNA% could either go up or go down depending on its strands. DCM% could also go either way depending on the magnitude of the figures involved. A word of caution is needed here. The Dr% is not affected in the long term but there will be an impact as the pricing decision works its way through the time warp.

We can now look at the magnitude of the initial impact on each of the eight dynamic indicators in the order presented in the table. As an example we will use the figures in the model business presented in the *Introduction to Part Two*.

Throughout this chapter we will assume that the effective price has decreased by 5 per cent, i.e. the amount of income has gone down to 95 per cent of its previous level without any decrease in the level of activity. We will look first at the initial impact of a decrease in price on GC%.

Cause Price down
Effect on GC%
Method Look-up

Not surprisingly, if you reduce your selling price and nothing else happens, your GC% must go down. But by how much? Table 8.1 allows you to look up the new GC%. The GC% is currently 40 per cent and we are, effectively, going to lower our price by 5 per cent. Looking up these figures in the table we see the new GC% will be 36.84 per cent.

Table 8.1 ● New GC% after a price decrease

Current GC%	% Decrease in price										
	1	3	5	7	9	10	12	14	16	18	20
10	9.09	7.22	5.26	3.23	1.10	0.00	N/A	N/A	N/A	N/A	N/A
15	14.14	12.37	10.53	8.60	6.59	5.56	3.41	1.16	N/A	N/A	N/A
20	19.19	17.53	15.79	13.98	12.09	11.11	9.09	6.98	4.76	2.44	0.00
25	24.24	22.68	21.05	19.35	17.58	16.67	14.77	12.79	10.71	8.54	6.25
30	29.29	27.84	26.32	24.73	23.08	22.22	20.45	18.60	16.67	14.63	12.50
35	34.34	32.99	31.58	30.11	28.57	27.78	26.14	24.42	22.62	20.73	18.75
40	39.39	38.14	**36.84**	35.48	34.07	33.33	31.82	30.23	28.57	26.83	25.00
45	44.44	43.30	42.11	40.86	39.56	38.89	37.50	36.05	34.52	32.93	31.25
50	49.49	48.45	47.37	46.24	45.05	44.44	43.18	41.86	40.48	39.02	37.50
55	54.55	53.61	52.63	51.61	50.55	50.00	48.86	47.67	46.43	45.12	43.75
60	59.60	58.76	57.89	56.99	56.04	55.56	54.55	53.49	52.38	51.22	50.00
65	64.65	63.92	63.16	62.37	61.54	61.11	60.23	59.30	58.33	57.32	56.25
70	69.70	69.07	68.42	67.74	67.03	66.67	65.91	65.12	64.29	63.41	62.50
75	74.75	74.23	73.68	73.12	72.53	72.22	71.59	70.93	70.24	69.51	68.75
80	79.80	79.38	78.95	78.49	78.02	77.78	77.27	76.74	76.19	75.61	75.00
85	84.85	84.54	84.21	83.87	83.52	83.33	82.95	82.56	82.14	81.71	81.25
90	89.90	89.69	89.47	89.25	89.01	88.89	88.64	88.37	88.10	87.80	87.50

What does this really mean to your business? For every £100 of income you used to earn £40 worth of gross contribution, £40 towards the static costs of the business. You now earn only £36.84 of gross contribution. Just checking this with the model business:

	Before	After
Income	£100.00	£95.00
Dynamic Costs	£60.00	£60.00
Gross Contribution	£40.00	£35.00
GC%	40.00%	36.84%

In reality, because the income has also fallen from £100 to £95, the value of gross contribution has fallen to £35. This is a 12 per cent drop in the value of gross contribution (£5/£40).

Cause Price down
Effect on DNC%
Method Look-up

In the model business the existing DNC% was 10 per cent. What will be the impact of the 5 per cent decrease in price? Table 8.2 gives the answer. The new DNC% is 5.26 per cent. This is an effective drop of 47 per cent in DNC% for a price decrease of only 5 per cent. If you were predicting sales of £1 million you would now return a DNC of only £52,600 instead of the original £100,000. Many managers mistakenly assume a 5 per cent decrease in price will be a 5 per cent decrease in contribution.

Table 8.2 ● **New DNC% after a price decrease**

Current					% Decrease in price						
DNC%	1	3	5	7	9	10	12	14	16	18	20
1	0.00	−2.06	−4.21	−6.45	−8.79	−10.00	−12.50	−15.12	−17.86	−20.73	−23.75
2	1.01	−1.03	−3.16	−5.38	−7.69	−8.89	−11.36	−13.95	−16.67	−19.51	−22.50
3	2.02	0.00	−2.11	−4.30	−6.59	−7.78	−10.23	−12.79	−15.48	−18.29	−21.25
4	3.03	1.03	−1.05	−3.23	−5.49	−6.67	−9.09	−11.63	−14.29	−17.07	−20.00
5	4.04	2.06	0.00	−2.15	−4.40	−5.56	−7.95	−10.47	−13.10	−15.85	−18.75
6	5.05	3.09	1.05	−1.08	−3.30	−4.44	−6.82	−9.30	−11.90	−14.63	−17.50
7	6.06	4.12	2.11	0.00	−2.20	−3.33	−5.68	−8.14	−10.71	−13.41	−16.25
8	7.07	5.15	3.16	1.08	−1.10	−2.22	−4.55	−6.98	−9.52	−12.20	−15.00
9	8.08	6.19	4.21	2.15	0.00	−1.11	−3.41	−5.81	−8.33	−10.98	−13.75
10	9.09	7.22	**5.26**	3.23	1.10	0.00	−2.27	−4.65	−7.14	−9.76	−12.50
12	11.11	9.28	7.37	5.38	3.30	2.22	0.00	−2.33	−4.76	−7.32	−10.00
14	13.13	11.34	9.47	7.53	5.49	4.44	2.27	0.00	−2.38	−4.88	−7.50
16	15.15	13.40	11.58	9.68	7.69	6.67	4.55	2.33	0.00	−2.44	−5.00
18	17.17	15.46	13.68	11.83	9.89	8.89	6.82	4.65	2.38	0.00	−2.50
20	19.19	17.53	15.79	13.98	12.09	11.11	9.09	6.98	4.76	2.44	0.00
25	24.24	22.68	21.05	19.35	17.58	16.67	14.77	12.79	10.71	8.54	6.25
30	29.29	27.84	26.32	24.73	23.08	22.22	20.45	18.60	16.67	14.63	12.50
35	34.34	32.99	31.58	30.11	28.57	27.78	26.14	24.42	22.62	20.73	18.75
40	39.39	38.14	36.84	35.48	34.07	33.33	31.82	30.23	28.57	26.83	25.00
50	49.49	48.45	47.37	46.24	45.05	44.44	43.18	41.86	40.48	39.02	37.50

Let us look at the new contribution statement for the model business:

	Before		After	
Income	£100.00	100.00%	£95.00	100.00%
Dynamic Costs	£60.00	60.00%	£60.00	63.16%
Gross Contribution	£40.00	40.00%	£35.00	36.84%
Static Costs	£30.00	30.00%	£30.00	31.58%
Dynamic Net Contribution	£10.00	10.00%	£5.00	5.26%

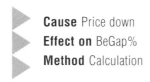

Cause Price down
Effect on BeGap%
Method Calculation

The basic calculation for the new BeGap% value is simple and is based upon the two previous results:

$$\text{New BeGap\%} = \frac{\text{New DNC\%}}{\text{New GC\%}}$$

$$\text{New BeGap\%} = \frac{5.26\%}{36.84\%}$$

$$\text{New BeGap\%} = 14.28\%$$

This has nearly halved the BeGap% from its original level of 25 per cent – thereby halving the safety factor of your business, doubling the risk.

As a summary so far, the dynamic indicators of contribution are:

GC%	was	40.00%	is now	36.84	
DNC%	was	10.00%	is now	5.26	
BeGap%	was	25.00%	is now	14.28	

But as we have seen, a price decrease also has an impact on two strands of our DNA%. So we now only need to consider the impact on Stock% and Cr% and, as a result of these, our new DNA% and DCM%.

Cause Price down
Effect on Stock%
Method Look-up

Look back at Fig 8.1 on p. 192. The arrow indicates that the Stock% is going up. We need to know the magnitude of the effect so that we can predict the impact on the radar chart. And again, this is as simple as looking it up in Table 8.3.

With a 5 per cent decrease in price with an existing Stock% of 50 per cent of the month's sales, we can simply read from the table the new Stock% of 52.63 per cent. This means you have now tied up an extra 2.63 per cent of income in the time warp, or to state this a bit more dramatically, an increase in your

Table 8.3 ● **New Stock% after a price decrease**

Current Stock%	1	3	5	7	9	10	12	14	16	18	20
						% Decrease in price					
10	10.10	10.31	10.53	10.75	10.99	11.11	11.36	11.63	11.90	12.20	12.50
20	20.20	20.62	21.05	21.51	21.98	22.22	22.73	23.26	23.81	24.39	25.00
30	30.30	30.93	31.58	32.26	32.97	33.33	34.09	34.88	35.71	36.59	37.50
40	40.40	41.24	42.11	43.01	43.96	44.44	45.45	46.51	47.62	48.78	50.00
50	50.51	51.55	**52.63**	53.76	54.95	55.56	56.82	58.14	59.52	60.98	62.50
60	60.61	61.86	63.16	64.52	65.93	66.67	68.18	69.77	71.43	73.17	75.00
70	70.71	72.16	73.68	75.27	76.92	77.78	79.55	81.40	83.33	85.37	87.50
80	80.81	82.47	84.21	86.02	87.91	88.89	90.91	93.02	95.24	97.56	100.00
90	90.91	92.78	94.74	96.77	98.90	100.00	102.27	104.65	107.14	109.76	112.50
100	101.01	103.09	105.26	107.53	109.89	111.11	113.64	116.28	119.05	121.95	125.00
110	111.11	113.40	115.79	118.28	120.88	122.22	125.00	127.91	130.95	134.15	137.50
120	121.21	123.71	126.32	129.03	131.87	133.33	136.36	139.53	142.86	146.34	150.00
130	131.31	134.02	136.84	139.78	142.86	144.44	147.73	151.16	154.76	158.54	162.50
140	141.41	144.33	147.37	150.54	153.85	155.56	159.09	162.79	166.67	170.73	175.00
150	151.52	154.64	157.89	161.29	164.84	166.67	170.45	174.42	178.57	182.93	187.50

effective stock levels. If you are hoping to increase your level of activity as a result of this decrease in price, you are going to have to find relatively more cash to support the increased Stock%. The amount of internal funding that will be available to help you grow has been diminished.

Cause Price down
Effect on Cr%
Method Look-up

If you have reduced your price, the initial impact assumes no other decreases. You might be selling for less but your costs are still the same. That means you have not negotiated any compensating differences in your dynamic costs, and your suppliers, who represent a major part of your dynamic costs, make up a substantial amount of your Cr%. As such they are bound to have increased as a percentage of the income figure if you have decreased your price. Another dynamic look-up table is available to simply find the new figure (*see* Table 8.4).

Table 8.4 ● New Cr% after a price decrease

Current						% Decrease in price					
Cr%	1	3	5	7	9	10	12	14	16	18	20
10	10.10	10.31	10.53	10.75	10.99	11.11	11.36	11.63	11.90	12.20	12.50
20	20.20	20.62	21.05	21.51	21.98	22.22	22.73	23.26	23.81	24.39	25.00
30	30.30	30.93	31.58	32.26	32.97	33.33	34.09	34.88	35.71	36.59	37.50
40	40.40	41.24	42.11	43.01	43.96	44.44	45.45	46.51	47.62	48.78	50.00
50	50.51	51.55	52.63	53.76	54.95	55.56	56.82	58.14	59.52	60.98	62.50
60	60.61	61.86	63.16	64.52	65.93	66.67	68.18	69.77	71.43	73.17	75.00
70	70.71	72.16	73.68	75.27	76.92	77.78	79.55	81.40	83.33	85.37	87.50
80	80.81	82.47	**84.21**	86.02	87.91	88.89	90.91	93.02	95.24	97.56	100.00
90	90.91	92.78	94.74	96.77	98.90	100.00	102.27	104.65	107.14	109.76	112.50
100	101.01	103.09	105.26	107.53	109.89	111.11	113.64	116.28	119.05	121.95	125.00
110	111.11	113.40	115.79	118.28	120.88	122.22	125.00	127.91	130.95	134.15	137.50
120	121.21	123.71	126.32	129.03	131.87	133.33	136.36	139.53	142.86	146.34	150.00
130	131.31	134.02	136.84	139.78	142.86	144.44	147.73	151.16	154.76	158.54	162.50
140	141.41	144.33	147.37	150.54	153.85	155.56	159.09	162.79	166.67	170.73	175.00
150	151.52	154.64	157.89	161.29	164.84	166.67	170.45	174.42	178.57	182.93	187.50

After a 5 per cent decrease in price with an existing Cr% of 80 per cent, we can see from the table the new Cr% of 84.21 per cent. But hold on, if we have reduced our price don't we want to delay the payment to our suppliers? This is not what the table is saying. The table is saying that the amount you owe your creditors as a percentage of income is more, yet the value will be the same. With a lower income figure you will have to pay more of this out to your suppliers. The time warp is swallowing your cash.

However, for every £100 of income this will give a new creditor value of £84.21 instead of the original value of £80. That is an extra £4.21 that will soon be leaking out of the time warp. The effect of decisions made 'today' will have to be paid for 'tomorrow'.

We now need to look at the overall effect on DNA% for the model business.

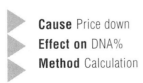

Cause Price down
Effect on DNA%
Method Calculation

In order to calculate the dynamic net assets as a result of this change we need to look at the strands of our static net assets imprisoned in the time warp before and after the anticipated change. This can be shown as:

DNA = SNA *after* Decrease – SNA *before* Decrease

For the model business the strands of the SNA, both in terms of value and percentage, are shown below:

	Before	After
Income	$100.00	$95.00
Stock	£50.00	£50.00
Debtors	£100.00	£95.00
Creditors	£80.00	£80.00
SNA	£70.00	£65.00
Stock%	50.00%	52.63%
Dr%	100.00%	100.00%
Cr%	80.00%	84.21%
SNA%	70.00%	68.42%

The DNA can now be calculated as:

$$\text{DNA} = £65.00 - £70.00 = £(5.00)$$

The DNA% is

$$\text{DNA\%} = \frac{\$(5.00)}{\$95.00} \times 100 = (5.26)\%$$

A negative DNA% is good for cash as cash has effectively been released from the time warp. Less real cash has moved into the time warp as a result of the initial impact.

The final dynamic indicator to consider is the DCM% and now we have the figures for DNC% and DNA% we can move on to look at this.

▶ **Cause** Price down
▶ **Effect on** DCM%
▶ **Method** Calculation

The final dynamic indicator is now very easy to calculate:

$$\text{DCM\%} = \text{DNC\%} - \text{DNA\%}$$

$$\text{DCM\%} = 5.26\% - (5.26)\% = 10.52\%$$

Your DCM% after the decrease is 10.52 per cent, compared with the 10 per cent you were forecasting before the decrease, which suggests you have released cash from the time warp. But when you are considering a decrease in price you have to think very carefully about this. The main reason that the DCM% is bigger is because the value of the debtors has fallen. This represents cash you will never get.

Think what will happen next month when the business stabilizes. With no movement in the static net assets, the DCM% will, like the DNC%, return to a stable level of 5.26 per cent, less real cash available to the business.

The new shape of your business

The eight dynamic indicators before and after the decrease in prices are:

Contribution statement			DNA statement		
	Before	**After**		**Before**	**After**
Income	£100.00	£95.00	Income	£100.00	£95.00
Dynamic Costs	£60.00	£60.00	Stock	£50.00	£50.00
Gross Contribution	£40.00	£35.00	Debtors	£100.00	£95.00
Static Costs	£30.00	£30.00	Creditors	£80.00	£80.00
Dynamic Net Contribution	£10.00	£5.00	Static Net Assets	£70.00	£65.00

Eight dynamic indicators

	Before	**After**
GC%	40.00%	36.84%
DNC%	10.00%	5.26%
BeGap%	25.00%	14.28%
Stock%	50.00%	52.63%
Dr%	100.00%	100.00%
Cr%	80.00%	84.21%
DNA%	0.00%	(5.26)%
DCM%	10.00%	10.52%

Figure 8.2 shows how this looks on the radar chart. As you can see, the contribution indicators for your business are shrinking!

For the model business the effect on GC% looks quite small on the radar chart.

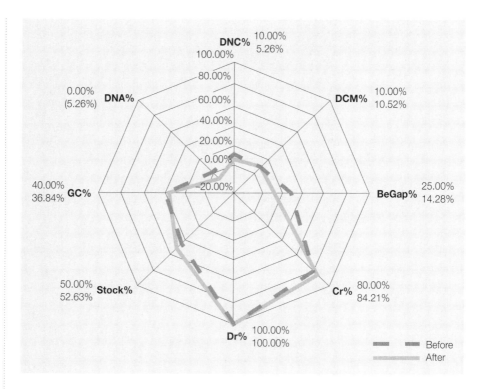

Fig 8.2 ● **Model business radar chart**

But look at the DNC% and BeGap%. They have been decimated. In the long run, DNC for reinvesting in the business has been reduced and because of the increased risk revealed in the BeGap% any future decisions or decreases in prices or costs are likely to start a vicious circle of decline. You are potentially on a downward spiral.

However, you still seem to be relatively cash rich. Many businesses in unmanaged decline are fooled by this inflow of cash. They believe the business is doing okay as 'cash is king'. It is only through the relationship of the dynamic indicators in the radar chart that the true shape of the business is revealed. The DCM% is higher because income, the anchor, is lower. Less money is tied up in debtors because you are charging them less, not because you are managing them better. Cash has not been released from the time warp – it never got there in the first place.

Actions for dynamic management of a decrease in income

Decreases in income are, as mentioned earlier, often directly under the control of managers. The initial impact is therefore of interest but it is rarely where the story ends. Price is often used as a strategy to prompt another event and it is the magnitude of these events that is of most interest. The magnitude with which dynamic financial management is particularly concerned is the secondary decrease needed:

'to return the DNC% to the same level as it was before the decrease.'

As we have shown, managers are usually left with three things they can do when they have made a decision to reduce the price:

Decrease		Appropriate action to regain DNC%
Decrease	⟶	Increase volume
in income	⟶	Decrease dynamic costs
	⟶	Decrease static costs

As possible reactions these are nothing new. They are fairly obvious things that you could do to regain your DNC%. The dynamic techniques we are using can predict the *magnitude* of each of the decreases that will be needed to compensate for the original decision.

Again we can look at the impact of these using a series of dynamic look-up tables and calculations and we will continue to assume we are responding to the initial impact of a 5 per cent decrease in income.

Cause Price down
Possible action Increase volume
Method Look-up/Look-up

If you increase volume, you increase the value of DNC. For every extra one you sell, you make extra GC, and if you can keep your static costs at the same level, this is extra DNC. What dynamic financial management reveals is the level of volume increase you need in your business to regain your original DNC%.

Increasing volume is probably one of the most anticipated consequences of a price decrease. Economics tells us there is a relationship between price and demand. But in reality the market does not always perform in the way the theories say it will. Customers are often less predictable. Dynamic financial management will tell us what needs to be done. Close co-operation is needed with marketing to assess whether this volume increase can actually be achieved.

Back to our model business where we were looking at a decrease of 5 per cent in our price. What volume increase does the model business need to regain its original DNC% of 10 per cent? There are two simple tables involved in discovering the volume increase needed. The first tells us the dynamic adjuster and the second tells us the Volume% increase needed (*see* Tables 8.5, 8.6 and 8.7).

Table 8.5 ● **Dynamic adjuster**

Current					% Decrease in price					
DNC%	2	4	6	8	10	12	14	16	18	20
1	1.98	3.96	5.94	7.92	9.90	11.88	13.86	15.84	17.82	19.80
2	1.96	3.92	5.88	7.84	9.80	11.76	13.72	15.68	17.64	19.60
3	1.94	3.88	5.82	7.76	9.70	11.64	13.58	15.52	17.46	19.40
4	1.92	3.84	5.76	7.68	9.60	11.52	13.44	15.36	17.28	19.20
5	1.90	3.80	5.70	7.60	9.50	11.40	13.30	15.20	17.10	19.00
6	1.88	3.76	5.64	7.52	9.40	11.28	13.16	15.04	16.92	18.80
7	1.86	3.72	5.58	7.44	9.30	11.16	13.02	14.88	16.74	18.60
8	1.84	3.68	5.52	7.36	9.20	11.04	12.88	14.72	16.56	18.40
9	1.82	3.64	5.46	7.28	9.10	10.92	12.74	14.56	16.38	18.20
10	1.80	3.60	5.40	7.20	9.00	10.80	12.60	14.40	16.20	18.00
12	1.76	3.52	5.28	7.04	8.80	10.56	12.32	14.08	15.84	17.60
14	1.72	3.44	5.16	6.88	8.60	10.32	12.04	13.76	15.48	17.20
16	1.68	3.36	5.04	6.72	8.40	10.08	11.76	13.44	15.12	16.80
18	1.64	3.28	4.92	6.56	8.20	9.84	11.48	13.12	14.76	16.40
20	1.60	3.20	4.80	6.40	8.00	9.60	11.20	12.80	14.40	16.00
25	1.50	3.00	4.50	6.00	7.50	9.00	10.50	12.00	13.50	15.00
30	1.40	2.80	4.20	5.60	7.00	8.40	9.80	11.20	12.60	14.00
35	1.30	2.60	3.90	5.20	6.50	7.80	9.10	10.40	11.70	13.00
40	1.20	2.40	3.60	4.80	6.00	7.20	8.40	9.60	10.80	12.00
50	1.00	2.00	3.00	4.00	5.00	6.00	7.00	8.00	9.00	10.00

If our anticipated price decrease is 5 per cent and our existing DNC% is 10 per cent, using Table 8.5 we can derive our dynamic adjuster of 4.50. This table then uses the two components of the dynamic adjuster and the existing SC% of 30 per cent for the model business. We can now use these figures in Tables 8.6 and 8.7. (You will see that 4.50 is not on the table below. Estimating halfway between 4 and 5 will give you the answer you need.) If your dynamic adjuster is between 1 and 10 use Table 8.6. And if your dynamic adjuster is between 11 and 20 use Table 8.7.

Table 8.6 ● New Volume% to maintain same DNC% with a price decrease

Static cost%	Dynamic adjuster									
	1	2	3	4	5	6	7	8	9	10
10	111.11	125.00	142.86	166.67	200.00	250.00	333.33	500.00		
15	107.14	115.38	125.00	136.36	150.00	166.67	187.50	214.29	250.00	300.00
20	105.26	111.11	117.65	125.00	133.33	142.86	153.85	166.67	181.82	200.00
25	104.17	108.70	113.64	119.05	125.00	131.58	138.89	147.06	156.25	166.67
30	103.45	107.14	111.11	115.38	120.00	125.00	130.43	136.36	142.86	150.00
35	102.94	106.06	109.38	112.90	116.67	120.69	125.00	129.63	134.62	140.00
40	102.56	105.26	108.11	111.11	114.29	117.65	121.21	125.00	129.03	133.33
45	102.27	104.65	107.14	109.76	112.50	115.38	118.42	121.62	125.00	128.57
50	102.04	104.17	106.38	108.70	111.11	113.64	116.28	119.05	121.95	125.00
55	101.85	103.77	105.77	107.84	110.00	112.24	114.58	117.02	119.57	122.22
60	101.69	103.45	105.26	107.14	109.09	111.11	113.21	115.38	117.65	120.00
65	101.56	103.17	104.84	106.56	108.33	110.17	112.07	114.04	116.07	118.18
70	101.45	102.94	104.48	106.06	107.69	109.38	111.11	112.90	114.75	116.67
75	101.35	102.74	104.17	105.63	107.14	108.70	110.29	111.94	113.64	115.38
80	101.27	102.56	103.90	105.26	106.67	108.11	109.59	111.11	112.68	114.29
85	101.19	102.41	103.66	104.94	106.25	107.59	108.97	110.39	111.84	113.33
90	101.12	102.27	103.45	104.65	105.88	107.14	108.43	109.76	111.11	112.50

Table 8.7 ● New Volume% to maintain same DNC% with a price decrease

Static cost%	Dynamic adjuster									
	11	12	13	14	15	16	17	18	19	20
10										
15	375.00									
20	222.22	250.00	285.71	333.33	400.00	500.00	666.67			
25	178.57	192.31	208.33	227.27	250.00	277.78	312.50	357.14	416.67	500.00
30	157.89	166.67	176.47	187.50	200.00	214.29	230.77	250.00	272.73	300.00
35	145.83	152.17	159.09	166.67	175.00	184.21	194.44	205.88	218.75	233.33
40	137.93	142.86	148.15	153.85	160.00	166.67	173.91	181.82	190.48	200.00
45	132.35	136.36	140.63	145.16	150.00	155.17	160.71	166.67	173.08	180.00
50	128.21	131.58	135.14	138.89	142.86	147.06	151.52	156.25	161.29	166.67
55	125.00	127.91	130.95	134.15	137.50	141.03	144.74	148.65	152.78	157.14
60	122.45	125.00	127.66	130.43	133.33	136.36	139.53	142.86	146.34	150.00
65	120.37	122.64	125.00	127.45	130.00	132.65	135.42	138.30	141.30	144.44
70	118.64	120.69	122.81	125.00	127.27	129.63	132.08	134.62	137.25	140.00
75	117.19	119.05	120.97	122.95	125.00	127.12	129.31	131.58	133.93	136.36
80	115.94	117.65	119.40	121.21	123.08	125.00	126.98	129.03	131.15	133.33
85	114.86	116.44	118.06	119.72	121.43	123.19	125.00	126.87	128.79	130.77
90	113.92	115.38	116.88	118.42	120.00	121.62	123.29	125.00	126.76	128.57

In the model business our static costs are 30 per cent and our dynamic adjuster is 4.50. This tells us that the sales volume needs to go up to a new volume of 117.65 per cent – in other words, a 17.65 per cent increase above the current volume of sales. This may seem a surprisingly large amount. All you have done is reduced the price by 5 per cent, yet you are now faced with trying to achieve a compensating volume increase of 17.65 per cent. How many businesses could achieve this with ease? And the lower the GC%, the higher the volume increase needed. Unfortunately it is often in low GC% companies operating in highly competitive markets that we are tempted (or forced) to reduce our price. So the contribution statement for the model business will have decreased as follows:

	Before	After initial impact	After volume increase	%
Income	£100.00	£95.00	£111.77	100.00
Dynamic Costs	£60.00	£60.00	£70.59	63.16
Gross Contribution	£40.00	£35.00	£41.18	36.84
Static Costs	£30.00	£30.00	£30.00	26.84
Dynamic Net Contribution	£10.00	£5.00	£11.18	10.00

Don't forget, if your volume has increased, so will the value of your dynamic costs. In this example we have increased volume by 17.65 per cent, therefore our dynamic costs will also go up by 17.65 per cent. If you recall, the initial impact of the decision to reduce price had increased the DC% in the model business from 60 per cent to 63.16 per cent. With a volume increase as a possible management action, it will stay at 63.16 per cent.

What about the other dynamic indicators? With a decrease in volume your GC% will stay the same as it was after the initial impact. But what about the rest of the dynamic indicators? We can start with the formula for calculating the BeGap%:

New BeGap% = New DNC% / New GC%

New BeGap% = 10.00% / 36.84% = 27.14%

And the impact on DNA% and DCM%? If the only decrease is one of volume, then as a percentage of sales the strands of your SNA should stay the same, that is, at the levels after the impact of the decrease in price. We are still suffering the associated adverse effect of the relatively increased costs tied up in our stock and the increasing amount we will have to pay out to our suppliers for the extra cost. The table after the initial impact was:

	Before	After initial impact	After volume increase
Income	£100.00	£95.00	£111.77
Stock	£50.00	£50.00	£58.82
Debtors	£100.00	£95.00	£111.77
Creditors	£80.00	£80.00	£94.12
SNA	£70.00	£65.00	£76.47
Stock%	50.00%	52.63%	52.63%
Dr%	100.00%	100.00%	100.00%
Cr%	80.00%	84.21%	84.21%
SNA%	70.00%	68.42%	68.42%

In addition, the increase in volume means we need to increase the value of SNA, from its original level of £70 to £76.47, a 9.24 per cent increase in the actual value of your SNA.

What does this mean for the DNA%?

DNA = SNA *after* Decision – SNA *before* Initial Impact

DNA = £76.47 – £70.00 = £6.47

And then DNA% is:

$$DNA\% = \frac{£6.47}{£111.77} \times 100$$

DNA% = 5.79%

So the DNA% is now positive, meaning that there has been a significant movement of money in the strands of the SNA due to the increase in volume. The final evaluation is to see whether this has been compensated for with the increase in DNC% and we will do this by looking at the DCM%:

DCM% = DNC% – DNA%

DCM% = 10.00% – 5.79% = 4.21%

The answer is no. The size of the increase in volume needed has drained cash from the business and the indicator of this is a lower DCM% after this decrease. To summarize this option:

Eight dynamic indicators

	Before	After initial impact	After volume increase
GC%	40.00%	36.84%	36.84%
DNC%	10.00%	5.26%	10.00%
BeGap%	25.00%	14.28%	27.14%
Stock%	50.00%	52.63%	52.63%
Dr%	100.00%	100.00%	100.00%
Cr%	80.00%	84.21%	84.21%
DNA%	0.00%	(5.26)%	5.79%
DCM%	10.00%	10.52%	4.21%

There is an improvement in the contribution indicators of DNC% and BeGap% but an adverse impact on the cash indicators of DNA% and DCM%. For the model business a 17.65 per cent increase in volume may be achievable but the business needs to consider how it will fund this growth and how long it will take to pay back that funding.

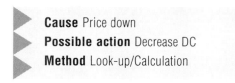

Cause Price down
Possible action Decrease DC
Method Look-up/Calculation

If our price decreases, then an alternative way of regaining our DNC% is to reduce the costs. We have two different types of costs that we can attempt to reduce. Each of these will produce a differently shaped business, or perhaps more importantly, a fundamentally different cost structure that will respond to future growth or decline in very different ways. Remember the discussion in *Chapter 2: What are dynamic indicators?* on the relationship of risk and reward to cost structure? We will first look at achieving the decrease through a decrease in our dynamic costs.

But getting back to the decreases in the model business, if our price decreases by 5 per cent, the compensating DC decrease can now be calculated. This requires two stages, the use of a dynamic look-up table followed by a simple calculation to find the required decrease in DC.

Table 8.8 ● Dynamic adjuster for new DC% with a price decrease

Current DC%	Existing SC%								
	10	20	30	40	50	60	70	80	90
10	2.00	3.00	4.00	5.00	6.00	7.00	8.00	9.00	10.00
15	1.67	2.33	3.00	3.67	4.33	5.00	5.67	6.33	7.00
20	1.50	2.00	2.50	3.00	3.50	4.00	4.50	5.00	5.50
25	1.40	1.80	2.20	2.60	3.00	3.40	3.80	4.20	4.60
30	1.33	1.67	2.00	2.33	2.67	3.00	3.33	3.67	4.00
35	1.29	1.57	1.86	2.14	2.43	2.71	3.00	3.29	3.57
40	1.25	1.50	1.75	2.00	2.25	2.50	2.75	3.00	3.25
45	1.22	1.44	1.67	1.89	2.11	2.33	2.56	2.78	3.00
50	1.20	1.40	1.60	1.80	2.00	2.20	2.40	2.60	2.80
55	1.18	1.36	1.55	1.73	1.91	2.09	2.27	2.45	2.64
60	1.17	1.33	**1.50**	1.67	1.83	2.00	2.17	2.33	2.50
65	1.15	1.31	1.46	1.62	1.77	1.92	2.08	2.23	2.38
70	1.14	1.29	1.43	1.57	1.71	1.86	2.00	2.14	2.29
75	1.13	1.27	1.40	1.53	1.67	1.80	1.93	2.07	2.20
80	1.13	1.25	1.38	1.50	1.63	1.75	1.88	2.00	2.13
85	1.12	1.24	1.35	1.47	1.59	1.71	1.82	1.94	2.06
90	1.11	1.22	1.33	1.44	1.56	1.67	1.78	1.89	2.00

In the model business the existing DC% is 60 per cent and the existing SC% is 30 per cent. Using Table 8.8 this would give us a dynamic adjuster of 1.50. We can use this in our calculation with a decrease in price of 5 per cent as follows:

% Decrease in DC = Price Decrease × Dynamic Adjuster

% Decrease in DC = 5.00 × 1.50 = 7.50%

This table has given you the actual decrease needed in the value of your dynamic costs. The dynamic costs were £60 before any decrease was made, i.e. before the initial impact – 7.5 per cent of this figure is £4.50 and reducing the original figure by £4.50 will give you the value £55.50, the figure we have used in the contribution statement.

	Before	After initial impact	After DC decrease	%
Income	£100.00	£95.00	£95.00	100.00
Dynamic Costs	£60.00	£60.00	£55.50	58.42
Gross Contribution	£40.00	£35.00	£39.50	41.58
Static Costs	£30.00	£30.00	£30.00	31.58
Dynamic Net Contribution	£10.00	£5.00	£9.50	10.00

And £55.50 as a percentage of the new income level of £95 gives you a DC% figure of 58.42 per cent and a GC% of 41.58 per cent – indeed, this is now higher than the figure before the price decrease. You need to be even more efficient than you were before the initial impact, not simply return to your original level of efficiency. Many businesses think that returning their DC% to 60 per cent will get the business back into shape. This is not so, you need to get your DC% even further down to 58.42 per cent.

What about the other dynamic indicators?

New BeGap% = New DNC% / New GC%

New BeGap% = 10.00% / 41.58%

New BeGap% = 24.05%

This action has resulted in a decrease in our dynamic costs of 7.5 per cent. This should also result in a decrease in Stock% and Cr%. This requires going through the initial impact tables for a decrease in dynamic costs. With a Stock% of 52.63 per cent after the initial impact, and a subsequent decrease in DC% of 7.5 per cent, the new Stock% will be 48.68 per cent. Similarly, with a Cr% of 84.21 per cent after the initial impact, the new Cr% will be 81.05 per cent. You can check these figures at your leisure using the tables. The Dr% will stay the same as we are not changing the price or the volume.

So the strands of the SNA at the various 'static' points in time of this analysis are:

	Before	After initial impact	After DC decrease
Income	£100.00	£95.00	£95.00
Stock	£50.00	£50.00	£46.25
Debtors	£100.00	£95.00	£95.00
Creditors	£80.00	£80.00	£77.00
SNA	£70.00	£65.00	£64.25
Stock%	50.00%	52.63%	48.68%
Dr%	100.00%	100.00%	100.00%
Cr%	80.00%	84.21%	81.05%
SNA%	70.00%	68.42%	67.63%

What does this mean for the DNA%?

$$\text{DNA} = \text{SNA } \textit{after} \text{ Decision} - \text{SNA } \textit{before} \text{ Initial Impact}$$

$$\text{DNA} = £64.25 - £70.00 = £(5.75)$$

And DNA% is:

$$\text{DNA\%} = \frac{£(5.75)}{£95.00} \times 100$$

$$\text{DNA\%} = (6.05)\%$$

So the DNA% is still negative, but again this is because of the lower value of debtors overall as a result of the initial impact of the price decrease. The impact on the DCM% is:

$$\text{DCM\%} = \text{DNC\%} - \text{DNA\%}$$

$$\text{DCM\%} = 10.00\% - (6.05)\% = 16.05\%$$

To summarize this option:

Eight dynamic indicators

	Before	After initial impact	After DC decrease
GC%	40.00%	36.84%	41.58%
DNC%	10.00%	5.26%	10.00%
BeGap%	25.00%	14.28%	24.05%
Stock%	50.00%	52.63%	48.68%
Dr%	100.00%	100.00%	100.00%
Cr%	80.00%	84.21%	81.05%
DNA%	0.00%	(5.26)%	(6.05)%
DCM%	10.00%	10.52%	16.05%

To compensate for the price decrease of 5 per cent we had to decrease our dynamic costs by 7.5 per cent. This has improved the performance of the dynamic indicators of contribution and has also had a beneficial impact on DNA%. Overall, therefore, we have a significant improvement in the DCM% of 16.05 per cent. If the model business can achieve a decrease in its DC of 7.5 per cent, it could even emerge as a leaner, meaner business. But in a low GC% business, reducing DC by 7.5 per cent is often too deep a cut.

> **Cause** Price down
> **Possible action** Decrease SC
> **Method** Look-up/Calculation

The alternative action to reducing your dynamic costs is, obviously, reducing your static costs. Again this will have a different impact on the cost structure and risk within the business.

In the model business, if our price decreases by 5 per cent the compensating SC decrease can be calculated. This requires two stages, the use of a dynamic look-up table (*see* Table 8.9) followed by a simple calculation to find the required decrease in DC.

Table 8.9 ● **Dynamic adjuster for new SC% with a price decrease**

Current SC%	Existing DC% 10	20	30	40	50	60	70	80	90
10	2.00	3.00	4.00	5.00	6.00	7.00	8.00	9.00	10.00
15	1.67	2.33	3.00	3.67	4.33	5.00	5.67	6.33	7.00
20	1.50	2.00	2.50	3.00	3.50	4.00	4.50	5.00	5.50
25	1.40	1.80	2.20	2.60	3.00	3.40	3.80	4.20	4.60
30	1.33	1.67	2.00	2.33	2.67	**3.00**	3.33	3.67	4.00
35	1.29	1.57	1.86	2.14	2.43	2.71	3.00	3.29	3.57
40	1.25	1.50	1.75	2.00	2.25	2.50	2.75	3.00	3.25
45	1.22	1.44	1.67	1.89	2.11	2.33	2.56	2.78	3.00
50	1.20	1.40	1.60	1.80	2.00	2.20	2.40	2.60	2.80
55	1.18	1.36	1.55	1.73	1.91	2.09	2.27	2.45	2.64
60	1.17	1.33	1.50	1.67	1.83	2.00	2.17	2.33	2.50
65	1.15	1.31	1.46	1.62	1.77	1.92	2.08	2.23	2.38
70	1.14	1.29	1.43	1.57	1.71	1.86	2.00	2.14	2.29
75	1.13	1.27	1.40	1.53	1.67	1.80	1.93	2.07	2.20
80	1.13	1.25	1.38	1.50	1.63	1.75	1.88	2.00	2.13
85	1.12	1.24	1.35	1.47	1.59	1.71	1.82	1.94	2.06
90	1.11	1.22	1.33	1.44	1.56	1.67	1.78	1.89	2.00

The dynamic adjuster for this decrease is 3.00. The calculation for a 5 per cent price decrease is therefore:

% Decrease in SC = Price Decrease × Dynamic Adjuster

% Decrease in SC = 5.00 × 3.00 = 15.00%

This table has given you the actual decrease needed in the value of your static costs. The static costs were £30 before any decrease was made, i.e. before the initial impact – 15 per cent of this figure is £4.50 and reducing the original figure by £4.50 will give you the value £25.50, the figure we have used in the contribution statement.

	Before	After initial impact	After SC decrease	%
Income	£100.00	£95.00	£95.00	100.00
Dynamic Costs	£60.00	£60.00	£60.00	63.16
Gross Contribution	£40.00	£35.00	£35.00	36.84
Static Costs	£30.00	£30.00	£25.50	26.84
Dynamic Net Contribution	£10.00	£5.00	£9.50	10.00

And £25.50 as a percentage of the new income level of £95 gives you a SC% figure of 26.84 per cent. Changing the static costs leaves the GC% unchanged at its new level after the initial impact, i.e. at 36.84 per cent. With this lower level of GC% there is an increased pressure on you to become more effective in your use of your static costs.

Let us see what happens with the rest of the dynamic indicators:

New BeGap% = New DNC% / New GC%

New BeGap% = 10.00% / 36.84%

New BeGap% = 27.14%

We could now go through the analysis of decreases in the strands of the DNA, the Stock%, the Dr% and the Cr%. However, in *Chapter 12: Decreases in your static costs* we identify that the strands of our DNA are not affected by decreases in the static costs. So there will be no decrease in SNA% as a result of this possible action. However, there is still the decrease in DNA as a result of the initial impact to consider.

	Before	**After initial impact**	**After SC decrease**
Income	£100.00	£95.00	£95.00
Stock	£50.00	£50.00	£50.00
Debtors	£100.00	£95.00	£95.00
Creditors	£80.00	£80.00	£80.00
SNA	£70.00	£65.00	£65.00
Stock%	50.00%	52.63%	52.63%
Dr%	100.00%	100.00%	100.00%
Cr%	80.00%	84.21%	84.21%
SNA%	70.00%	68.42%	68.42%

As you can see, the SNA values and percentage are the same as after the initial impact. What does this mean for the DNA%?

DNA = SNA *after* Decision – SNA *before* Initial Impact

DNA = £65.00 – £70.00 = £(5.00)

And then DNA% remains as:

$$\text{DNA\%} = \frac{£(5.00)}{£95.00} \times 100$$

DNA% = (5.26)%

So the DNA% is negative and the impact on the DCM% is:

DCM% = DNC% – DNA%

DCM% = 10.00% – (5.26)% = 15.26%

To summarize this option:

Eight dynamic indicators

	Before	**After initial impact**	**After SC decrease**
GC%	40.00%	36.84%	36.84%
DNC%	10.00%	5.26%	10.00%
BeGap%	25.00%	14.28%	27.14%
Stock%	50.00%	52.63%	52.63%
Dr%	100.00%	100.00%	100.00%
Cr%	80.00%	84.21%	84.21%
DNA%	0.00%	(5.26)%	(5.26)%
DCM%	10.00%	10.52%	15.26%

Again this has achieved a huge growth in the anticipated DCM%. But SC% needs to be reduced from 30 per cent to 26.84 per cent. With the same level of volume as before the price decrease this seems unlikely – a 15 per cent cut, an even deeper cut than needed in DC. This is due to the cost structure within the model business. For your business the situation could be reversed.

chapter 9

Increases in your dynamic costs

Why do dynamic costs increase?

Increases in your dynamic costs need to be managed and there are two stages in understanding the impact on your business:

1 The initial impact of the increase.

2 The alternative actions you could take to dynamically manage this increase.

The initial impact of any increase in dynamic costs can be most successfully visualized using the eight dynamic indicators on the radar chart. The trends you will be monitoring using the dynamic breakeven graph and the dynamic cash graph will put these increases into context – do you need to react or is it simply a momentary blip?

However, we should be managing the increase dynamically. From our understanding of the increase, monitored in the three charts we are using to visualize the business, we can begin to select the most appropriate action to take to get the business back into shape.

An example of this for dynamic costs could be responding to a proposed increase in materials costs from your supplier. A dynamic response would be to negotiate with your supplier for, say, a decrease in the cost of materials in exchange for an increase in the amount you will buy from them, making them a preferred supplier. Another, less palatable example could be decreasing the wages of your employees. How else could you get back into shape? Can you pass this increase on to your customers? If so, what price increase would this require? This is the chapter in which we will give you the power to answer all these questions. And you will not need to be a mathematician or an accountant to do it.

In dynamic financial management we have a specific way of defining dynamic management of these increases. In terms of our dynamic indicators we do not know what will happen as a result of these increases, but with dynamic financial management techniques we can predict very accurately what needs to be done to keep your business fit and healthy.

What do we mean by fit and healthy? Ideally we would like our radar to be in at least the same shape that it was in before the increase. We will soon see that in the initial impact of an increase in dynamic costs is reflected in the shape of your business. The shape changes, often in unexpected ways. Getting everything back into shape with one dynamic decision is, in fact, too ambitious. In dynamic financial management a meaningful definition of getting back into shape – being fit and healthy – is returning the DNC% to the level it was before the initial management decision.

For example, let us look at the model business. If dynamic costs go up to 65 per cent, the initial impact on the contribution statement would be to reduce the DNC to 5 per cent. We need to know what the alternative ways are of getting your DNC% back up to its original level of 10 per cent.

This chapter will present the effect of an increase in your dynamic costs. We will do this in the two stages mentioned earlier, i.e. look at the simple impact of the increase and then the measures available to us to manage these dynamically and regain our level of fitness, i.e. regain our original DNC%.

Increases in your dynamic costs

Let us begin with a summary of what could happen if your business incurred an increase in its dynamic costs. For the model business, if dynamic costs were to increase by 5 per cent, from 60 per cent to 63 per cent, the possible actions to compensate are:

Change		Appropriate action to regain DNC%	Amount
Increase in	⭢	Increase volume	By 11.11%
dynamic costs	⭢	Increase price	By 3.34%
of 5%	⭢	Decrease static costs	By 10.00%

And the shape of your business after these changes will be:

Eight dynamic indicators

	Before any change	After initial impact DC increase 5.00%	After volume increase 11.11%	After price increase 3.34%	After SC decrease 10.00%
GC%	40.00%	37.00%	37.00%	39.04%	37.00%
DNC%	10.00%	7.00%	10.00%	10.00%	10.00%
BeGap%	25.00%	18.92%	27.03%	25.61%	27.03%
Stock%	50.00%	52.50%	52.50%	50.80%	52.50%
Dr%	100.00%	100.00%	100.00%	100.00%	100.00%
Cr%	80.00%	82.00%	82.00%	79.35%	82.00%
DNA%	0.00%	0.50%	7.50%	3.72%	0.50%
DCM%	10.00%	6.50%	2.50%	6.28%	9.50%

The decision is now yours:

● accept the new shape of your business after the initial impact and change your targets accordingly;

● work dynamically towards one of the above possible actions;

● somewhere in between.

Whatever your decision, you can predict its impact before you are committed to any changes – managing tomorrow today.

How did we get to these results? First we need to find out the result of the initial impact, then we need to look at all the possible actions that could be taken to compensate for this increase in dynamic costs.

The initial impact

Sometimes you are faced with an increase in your dynamic costs. These may be unavoidable. Annual pay rises, costs of materials rising, unfavourable exchange rates, subcontract costs increasing. You need to understand and manage these changes. Figure 9.1 shows the effect of the initial impact of an increase in your dynamic costs on the eight dynamic indicators.

With an increase in dynamic costs, Stock% and Cr% increase as a percentage of income. As indicated, there should be no impact on the Dr%. Your dynamic

The eight dynamic indicators	Increase dynamic costs
	Tool
GC%	Look-up and calculation
DNC%	Look-up and calculation
BeGap%	Calculation
Stock%	Look-up
Dr%	
Cr%	Look-up
DNA%	Calculation
DCM%	Calculation

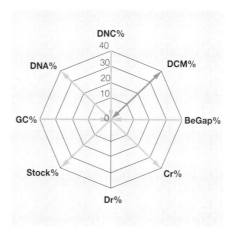

Fig 9.1 ●
Radar chart of dynamic indicators

indicators of contribution, the GC%, BeGap% and DNC%, will decrease. Finally, DNA% will most probably go up, and DCM% could go either way depending on the magnitude of the figures involved. This radar chart illustration will be used to show the effects of all the decisions we are considering in these sections.

Throughout this chapter we will assume that the dynamic costs have increased by 5 per cent, i.e. they have gone up to 63 per cent. We will now look at these effects individually, the first being change to GC%.

Cause DC up

Effect on GC%

Method Look-up/Calculation

In the model business the existing GC% was 40 per cent. What will be the impact of the 5 per cent increase in dynamic costs? There are actually two ways to approach this one.

Adjuster method

The basic calculation for the new GC% value is:

New GC% = Existing GC% – 'Dynamic Adjuster'

The dynamic look-up table that gives this dynamic adjuster is shown in Table 9.1. So how does it work? Let us look back at the contribution statement of our model business to answer this. The DC% is currently 60 per cent and we are going to increase our dynamic costs by 5 per cent. Taking these figures and looking up in the table the dynamic adjuster, you will get 3.00.

Table 9.1 ● **Dynamic adjuster for new GC% after a DC increase**

Current	% Increase in DC										
DC%	1	3	5	7	9	10	12	14	16	18	20
10	0.10	0.30	0.50	0.70	0.90	1.00	1.20	1.40	1.60	1.80	2.00
15	0.15	0.45	0.75	1.05	1.35	1.50	1.80	2.10	2.40	2.70	3.00
20	0.20	0.60	1.00	1.40	1.80	2.00	2.40	2.80	3.20	3.60	4.00
25	0.25	0.75	1.25	1.75	2.25	2.50	3.00	3.50	4.00	4.50	5.00
30	0.30	0.90	1.50	2.10	2.70	3.00	3.60	4.20	4.80	5.40	6.00
35	0.35	1.05	1.75	2.45	3.15	3.50	4.20	4.90	5.60	6.30	7.00
40	0.40	1.20	2.00	2.80	3.60	4.00	4.80	5.60	6.40	7.20	8.00
45	0.45	1.35	2.25	3.15	4.05	4.50	5.40	6.30	7.20	8.10	9.00
50	0.50	1.50	2.50	3.50	4.50	5.00	6.00	7.00	8.00	9.00	10.00
55	0.55	1.65	2.75	3.85	4.95	5.50	6.60	7.70	8.80	9.90	11.00
60	0.60	1.80	**3.00**	4.20	5.40	6.00	7.20	8.40	9.60	10.80	12.00
65	0.65	1.95	3.25	4.55	5.85	6.50	7.80	9.10	10.40	11.70	13.00
70	0.70	2.10	3.50	4.90	6.30	7.00	8.40	9.80	11.20	12.60	14.00
75	0.75	2.25	3.75	5.25	6.75	7.50	9.00	10.50	12.00	13.50	15.00
80	0.80	2.40	4.00	5.60	7.20	8.00	9.60	11.20	12.80	14.40	16.00
85	0.85	2.55	4.25	5.95	7.65	8.50	10.20	11.90	13.60	15.30	17.00
90	0.90	2.70	4.50	6.30	8.10	9.00	10.80	12.60	14.40	16.20	18.00

The current GC% in the contribution statement is 40 per cent and to arrive at the new GC% we use the following formula:

New GC% = Existing GC% – 'Dynamic Adjuster'

New GC% = 40.00% – '3.00' = 37.00%

Mathematical method

If you are OK with a bit of mathematics, the new GC% can be calculated even more quickly as follows:

New GC% = Existing GC% – (Increase in DC × DC%)

New GC% = 40.00% – (5.00 × 60%)

New GC% = 40.00% – 3.00% = 37.00%

Your GC% is very important – it is one measure of your efficiency and also, on activity above the breakeven point, it is the amount of contribution you will make. This key measure has reduced from 40 per cent to 37 per cent. For every $1,000 extra income you will now receive $30 less in gross contribution.

Cause DC up
Effect on DNC%
Method Look-up/Calculation

In the model business the existing DNC% was 10 per cent. What will be the impact of the 5 per cent increase in dynamic costs? Again there are two ways to approach this.

Adjuster method

The basic calculation for the new DNC% value is similar to the one for the GC%:

New DNC% = Existing DNC% – 'Dynamic Adjuster'

The dynamic look-up table that gives this dynamic adjuster is shown in Table 9.2. Again referring to the model business, the DC% is currently 60 per cent and we are going to increase our dynamic costs by 5 per cent. Taking these figures and looking up in the table the dynamic adjuster, you will get 3.00 (the same adjuster as for GC%).

Table 9.2 ● Dynamic adjuster for new DNC% after a DC increase

Current	% Increase in DC										
DC%	1	3	5	7	9	10	12	14	16	18	20
10	0.10	0.30	0.50	0.70	0.90	1.00	1.20	1.40	1.60	1.80	2.00
15	0.15	0.45	0.75	1.05	1.35	1.50	1.80	2.10	2.40	2.70	3.00
20	0.20	0.60	1.00	1.40	1.80	2.00	2.40	2.80	3.20	3.60	4.00
25	0.25	0.75	1.25	1.75	2.25	2.50	3.00	3.50	4.00	4.50	5.00
30	0.30	0.90	1.50	2.10	2.70	3.00	3.60	4.20	4.80	5.40	6.00
35	0.35	1.05	1.75	2.45	3.15	3.50	4.20	4.90	5.60	6.30	7.00
40	0.40	1.20	2.00	2.80	3.60	4.00	4.80	5.60	6.40	7.20	8.00
45	0.45	1.35	2.25	3.15	4.05	4.50	5.40	6.30	7.20	8.10	9.00
50	0.50	1.50	2.50	3.50	4.50	5.00	6.00	7.00	8.00	9.00	10.00
55	0.55	1.65	2.75	3.85	4.95	5.50	6.60	7.70	8.80	9.90	11.00
60	0.60	1.80	**3.00**	4.20	5.40	6.00	7.20	8.40	9.60	10.80	12.00
65	0.65	1.95	3.25	4.55	5.85	6.50	7.80	9.10	10.40	11.70	13.00
70	0.70	2.10	3.50	4.90	6.30	7.00	8.40	9.80	11.20	12.60	14.00
75	0.75	2.25	3.75	5.25	6.75	7.50	9.00	10.50	12.00	13.50	15.00
80	0.80	2.40	4.00	5.60	7.20	8.00	9.60	11.20	12.80	14.40	16.00
85	0.85	2.55	4.25	5.95	7.65	8.50	10.20	11.90	13.60	15.30	17.00
90	0.90	2.70	4.50	6.30	8.10	9.00	10.80	12.60	14.40	16.20	18.00

The current DNC% in the contribution statement is 10 per cent and to arrive at the new DNC% we use the formula:

New DNC% = Existing DNC% – 'Dynamic Adjuster'

New DNC% = 10.00% – '3.00' = 7.00%

The simplicity of this calculation is brought to life by the use of the dynamic adjuster. Indeed, many readers may now see that this is an obvious result, but did you know it before you started on this journey?

Mathematical method

New DNC% = Existing DNC% – (Increase in DC × DC%)

New DNC% = 10.00% – (5.00 × 60.00%)

New DNC% = 10.00% – 3.00% = 7.00%

Your DNC% is the most important dynamic indicator – it is the measure of your effectiveness, the amount of overall contribution you make on your activities. Your contribution towards future development has reduced significantly. This is effectively a 30 per cent reduction in DNC for a 5 per cent increase in DC.

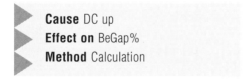

Cause DC up

Effect on BeGap%

Method Calculation

The basic calculation for the new BeGap% value is simple and is based upon the two previous results:

$$\text{New BeGap\%} = \frac{\text{New DNC\%}}{\text{New GC\%}}$$

$$\text{New BeGap\%} = \frac{7.00\%}{37.00\%}$$

New BeGap% = 18.92%

This is a significantly more risky business as a result of the increase in your DC.

We can summarize the dynamic indicators of contribution as:

GC%	was	40.00%	is now	37.00%
DNC%	was	10.00%	is now	7.00%
BeGap%	was	25.00%	is now	18.92%

Imagine the power of this for the managers of the model business in their management meeting. They know there is a dynamic cost increase due and they can now see at a glance the impact of this on the dynamic indicators of contribution. They could move on to consider a dynamic decision – what are they going to do to get back into shape?

This is what dynamic financial management is all about. There is no need to go into a lengthy recalculation of the standard financial statements, or indeed if need be, to call the accountant in. With your finger on the pulse of the business using the dynamic indicators and these dynamic techniques, you can manage tomorrow today.

But we should not become complacent. We have looked at the impact of an increase in DC% on only three of the eight dynamic indicators. We have not seen the full impact on the model business. We need to look at it in relation to the effect on the strands of the DNA.

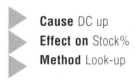

Cause DC up
Effect on Stock%
Method Look-up

As a result of an increase in dynamic costs, Stock% goes up. Why is this? And is it good or bad? We will tackle these questions in order.

What is stock? It is the dynamic costs that are imprisoned in your time warp. For a consultancy or service company it is the value of work in progress, not yet paid for. In a manufacturing company, it is the value of your material purchases plus the value added to them by the work you have carried out to make your products, including work in progress and finished products awaiting sale.

Is a higher Stock% good or bad? It is money imprisoned in the time warp, so fundamentally it must be bad. Therefore we need to know the magnitude of the effect. This is where the look-up table comes in (*see* Table 9.3).

The end result – the new Stock% – is given directly from the table. It is so simple – you do not need to calculate anything. In the model business, stock as a percentage of a month's income was 50 per cent. With a 5 per cent increase in dynamic costs, the Stock% would go up to 52.5 per cent.

What does this mean? A new Stock% of 52.50 per cent multiplied by the income value of $100 will give a stock value of $52.50 instead of the original value of $50. An extra $2.50 imprisoned in the time warp! 'So what?', you may say, but add a few zeros to these figures and it really gets serious.

Table 9.3 ● **New Stock% after a DC increase**

Current Stock%					% Increase in DC						
	1	3	5	7	9	10	12	14	16	18	20
10	10.10	10.30	10.50	10.70	10.90	11.00	11.20	11.40	11.60	11.80	12.00
20	20.20	20.60	21.00	21.40	21.80	22.00	22.40	22.80	23.20	23.60	24.00
30	30.30	30.90	31.50	32.10	32.70	33.00	33.60	34.20	34.80	35.40	36.00
40	40.40	41.20	42.00	42.80	43.60	44.00	44.80	45.60	46.40	47.20	48.00
50	50.50	51.50	**52.50**	53.50	54.50	55.00	56.00	57.00	58.00	59.00	60.00
60	60.60	61.80	63.00	64.20	65.40	66.00	67.20	68.40	69.60	70.80	72.00
70	70.70	72.10	73.50	74.90	76.30	77.00	78.40	79.80	81.20	82.60	84.00
80	80.80	82.40	84.00	85.60	87.20	88.00	89.60	91.20	92.80	94.40	96.00
90	90.90	92.70	94.50	96.30	98.10	99.00	100.80	102.60	104.40	106.20	108.00
100	101.00	103.00	105.00	107.00	109.00	110.00	112.00	114.00	116.00	118.00	120.00
110	111.10	113.30	115.50	117.70	119.90	121.00	123.20	125.40	127.60	129.80	132.00
120	121.20	123.60	126.00	128.40	130.80	132.00	134.40	136.80	139.20	141.60	144.00
130	131.30	133.90	136.50	139.10	141.70	143.00	145.60	148.20	150.80	153.40	156.00
140	141.40	144.20	147.00	149.80	152.60	154.00	156.80	159.60	162.40	165.20	168.00
150	151.50	154.50	157.50	160.50	163.50	165.00	168.00	171.00	174.00	177.00	180.00

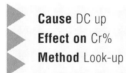

Cause DC up
Effect on Cr%
Method Look-up

Note: This is applicable only if the increase in dynamic costs is attributable to an increase in the cost of the things you buy on credit.

If the increase in dynamic costs is attributable to things you buy on credit, an increase in the cost must be followed by an increase in creditors. To complete the picture you need to have an idea of the proportion of your dynamic costs represented by things you buy. As a good rule of thumb 50 per cent is a reasonable split. This is the assumption used in Table 9.4.

Table 9.4 ● New Cr% after a DC increase

Current Cr%	% Increase in DC										
	1	3	5	7	9	10	12	14	16	18	20
10	10.05	10.15	10.25	10.35	10.45	10.50	10.60	10.70	10.80	10.90	11.00
20	20.10	20.30	20.50	20.70	20.90	21.00	21.20	21.40	21.60	21.80	22.00
30	30.15	30.45	30.75	31.05	31.35	31.50	31.80	32.10	32.40	32.70	33.00
40	40.20	40.60	41.00	41.40	41.80	42.00	42.40	42.80	43.20	43.60	44.00
50	50.25	50.75	51.25	51.75	52.25	52.50	53.00	53.50	54.00	54.50	55.00
60	60.30	60.90	61.50	62.10	62.70	63.00	63.60	64.20	64.80	65.40	66.00
70	70.35	71.05	71.75	72.45	73.15	73.50	74.20	74.90	75.60	76.30	77.00
80	80.40	81.20	**82.00**	82.80	83.60	84.00	84.80	85.60	86.40	87.20	88.00
90	90.45	91.35	92.25	93.15	94.05	94.50	95.40	96.30	97.20	98.10	99.00
100	100.50	101.50	102.50	103.50	104.50	105.00	106.00	107.00	108.00	109.00	110.00
110	110.55	111.65	112.75	113.85	114.95	115.50	116.60	117.70	118.80	119.90	121.00
120	120.60	121.80	123.00	124.20	125.40	126.00	127.20	128.40	129.60	130.80	132.00
130	130.65	131.95	133.25	134.55	135.85	136.50	137.80	139.10	140.40	141.70	143.00
140	140.70	142.10	143.50	144.90	146.30	147.00	148.40	149.80	151.20	152.60	154.00
150	150.75	152.25	153.75	155.25	156.75	157.50	159.00	160.50	162.00	163.50	165.00

The end result – the new Cr% – is again given to you straight from the table. After a 5 per cent increase in dynamic costs with an existing Cr% of 80 per cent, we can see from the table the new Cr% of 82 per cent.

What does this mean in cash terms? With a new Cr% in the model business of 82 per cent multiplied by the income of $100, this will give a new creditor value of $82 instead of the original value of $80. This is an extra $2 that we will have to find to pay our creditors. For example, if you were in a business with annual sales of $1 million, you would have to find an extra $20,000 of cash in the month that the increase in dynamic costs was made.

The effect of decisions made 'today' will have to be paid for 'tomorrow'.

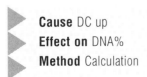

Cause DC up
Effect on DNA%
Method Calculation

In order to calculate the dynamic net assets as a result of this change we need to look at the strands of our static net assets imprisoned in the time warp before and after the anticipated change. This can be shown as:

$$\text{DNA} = \text{SNA } after \text{ Change} - \text{SNA } before \text{ Change}$$

And then DNA% will be:

$$\text{DNA\%} = \frac{\text{DNA}}{\text{Income}} \times 100$$

The DNA structure is shown below:

	Before	After
Income	$100.00	$100.00
Stock	$50.00	$52.50
Debtors	$100.00	$100.00
Creditors	$80.00	$82.00
SNA	$70.00	$70.50
Stock%	50.00%	52.50%
Dr%	100.00%	100.00%
Cr%	80.00%	82.00%
SNA%	70.00%	70.50%

The DNA can now be calculated as:

$$\text{DNA} = \$70.50 - \$70.00 = \$0.50$$

And the DNA% is:

$$\text{DNA\%} = \frac{\$0.50}{\$100.00} \times 100 = 0.50\%$$

The overall effect on DNA% shows a small outflow of money, extra money tied up in the strands of the DNA. The additional money tied up in the new Stock% is higher than the additional money to be paid in the future as Cr%. But the real measure has got to be the overall impact on the DCM%.

> **Cause** DC up
> **Effect on** DCM%
> **Method** Calculation

The final dynamic indicator is now very easy to calculate:

$$\text{DCM\%} = \text{DNC\%} - \text{DNA\%}$$

$$\text{DCM\%} = 7.00\% - 0.50\% = 6.50\%$$

The combined effect of the reduction in DNC% and the apparently small amount of extra cash tied up in the time warp has decreased your DCM% to 6.5 per cent. It is not too bad for the model business, as DCM% is still positive. Would the result be the same in your business given your figures for DNC% and DNA%?

But look to the long term. The best DCM% the model business can get now is 7 per cent, the new level of the DNC%. Any plans for investing in the business may have to be delayed or alternative funding found.

The new shape of your business

The eight dynamic indicators before and after the increase in dynamic costs are:

Contribution statement			DNA statement		
	Before	**After**		**Before**	**After**
Income	$100.00	$100.00	Income	$100.00	$100.00
Dynamic Costs	$60.00	$63.00	Stock	$50.00	$52.50
Gross Contribution	$40.00	$37.00	Debtors	$100.00	$100.00
Static Costs	$30.00	$30.00	Creditors	$80.00	$82.00
Dynamic Net Contribution	$10.00	$7.00	Static Net Assets	$70.00	$70.50

Eight dynamic indicators

	Before	**After**
GC%	40.00%	37.00%
DNC%	10.00%	7.00%
BeGap%	25.00%	18.92%
Stock%	50.00%	52.50%
Dr%	100.00%	100.00%
Cr%	80.00%	82.00%
DNA%	0.00%	0.50%
DCM%	10.00%	6.50%

The real goal of this exercise is reflected in the changing shape of the business as shown in Fig 9.2. As you can see, your business is quite literally shrinking!

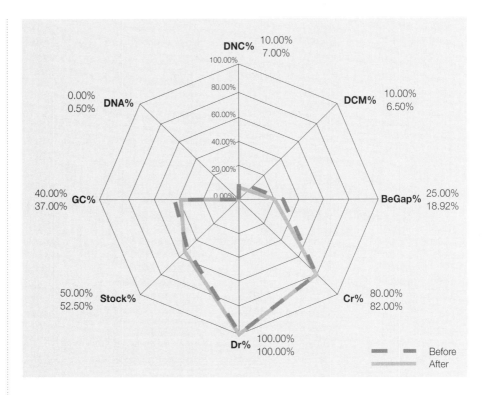

Fig 9.2 ● Model business radar chart

Actions for dynamic management of an increase in dynamic costs

We have now considered the initial step. As we mentioned at the start of this chapter there are a number of actions you could take to dynamically manage this change so that we maintain our DNC%. These can be summarized as follows:

Change		Appropriate action to regain DNC%
Increase	⯈	Increase volume
in dynamic	⯈	Increase price
costs	⯈	Decrease static costs

These seem obvious; you can try to sell more, put up your price or reduce your other costs – the static costs. The results of a dynamic analysis will help you decide the option most appropriate for your business. The dynamic financial management definition of back into shape is:

'returning the DNC% to the same level as it was before the change.'

Again we can look at the impact of these using a series of dynamic look-up tables, dynamic adjusters and calculations. The power of dynamic financial management is that it will give you the exact magnitude of the actions you need to take.

Cause DC up
Possible action Increase volume
Method Calculation/Look-up

The first possible action to look at is increasing the volume or level of activity in order to increase your DNC%. What does an increase in volume or level of activity really mean? In a manufacturing, service or retail business it is additional sales volume – you do not just make or provide more, you sell more. For a budget holder it means negotiating an increase in budget because of an increase in the level of activity within your department.

Back to our model business where we were looking at an increase of 5 per cent in our DC. What volume increase does the model business need to regain its original DNC% of 10 per cent? Again we can find the figure using a dynamic adjuster and a figure extracted from a table. The volume increase needed is shown in Table 9.5. But in order to use the table we first need to calculate a dynamic adjuster:

Dynamic Adjuster = Increase in DC × Original DC%

Dynamic Adjuster = 5.00 × 60.00%

Dynamic Adjuster = 3.00

We can now use this figure as part of the table. The original SC% was 30 per cent and the dynamic adjuster is 3.00. This means we need to attain a new volume of 111.11 per cent of current levels to regain our DNC%, an increase in volume of 11.11 per cent.

Table 9.5 ● New Volume% to maintain same DNC% after a DC increase

Current SC%	Dynamic adjuster											
	2	3	4	5	6	7	8	9	10	12	14	16
10	125.00	142.86	166.67	200.00	250.00	333.33	500.00					
15	115.38	125.00	136.36	150.00	166.67	187.50	214.29	250.00	300.00	500.00		
20	111.11	117.65	125.00	133.33	142.86	153.85	166.67	181.82	200.00	250.00	333.33	500.00
25	108.70	113.64	119.05	125.00	131.58	138.89	147.06	156.25	166.67	192.31	227.27	277.78
30	107.14	**111.11**	115.38	120.00	125.00	130.43	136.36	142.86	150.00	166.67	187.50	214.29
35	106.06	109.38	112.90	116.67	120.69	125.00	129.63	134.62	140.00	152.17	166.67	184.21
40	105.26	108.11	111.11	114.29	117.65	121.21	125.00	129.03	133.33	142.86	153.85	166.67
45	104.65	107.14	109.76	112.50	115.38	118.42	121.62	125.00	128.57	136.36	145.16	155.17
50	104.17	106.38	108.70	111.11	113.64	116.28	119.05	121.95	125.00	131.58	138.89	147.06
55	103.77	105.77	107.84	110.00	112.24	114.58	117.02	119.57	122.22	127.91	134.15	141.03
60	103.45	105.26	107.14	109.09	111.11	113.21	115.38	117.65	120.00	125.00	130.43	136.36
65	103.17	104.84	106.56	108.33	110.17	112.07	114.04	116.07	118.18	122.64	127.45	132.65
70	102.94	104.48	106.06	107.69	109.38	111.11	112.90	114.75	116.67	120.69	125.00	129.63
75	102.74	104.17	105.63	107.14	108.70	110.29	111.94	113.64	115.38	119.05	122.95	127.12
80	102.56	103.90	105.26	106.67	108.11	109.59	111.11	112.68	114.29	117.65	121.21	125.00
85	102.41	103.66	104.94	106.25	107.59	108.97	110.39	111.84	113.33	116.44	119.72	123.19
90	102.27	103.45	104.65	105.88	107.14	108.43	109.76	111.11	112.50	115.38	118.42	121.62

The progress of the contribution statement can be tracked below:

	Before	After initial impact	After volume increase	%
Income	$100.00	$100.00	$111.11	100.00
Dynamic Costs	$60.00	$63.00	$70.00	63.00
Gross Contribution	$40.00	$37.00	$41.11	37.00
Static Costs	$30.00	$30.00	$30.00	27.00
Dynamic Net Contribution	$10.00	$7.00	$11.11	10.00

So, if we increase our volume by 11.11 per cent we regain DNC% at 10 per cent – the level it was before any of the decisions were made. It is worthwhile considering the other dynamic indicators here. The volume increase has made no difference to the GC% as we calculated it after the initial impact.

We can quickly calculate the impact of the volume increase on our BeGap%:

New BeGap% = New DNC% / New GC%

New BeGap% = 10.00% / 37.00% = 27.03%

Overall the option makes the business slightly less risky than before any change was envisaged.

We must also consider the impact on DNA% as shown below:

	Before	After initial impact	After volume increase
Income	$100.00	$100.00	$111.11
Stock	$50.00	$52.50	$58.33
Debtors	$100.00	$100.00	$111.11
Creditors	$80.00	$82.00	$91.11
SNA	$70.00	$70.50	$78.33
Stock%	50.00%	52.50%	52.50%
Dr%	100.00%	100.00%	100.00%
Cr%	80.00%	82.00%	82.00%
SNA%	70.00%	70.50%	70.50%

If the only change is one of volume, then as a percentage of sales, the indicators that make up the strands of the SNA should stay the same, that is, at the levels after the impact of the change in dynamic costs. We are still suffering the associated adverse effect of the increased costs tied up in our stock and the increasing amount we will have to pay out to our suppliers for the extra cost. In addition, the increase in volume means we need to increase the value of SNA, so what does this mean for the DNA%?

DNA = SNA *after* Decision – SNA *before* Initial Impact

DNA = $78.33 – $70.00 = $8.33

Then DNA% calculates as:

$$\text{DNA\%} = \frac{\$8.33}{\$111.11} \times 100 = 7.50\%$$

This seems to be a fairly large movement of cash into the SNA. Has the DNC% component of the DCM% compensated for it?

DCM% = DNC% – DNA%

DCM% = 10.00% – 7.50% = 2.50%

Just about! There is a small inflow of cash for the model business with this option, but much less than anticipated before the changes.

We now know the change in volume needed (11.11 per cent), we only need to know if that is really feasible in the current market environment, and whether we can find the cash available to fund the decrease in DCM%. This option can be summarized as:

Eight dynamic indicators

	Before	After initial impact	After volume increase
GC%	40.00%	37.00%	37.00%
DNC%	10.00%	7.00%	10.00%
BeGap%	25.00%	18.92%	27.03%
Stock%	50.00%	52.50%	52.50%
Dr%	100.00%	100.00%	100.00%
Cr%	80.00%	82.00%	82.00%
DNA%	0.00%	0.50%	7.50%
DCM%	10.00%	6.50%	2.50%

The bigger the increase in DC% we have to cope with, the higher the volume increase needed to compensate. Controlling DC% in a shrinking or highly competitive market is, therefore, a must. Efficiency should be a key driver within these types of markets. However, if we can increase volume to compensate, we will also be more effective – getting more volume out of the same static costs.

Cause DC up
Possible action Increase price
Method Look-up/Calculation

The next possible action to look at is increasing your price in order to increase your DNC%. Unlike the volume increase we talked about earlier, you have not sold any more but every sale has made more money. A price increase does not affect the value of dynamic costs. They stay the same. Therefore any increase in price will go straight down to your bottom line – your DNC.

But how much do you need to go down to the bottom line to regain your DNC%? Remember, what we are talking about in this section is using a price increase as a way of compensating for an increase in dynamic costs. What you need to know, and what dynamic financial management tells you, is the actual price increase you need in *your* business to regain your original DNC%.

What does an increase in price really mean? In a manufacturing, service or retail business it is fairly obvious – you put up the price of the products or services that you provide. When dynamic costs go up, we often try to pass on these increases to our customers. But we often pass on the wrong increase and too high a price can result in a loss of customers.

For a budget holder, a price increase simply means an increase in budget allocation, without an increase in the level of activity within your department, an increase that needs to be negotiated.

Back to our model business where we were looking at an increase of 5 per cent in our DC. What price increase does the model business need to implement in order to regain its original DNC% of 10 per cent? In dynamic financial management the formula for this is:

% Price Increase = Increase in DC × Dynamic Adjuster

But first we need to find the dynamic adjuster using a dynamic look-up table (*see* Table 9.6).

Table 9.6 ● Dynamic adjuster for price increase after increase in DC%

Existing DNC%	10	15	20	25	30	35	40	45	50	55	60	65	70	75	80
1	0.101	0.152	0.202	0.253	0.303	0.354	0.404	0.455	0.505	0.556	0.606	0.657	0.707	0.758	0.808
2	0.102	0.153	0.204	0.255	0.306	0.357	0.408	0.459	0.510	0.561	0.612	0.663	0.714	0.765	0.816
3	0.103	0.155	0.206	0.258	0.309	0.361	0.412	0.464	0.515	0.567	0.619	0.670	0.722	0.773	0.825
4	0.104	0.156	0.208	0.260	0.313	0.365	0.417	0.469	0.521	0.573	0.625	0.677	0.729	0.781	0.833
5	0.105	0.158	0.211	0.263	0.316	0.368	0.421	0.474	0.526	0.579	0.632	0.684	0.737	0.789	0.842
6	0.106	0.160	0.213	0.266	0.319	0.372	0.426	0.479	0.532	0.585	0.638	0.691	0.745	0.798	0.851
7	0.108	0.161	0.215	0.269	0.323	0.376	0.430	0.484	0.538	0.591	0.645	0.699	0.753	0.806	0.860
8	0.109	0.163	0.217	0.272	0.326	0.380	0.435	0.489	0.543	0.598	0.652	0.707	0.761	0.815	0.870
9	0.110	0.165	0.220	0.275	0.330	0.385	0.440	0.495	0.549	0.604	0.659	0.714	0.769	0.824	0.879
10	0.111	0.167	0.222	0.278	0.333	0.389	0.444	0.500	0.556	0.611	**0.667**	0.722	0.778	0.833	0.889
12	0.114	0.170	0.227	0.284	0.341	0.398	0.455	0.511	0.568	0.625	0.682	0.739	0.795	0.852	0.909
14	0.116	0.174	0.233	0.291	0.349	0.407	0.465	0.523	0.581	0.640	0.698	0.756	0.814	0.872	0.930
16	0.119	0.179	0.238	0.298	0.357	0.417	0.476	0.536	0.595	0.655	0.714	0.774	0.833	0.893	0.952
18	0.122	0.183	0.244	0.305	0.366	0.427	0.488	0.549	0.610	0.671	0.732	0.793	0.854	0.915	0.976
20	0.125	0.188	0.250	0.313	0.375	0.438	0.500	0.563	0.625	0.688	0.750	0.813	0.875	0.938	1.000
25	0.133	0.200	0.267	0.333	0.400	0.467	0.533	0.600	0.667	0.733	0.800	0.867	0.933	1.000	1.067
30	0.143	0.214	0.286	0.357	0.429	0.500	0.571	0.643	0.714	0.786	0.857	0.929	1.000	1.071	1.143
35	0.154	0.231	0.308	0.385	0.462	0.538	0.615	0.692	0.769	0.846	0.923	1.000	1.077	1.154	1.231
40	0.167	0.250	0.333	0.417	0.500	0.583	0.667	0.750	0.833	0.917	1.000	1.083	1.167	1.250	1.333
50	0.200	0.300	0.400	0.500	0.600	0.700	0.800	0.900	1.000	1.100	1.200	1.300	1.400	1.500	1.600

Referring to the model business, the existing DC% is 60 per cent and the existing DNC% is 10 per cent. So, using Table 9.6 gives you the dynamic adjuster figure of 0.667.

With a dynamic cost increase of 5 per cent we can now use the formula:

% Price Increase = Increase in DC × Dynamic Adjuster

% Price Increase = 5.00 × 0.667 = 3.34%

So if my current price is $100, the increase will be $3.34 (a 3.34 per cent price increase), therefore my new price will be $103.34.

	Before	After initial impact	After price increase	%
Income	$100.00	$100.00	$103.34	100.00
Dynamic Costs	$60.00	$63.00	$63.00	60.96
Gross Contribution	$40.00	$37.00	$40.34	39.04
Static Costs	$30.00	$30.00	$30.00	29.04
Dynamic Net Contribution	$10.00	$7.00	$10.34	10.00

In order to compensate for a DC increase of 5 per cent we need to increase our price by 3.34 per cent to regain DNC% at 10 per cent – the level it was before any of the decisions were made. That means the model business need only pass on an increase of 3.34 per cent, not the 5 per cent dynamic cost increase it has experienced.

We now know the price increase needed, but we still need to know how this will change the shape of the model business – the effect on all eight dynamic indicators. As we have instigated a price increase there will be no change in the value of dynamic costs – they will stay at $63. This can be worked through the contribution statement to calculate a new value for GC and a new GC% of 39.04 per cent.

We can quickly calculate the impact of the price increase on our BeGap%:

New BeGap% = New DNC% / New GC%

New BeGap% = 10.00% / 39.04% = 25.61%

And we must also consider the impact on DNA%. If the only change is price, then as a value, stock and creditors will stay the same. However, this means that the Stock% and Cr% go down as a percentage of the higher income value. The Dr% will stay at the same percentage of income, meaning the value has gone up. As the combined results of these changes, the SNA value and percentage will also change as shown below:

	Before	After initial impact	After price increase
Income	$100.00	$100.00	$103.34
Stock	$50.00	$52.50	$52.50
Debtors	$100.00	$100.00	$103.34
Creditors	$80.00	$82.00	$82.00
SNA	$70.00	$70.50	$73.84
Stock%	50.00%	52.50%	50.80%
Dr%	100.00%	100.00%	100.00%
Cr%	80.00%	82.00%	79.35%
SNA%	70.00%	70.50%	71.45%

And as there is an impact on the DNC% and SNA% there must also be an impact on DCM%.

DNA = SNA *after* Decision – SNA *before* Initial Impact

DNA = $73.84 – $70.00 = $3.84

Then DNA% remains as:

$$DNA\% = \frac{\$3.84}{\$103.34} \times 100 = 3.72\%$$

So the DNA% is positive, meaning there has been a movement of money into the strands of the SNA due to the increase in sales price. But again, when the movement is in price – beware. This could simply be more debtors because each customer is now paying us relatively more income. The final evaluation is to see whether this has been compensated for with the increase in DNC% and we will do this by looking at the DCM%:

DCM% = DNC% – DNA%

DCM% = 10.00% – 3.72% = 6.28%

This option has not eliminated the DCM% but it has reduced it. Let us summarize this option:

Eight dynamic indicators

	Before	After initial impact	After price increase
GC%	40.00%	37.00%	39.04%
DNC%	10.00%	7.00%	10.00%
BeGap%	25.00%	18.92%	25.61%
Stock%	50.00%	52.50%	50.80%
Dr%	100.00%	100.00%	100.00%
Cr%	80.00%	82.00%	79.35%
DNA%	0.00%	0.50%	3.72%
DCM%	10.00%	6.50%	6.28%

Your DCM% is 6.28 per cent, which means you have released cash from your time warp equivalent to 6.28 per cent of your current period's income, less than the 10 per cent you were predicting before the change.

You now know the price increase needed to compensate for this increase in your dynamic costs. The question only you can answer is whether this size of price increase is really feasible in your market environment.

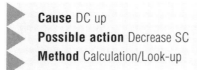

Cause DC up
Possible action Decrease SC
Method Calculation/Look-up

If one set of costs go up, you may need to look for savings elsewhere. Maybe you need to become more effective in what you do and therefore the decreases have to come from reducing your static costs. You may know the value you need to reduce the static costs by, but you also need to know what percentage this represents so that you can again start to examine the changed shape of our business.

We need to use the dynamic adjuster we looked at earlier:

Dynamic Adjuster = Increase in DC × Original DC%

Dynamic Adjuster = 5.00 × 60.00%

Dynamic Adjuster = 3.00

We can use this dynamic adjuster to use Table 9.7. Reading from the table, our original SC% was 30 per cent and our dynamic adjuster is 3.00. This means we need to decrease our static costs by 10 per cent to regain our DNC%.

Table 9.7 ● **Decrease in SC% to maintain same DNC% after a DC increase**

Current SC%	Dynamic adjuster											
	2	3	4	5	6	7	8	9	10	12	14	16
10	20.00	30.00	40.00	50.00	60.00	70.00	80.00	90.00	100.00	120.00	140.00	160.00
15	13.33	20.00	26.67	33.33	40.00	46.67	53.33	60.00	66.67	80.00	93.33	106.67
20	10.00	15.00	20.00	25.00	30.00	35.00	40.00	45.00	50.00	60.00	70.00	80.00
25	8.00	12.00	16.00	20.00	24.00	28.00	32.00	36.00	40.00	48.00	56.00	64.00
30	6.67	**10.00**	13.33	16.67	20.00	23.33	26.67	30.00	33.33	40.00	46.67	53.33
35	5.71	8.57	11.43	14.29	17.14	20.00	22.86	25.71	28.57	34.29	40.00	45.71
40	5.00	7.50	10.00	12.50	15.00	17.50	20.00	22.50	25.00	30.00	35.00	40.00
45	4.44	6.67	8.89	11.11	13.33	15.56	17.78	20.00	22.22	26.67	31.11	35.56
50	4.00	6.00	8.00	10.00	12.00	14.00	16.00	18.00	20.00	24.00	28.00	32.00
55	3.64	5.45	7.27	9.09	10.91	12.73	14.55	16.36	18.18	21.82	25.45	29.09
60	3.33	5.00	6.67	8.33	10.00	11.67	13.33	15.00	16.67	20.00	23.33	26.67
65	3.08	4.62	6.15	7.69	9.23	10.77	12.31	13.85	15.38	18.46	21.54	24.62
70	2.86	4.29	5.71	7.14	8.57	10.00	11.43	12.86	14.29	17.14	20.00	22.86
75	2.67	4.00	5.33	6.67	8.00	9.33	10.67	12.00	13.33	16.00	18.67	21.33
80	2.50	3.75	5.00	6.25	7.50	8.75	10.00	11.25	12.50	15.00	17.50	20.00
85	2.35	3.53	4.71	5.88	7.06	8.24	9.41	10.59	11.76	14.12	16.47	18.82
90	2.22	3.33	4.44	5.56	6.67	7.78	8.89	10.00	11.11	13.33	15.56	17.78

Let's see if it works:

	Before	After initial impact	After SC decrease	%
Income	$100.00	$100.00	$100.00	100.00
Dynamic Costs	$60.00	$63.00	$63.00	63.00
Gross Contribution	$40.00	$37.00	$37.00	37.00
Static Costs	$30.00	$30.00	$27.00	27.00
Dynamic Net Contribution	$10.00	$7.00	$10.00	10.00

What about the impact on the eight dynamic indicators? A decrease in static costs has no impact on the GC%. It has not changed since the initial impact and remains at the reduced level of 37 per cent. We can now quickly calculate the impact on our BeGap%:

New BeGap% = New DNC% / New GC%

New BeGap% = 10.00% / 37.00% = 27.03%

In *Chapter 12: Decreases in your static costs* we identify that the components of our SNA are not affected. However, the increase in DC had an initial impact on SNA and this still needs to be considered.

	Before	After initial impact	After SC decrease
Income	$100.00	$100.00	$100.00
Stock	$50.00	$52.50	$52.50
Debtors	$100.00	$100.00	$100.00
Creditors	$80.00	$82.00	$82.00
SNA	$70.00	$70.50	$70.50
Stock%	50.00%	52.50%	52.50%
Dr%	100.00%	100.00%	100.00%
Cr%	80.00%	82.00%	82.00%
SNA%	70.00%	70.50%	70.50%

The overall impact on DNA% can now be calculated along with DCM%:

DNA = SNA *after* Decision – SNA *before* Initial Impact

DNA = $70.50 – $70.00 = $0.50

Then DNA% is:

$$\text{DNA\%} = \frac{\$0.50}{\$100} \times 100 = 0.50\%$$

So the DNA% is now slightly positive, meaning that there has been a marginal movement of money into the strands of your SNA. The size and the direction of this movement will depend on the relationship between the Stock% and Cr% in your business.

The overall effect on the DCM% is:

DCM% = DNC% – DNA%

DCM% = 10.00% – 0.50% = 9.50%

Your DCM% is 9.5 per cent, which means you have released cash from your time warp equivalent to 9.5 per cent of your current period's income, slightly less than the anticipated 10 per cent.

Eight dynamic indicators

	Before	After initial impact	After SC decrease
GC%	40.00%	37.00%	37.00%
DNC%	10.00%	7.00%	10.00%
BeGap%	25.00%	18.90%	27.03%
Stock%	50.00%	52.50%	52.50%
Dr%	100.00%	100.00%	100.00%
Cr%	80.00%	82.00%	82.00%
DNA%	0.00%	0.50%	0.50%
DCM%	10.00%	6.50%	9.50%

Moving costs within the cost structure of the model business has a positive effect. You need to do the analysis on your cost structure to see if this is a possible action for you in your business.

chapter 10

Decreases in your dynamic costs

Why do dynamic costs decrease?

Decreases in your dynamic costs need to be managed and there are two stages in understanding the impact on your business:

1 The initial impact of the decrease.

2 The alternative actions you could take to dynamically manage this decrease.

The initial impact of any decrease can be most successfully visualized using the eight dynamic indicators on the radar chart. The trends you will be monitoring using the dynamic breakeven graph and the dynamic cash graph will put these decreases into context – what freedom this has given you to develop your business.

However, we should still be managing a decrease dynamically. From our understanding of the decrease, monitored in the three charts we are using to visualize the business, we can begin to select any benefits we can take advantage of.

In dynamic financial management we have a specific way of defining dynamic management of these decreases. In terms of our dynamic indicators we do not know what will happen as a result of these decreases, but with dynamic financial management techniques we can predict very accurately what needs to be done to keep your business fit and healthy.

What do we mean by fit and healthy? Ideally we would like our radar to be in at least the same shape that it was in before the decrease. We will soon see that the initial impact of a decrease in dynamic costs is reflected in the shape of your business. The shape changes, often in unexpected ways. Getting everything back into shape with one dynamic decision is, in fact, too ambitious. In dynamic financial management, a meaningful definition of getting back into shape – being fit and healthy – is returning the DNC% to the same level as it was before the initial management decision.

For example, let us look at the model business. If dynamic costs go down to 55 per cent, the initial impact on the contribution statement would be to increase the DNC to 15 per cent. We need to know what freedom we have got within the business while keeping the DNC% at its original level of 10 per cent.

This chapter will present the effect of a decrease in your dynamic costs. We will do this in the two stages mentioned in the introduction, i.e. look at the simple impact of the decrease and then the measures available to us to manage these dynamically and regain our level of fitness, i.e. regain our original DNC%.

Decreases in your dynamic costs

For the model business, if dynamic costs go down by 5 per cent from 60 per cent to 57 per cent, the alternative freedoms created are:

Change		Appropriate action to regain DNC%	Amount
Decrease in	⯮	Decrease volume	By 9.09%
dynamic costs	⯮	Decrease price	By 3.34%
of 5%	⯮	Increase static costs	By 10.00%

The shape of your business after these changes will be:

Eight dynamic indicators

	Before any change	After initial impact DC decrease 5%	After volume decrease 9.09%	After price decrease 3.34%	After SC increase 10.00%
GC%	40.00%	43.00%	43.00%	41.03%	43.00%
DNC%	10.00%	13.00%	10.00%	10.00%	10.00%
BeGap%	25.00%	30.23%	23.26%	24.37%	23.26%
Stock%	50.00%	47.50%	47.50%	49.14%	47.50%
Dr%	100.00%	100.00%	100.00%	100.00%	100.00%
Cr%	80.00%	78.00%	78.00%	80.70%	78.00%
DNA%	0.00%	(0.50)%	(7.50)%	(3.97)%	(0.50)%
DCM%	10.00%	13.50%	17.50%	13.97%	10.50%

The decision is now yours:

- work strategically towards one of the above;
- accept the new shape of your business as it is and change your targets accordingly;
- somewhere in between.

Whatever your decision, you can predict its impact before you are committed to any changes – managing tomorrow today.

How did we get to these results? First we need to find out the result of the initial impact, then we need to look at all the possible actions that could be taken to compensate for this decrease in dynamic costs.

The initial impact

The initial impact of a decrease in your dynamic costs will affect the eight dynamic indicators as shown in Fig 10.1. How can you reduce dynamic costs? You could be more efficient with your materials – lower the scrap rate – your people could be more productive – multi-skilling and empowerment – and you could be more efficient in your processes. Efficiency is the key to reducing dynamic costs.

With a decrease in dynamic costs, BeGap%, GC% and DNC% all increase as a percentage of income, while the Stock%, Cr% and DNA% will decrease. There should be no impact on the Dr%, as indicated in the table above. Finally, DCM% could go either way depending on the size of the figures involved.

The eight dynamic indicators	Decrease in dynamic costs
	Tool
GC%	Look-up and calculation
DNC%	Look-up and calculation
BeGap%	Calculation
Stock%	Look-up
Dr%	
Cr%	Look-up
DNA%	Calculation
DCM%	Calculation

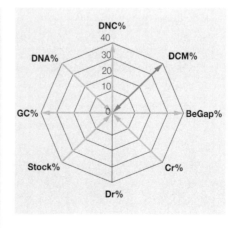

Fig 10.1 ●
Radar chart of dynamic indicators

We can now look at the magnitude of the initial impact on each of the eight dynamic indicators. Throughout this chapter we will assume that the dynamic costs have decreased by 5 per cent, i.e. they have gone down to 57 per cent. We will look at these effects individually, the first being change to GC%.

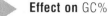

Cause DC down

Effect on GC%

Method Look-up/Calculation

In the model business the existing GC% was 40 per cent. What will be the impact of the 5 per cent decrease in dynamic costs? There are actually two ways to approach this one.

Adjuster method

The basic calculation for the new GC% value is:

New GC% = Existing GC% + 'Dynamic Adjuster'

The dynamic look-up table that gives this dynamic adjuster is shown in Table 10.1. So how does it work? Let us look back at the contribution statement of our model business to answer this.

Table 10.1 ● Dynamic adjuster for new GC% after a DC decrease

Current DC%	% Decrease in DC										
	1	3	5	7	9	10	12	14	16	18	20
10	0.10	0.30	0.50	0.70	0.90	1.00	1.20	1.40	1.60	1.80	2.00
15	0.15	0.45	0.75	1.05	1.35	1.50	1.80	2.10	2.40	2.70	3.00
20	0.20	0.60	1.00	1.40	1.80	2.00	2.40	2.80	3.20	3.60	4.00
25	0.25	0.75	1.25	1.75	2.25	2.50	3.00	3.50	4.00	4.50	5.00
30	0.30	0.90	1.50	2.10	2.70	3.00	3.60	4.20	4.80	5.40	6.00
35	0.35	1.05	1.75	2.45	3.15	3.50	4.20	4.90	5.60	6.30	7.00
40	0.40	1.20	2.00	2.80	3.60	4.00	4.80	5.60	6.40	7.20	8.00
45	0.45	1.35	2.25	3.15	4.05	4.50	5.40	6.30	7.20	8.10	9.00
50	0.50	1.50	2.50	3.50	4.50	5.00	6.00	7.00	8.00	9.00	10.00
55	0.55	1.65	2.75	3.85	4.95	5.50	6.60	7.70	8.80	9.90	11.00
60	0.60	1.80	**3.00**	4.20	5.40	6.00	7.20	8.40	9.60	10.80	12.00
65	0.65	1.95	3.25	4.55	5.85	6.50	7.80	9.10	10.40	11.70	13.00
70	0.70	2.10	3.50	4.90	6.30	7.00	8.40	9.80	11.20	12.60	14.00
75	0.75	2.25	3.75	5.25	6.75	7.50	9.00	10.50	12.00	13.50	15.00
80	0.80	2.40	4.00	5.60	7.20	8.00	9.60	11.20	12.80	14.40	16.00
85	0.85	2.55	4.25	5.95	7.65	8.50	10.20	11.90	13.60	15.30	17.00
90	0.90	2.70	4.50	6.30	8.10	9.00	10.80	12.60	14.40	16.20	18.00

The DC% is currently 60 per cent and we are going to decrease our dynamic costs by 5 per cent. Take these figures and look up in the table the dynamic adjuster, and you will get the highlighted figure of 3.00. The current GC% in the contribution statement is 40 per cent and to arrive at the new GC% we use the following formula:

New GC% = Existing GC% + 'Dynamic Adjuster'

New GC% = 40.00% + '3.00' = 43.00%

Mathematical method

If you are OK with a bit of mathematics, the new GC% can be quickly calculated as follows:

New GC% = Existing GC% + (Decrease in DC × DC%)

New GC% = 40.00% + (5.00 × 60.00%)

New GC% = 40.00% + 3.00% = 43.00%

Your GC% is very important – it is one measure of your efficiency and also, on activity above the breakeven point, it is the amount of contribution you will make.

Whichever method you use, the improvement in your GC% is significant. For every extra €100 you sell, you will get an extra €3 towards making your business more effective.

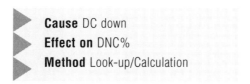

Cause DC down
Effect on DNC%
Method Look-up/Calculation

In the model business the existing DNC% was 10 per cent. What will be the impact of the 5 per cent decrease in dynamic costs? Again there are two ways to approach this.

Adjuster method

The basic calculation for the new DNC% value is similar to the one for the GC%:

New DNC% = Existing DNC% – 'Dynamic Adjuster'

The dynamic look-up table that gives this dynamic adjuster is shown in Table 10.2. Referring to the model business, the DC% is currently 60 per cent and we are going to decrease our dynamic costs by 5 per cent. Take these figures and look up in the table the dynamic adjuster, and you will get the highlighted figure of 3.00 (the same adjuster as for GC%).

Table 10.2 ● **Dynamic adjuster for new DNC% after a DC decrease**

Current						% Decrease in DC					
DC%	1	3	5	7	9	10	12	14	16	18	20
10	0.10	0.30	0.50	0.70	0.90	1.00	1.20	1.40	1.60	1.80	2.00
15	0.15	0.45	0.75	1.05	1.35	1.50	1.80	2.10	2.40	2.70	3.00
20	0.20	0.60	1.00	1.40	1.80	2.00	2.40	2.80	3.20	3.60	4.00
25	0.25	0.75	1.25	1.75	2.25	2.50	3.00	3.50	4.00	4.50	5.00
30	0.30	0.90	1.50	2.10	2.70	3.00	3.60	4.20	4.80	5.40	6.00
35	0.35	1.05	1.75	2.45	3.15	3.50	4.20	4.90	5.60	6.30	7.00
40	0.40	1.20	2.00	2.80	3.60	4.00	4.80	5.60	6.40	7.20	8.00
45	0.45	1.35	2.25	3.15	4.05	4.50	5.40	6.30	7.20	8.10	9.00
50	0.50	1.50	2.50	3.50	4.50	5.00	6.00	7.00	8.00	9.00	10.00
55	0.55	1.65	2.75	3.85	4.95	5.50	6.60	7.70	8.80	9.90	11.00
60	0.60	1.80	**3.00**	4.20	5.40	6.00	7.20	8.40	9.60	10.80	12.00
65	0.65	1.95	3.25	4.55	5.85	6.50	7.80	9.10	10.40	11.70	13.00
70	0.70	2.10	3.50	4.90	6.30	7.00	8.40	9.80	11.20	12.60	14.00
75	0.75	2.25	3.75	5.25	6.75	7.50	9.00	10.50	12.00	13.50	15.00
80	0.80	2.40	4.00	5.60	7.20	8.00	9.60	11.20	12.80	14.40	16.00
85	0.85	2.55	4.25	5.95	7.65	8.50	10.20	11.90	13.60	15.30	17.00
90	0.90	2.70	4.50	6.30	8.10	9.00	10.80	12.60	14.40	16.20	18.00

The current DNC% in the contribution statement is 10 per cent and to arrive at the new DNC% we use the following formula:

New DNC% = Existing DNC% + 'Dynamic Adjuster'

New DNC% = 10.00% + '3.00' = 13.00%

As with the table for GC%, the simplicity of this calculation is brought to life by the use of the dynamic adjuster, but did you know the answer before you started on this journey?

Mathematical method

New DNC% = Existing DNC% + (Decrease in DC × DC%)

New DNC% = 10.00% + (5.00 × 60.00%)

New DNC% = 10.00% + 3.00% = 13.00%

Your DNC% is the most important – you will recall that it is the measure of your effectiveness, the amount of overall contribution you make to your activities. You now have extra money to invest in the future of your business. A 5 per cent decrease in your dynamic costs has increased your DNC by 30 per cent!

Cause DC down

Effect on BeGap%

Method Calculation

The basic calculation for the new BeGap% value is simple and is based upon the two previous results:

$$\text{New BeGap\%} = \frac{\text{New DNC\%}}{\text{New GC\%}}$$

$$\text{New BeGap\%} = \frac{13.00\%}{43.00\%} = 30.23\%$$

We can summarize the dynamic indicators of contribution as:

GC%	was	40.00%	is now	43.00%
DNC%	was	10.00%	is now	13.00%
BeGap%	was	25.00%	is now	30.23%

Imagine the power of this for the managers of the model business in their management meeting. If they know they can achieve a dynamic cost decrease, they can see at a glance the impact of this on the dynamic indicators of contribution.

This is what dynamic financial management is all about. No need to go into a lengthy recalculation of the financial statements, or indeed, to call the accountant in. With your finger on the pulse of the dynamic indicators and the use of these dynamic techniques, you can manage tomorrow today.

We have looked at the impact of a decrease in DC% on only three of the eight dynamic indicators. We need to look at it in relation to the effect on the strands of your DNA and see if this benefit in contribution can also been seen in cash – in your DCM%, and if so by how much.

Cause DC down
Effect on Stock%
Method Look-up

The Stock% is going down. Why is this? And is it good or bad for your business? What is stock? It is your dynamic costs imprisoned in the time warp. In a manufacturing company, it is the value of your material purchases plus the value added to them by the work you have carried out in making your products, including work in progress and finished products awaiting sale.

Is a lower Stock% good or bad? It is money released from the time warp so fundamentally it is good. Now we need to know the magnitude of the effect that a 10 per cent decrease in dynamic costs will have on the Stock% of the model business. This is where the table comes in (*see* Table 10.3).

Table 10.3 ● **New Stock% after a DC decrease**

Current Stock%	% Decrease in DC										
	1	3	5	7	9	10	12	14	16	18	20
10	9.90	9.70	9.50	9.30	9.10	9.00	8.80	8.60	8.40	8.20	8.00
20	19.80	19.40	19.00	18.60	18.20	18.00	17.60	17.20	16.80	16.40	16.00
30	29.70	29.10	28.50	27.90	27.30	27.00	26.40	25.80	25.20	24.60	24.00
40	39.60	38.80	38.00	37.20	36.40	36.00	35.20	34.40	33.60	32.80	32.00
50	49.50	48.50	**47.50**	46.50	45.50	45.00	44.00	43.00	42.00	41.00	40.00
60	59.40	58.20	57.00	55.80	54.60	54.00	52.80	51.60	50.40	49.20	48.00
70	69.30	67.90	66.50	65.10	63.70	63.00	61.60	60.20	58.80	57.40	56.00
80	79.20	77.60	76.00	74.40	72.80	72.00	70.40	68.80	67.20	65.60	64.00
90	89.10	87.30	85.50	83.70	81.90	81.00	79.20	77.40	75.60	73.80	72.00
100	99.00	97.00	95.00	93.00	91.00	90.00	88.00	86.00	84.00	82.00	80.00
110	108.90	106.70	104.50	102.30	100.10	99.00	96.80	94.60	92.40	90.20	88.00
120	118.80	116.40	114.00	111.60	109.20	108.00	105.60	103.20	100.80	98.40	96.00
130	128.70	126.10	123.50	120.90	118.30	117.00	114.40	111.80	109.20	106.60	104.00
140	138.60	135.80	133.00	130.20	127.40	126.00	123.20	120.40	117.60	114.80	112.00
150	148.50	145.50	142.50	139.50	136.50	135.00	132.00	129.00	126.00	123.00	120.00

The end result – the new Stock% – is given to you directly from the table. It is simple – you do not need to calculate anything. In the model business, stock as a percentage of a month's income was 50 per cent. With a 5 per cent decrease in dynamic costs, the Stock% would go down to 47.5 per cent.

What does this mean? A new Stock% of 47.5 per cent multiplied by the income value of €100 will give a stock value of €47.50 instead of the original value of

€50. An extra €2.50 released from the time warp! 'So what?', you may say, but add a few zeros to these figures and it really becomes beneficial.

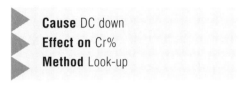

Cause DC down

Effect on Cr%

Method Look-up

Note: This is applicable only if the decrease in dynamic costs is attributable to a decrease in the cost of the things you buy on credit.

If the decrease in dynamic costs is attributable to things you buy on credit, a decrease in the cost must be followed by a decrease in creditors. To complete the picture you need to have an idea of the proportion of your dynamic costs represented by things you buy. As a good rule of thumb, 50 per cent is a reasonable split. This is the assumption used in Table 10.4.

Table 10.4 ● New Cr% after a DC decrease

Current Cr%	% Decrease in DC										
	1	3	5	7	9	10	12	14	16	18	20
10	9.95	9.85	9.75	9.65	9.55	9.50	9.40	9.30	9.20	9.10	9.00
20	19.90	19.70	19.50	19.30	19.10	19.00	18.80	18.60	18.40	18.20	18.00
30	29.85	29.55	29.25	28.95	28.65	28.50	28.20	27.90	27.60	27.30	27.00
40	39.80	39.40	39.00	38.60	38.20	38.00	37.60	37.20	36.80	36.40	36.00
50	49.75	49.25	48.75	48.25	47.75	47.50	47.00	46.50	46.00	45.50	45.00
60	59.70	59.10	58.50	57.90	57.30	57.00	56.40	55.80	55.20	54.60	54.00
70	69.65	68.95	68.25	67.55	66.85	66.50	65.80	65.10	64.40	63.70	63.00
80	79.60	78.80	**78.00**	77.20	76.40	76.00	75.20	74.40	73.60	72.80	72.00
90	89.55	88.65	87.75	86.85	85.95	85.50	84.60	83.70	82.80	81.90	81.00
100	99.50	98.50	97.50	96.50	95.50	95.00	94.00	93.00	92.00	91.00	90.00
110	109.45	108.35	107.25	106.15	105.05	104.50	103.40	102.30	101.20	100.10	99.00
120	119.40	118.20	117.00	115.80	114.60	114.00	112.80	111.60	110.40	109.20	108.00
130	129.35	128.05	126.75	125.45	124.15	123.50	122.20	120.90	119.60	118.30	117.00
140	139.30	137.90	136.50	135.10	133.70	133.00	131.60	130.20	128.80	127.40	126.00
150	149.25	147.75	146.25	144.75	143.25	142.50	141.00	139.50	138.00	136.50	135.00

The end result – the new Cr% – is given to you from the table. As with Stock% you do not need to calculate anything. After a 5 per cent decrease in dynamic costs with an existing Cr% of 80 per cent, we can read from the table the new Cr% of 78 per cent.

What does this mean in cash terms? With a new Cr% in the model business of 78 per cent multiplied by the monthly income of €100, this will give a new creditor value of €78 instead of the original value of €80. A reduction of €2 in the amount we will have to find to pay our creditors. For example, if you were in a business with annual sales of €1 million, you would have saved €20,000 of cash in the month that the decrease in dynamic costs was made.

The positive effects of changes sown 'today' will also be reaped 'tomorrow'.

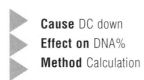

Cause DC down
Effect on DNA%
Method Calculation

In order to calculate the dynamic net assets as a result of this change we need to look at the strands of our static net assets imprisoned in the time warp before and after the anticipated change. This can be shown as:

DNA = SNA *after* Change – SNA *before* Change

Then DNA% will be:

$$\text{DNA\%} = \frac{\text{DNA}}{\text{Income}} \times 100$$

The strands of the SNA are shown below:

	Before	After
Income	€100.00	€100.00
Stock	€50.00	€47.50
Debtors	€100.00	€100.00
Creditors	€80.00	€78.00
SNA	€70.00	€69.50
Stock%	50.00%	47.50%
Dr%	100.00%	100.00%
Cr%	80.00%	78.00%
SNA%	70.00%	69.50%

The DNA can now be calculated as:

DNA = €69.50 – €70.00 = €(0.50)

And the DNA% is

$$\text{DNA\%} = \frac{\text{€}0.50}{\text{€}100.00} \times 100 = (0.50)\%$$

The overall effect on DNA% shows a small inflow of money, extra money freed from the strands of the DNA. But the real measure has got to be the overall impact on the DCM%.

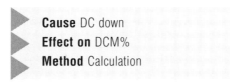

Cause DC down

Effect on DCM%

Method Calculation

The final dynamic indicator is now easy to calculate:

DCM% = DNC% – DNA%

DCM% = 13.00% – (0.50)% = 13.50%

The combined effect of the decrease in DNC% and the apparently small amount of extra cash released from the time warp has decreased your DCM% to 13.5 per cent. It is an excellent position for the model business as DCM% is a much larger percentage of the month's income. Would the result be the same in your business given your figures for DNC% and DNA%?

Looking to the long term, the future DCM% the model business can get now is the same as the new, increased level of the DNC% – 13 per cent. Any plans for investing in the business may be brought forward or additional external funding dispensed with.

The new shape of your business

The eight dynamic indicators before and after the decrease in dynamic costs are:

Contribution statement			DNA statement		
	Before	**After**		**Before**	**After**
Income	€100.00	€100.00	Income	€100.00	€100.00
Dynamic Costs	€60.00	€57.00	Stock	€50.00	€47.50
Gross Contribution	€40.00	€43.00	Debtors	€100.00	€100.00
Static Costs	€30.00	€30.00	Creditors	€80.00	€78.00
Dynamic Net Contribution	€10.00	€13.00	Static Net Assets	€70.00	€69.50

Eight dynamic indicators

	Before	After
GC%	40.00%	43.00%
DNC%	10.00%	13.00%
BeGap%	25.00%	30.23%
Stock%	50.00%	47.50%
Dr%	100.00%	100.00%
Cr%	80.00%	78.00%
DNA%	0.00%	(0.50)%
DCM%	10.00%	13.50%

To look at the impact on the visual representation of the business, we can look at Fig 10.2. As you can see, your business is quite literally developing! But this could take cash.

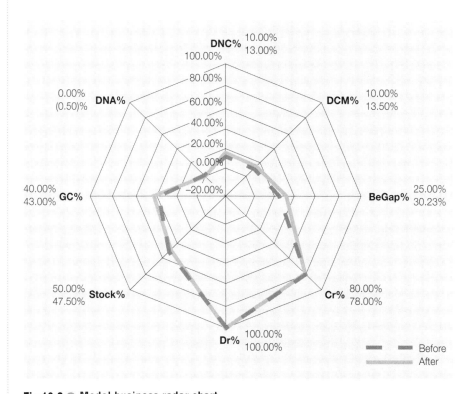

Fig 10.2 ● Model business radar chart

Actions for dynamic management of a decrease in dynamic costs

As we have said, you need to manage change dynamically, and even beneficial changes can be taken advantage of. You now have the freedom that may enable you to improve the quality of your business, or even to allow yourself to take more time off to relax.

The options open to you to take advantage of a decrease in dynamic costs are shown below:

Change		Appropriate action to regain DNC%
Decrease	⟹	Decrease volume
in dynamic	⟹	Decrease price
costs	⟹	Increase static costs

These seem obvious: you can choose to sell less, reduce your price, or decrease your other costs – the static costs. The results of a dynamic analysis will help you decide the maximum benefit for your business. The dynamic financial management definition of back into shape is:

'maintaining the DNC% at the same level as it was before the change.'

i.e. being as effective as we were before the change.

Again, with the dynamic techniques we are using, we can predict the magnitude of the freedom we now have and still maintain our original DNC%.

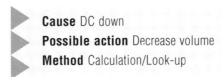

Cause DC down
Possible action Decrease volume
Method Calculation/Look-up

So what does a decrease in volume or level of activity really mean? In a manufacturing, service or retail business it is less sales volume – you don't just sell less, you make less. This can mean easing back on the accelerator, which may not be a bad thing, creating time to see the wood for the trees, to look to the future, to plan for a business that will survive in the long term. For a budget holder it may mean a smaller budget because of a decrease in the level of activity within your department. In political organizations that may mean your empire has been taken away. But it may simply mean you are running a more professional department that fulfils all its requirements, to time, and to the accepted standards.

In our model business, if our DC decreases by 5 per cent and we want to retain a DNC% of 10 per cent, the volume decrease allowed is shown in Table 10.5. But in order to use the table we first need to calculate a dynamic adjuster. For this change the adjuster is calculated as follows:

Dynamic Adjuster = Decrease in DC × Original DC%

Dynamic Adjuster = 5.00 × 60.00%

Dynamic Adjuster = 3.00

Reading from Table 10.5, in the model business the original SC% was 30 per cent and our dynamic adjuster is 3.00. This means we could decrease our volume to 90.91 per cent of current levels and retain our existing DNC% of 10 per cent, a decrease of 9.09 per cent. Let's see if it works:

Table 10.5 ● New Volume% to maintain same DNC% after a DC decrease

Current SC%	2	3	4	5	6	7	8	9	10	12	14	16
10	83.33	76.92	71.43	66.67	62.50	58.82	55.56	52.63	50.00	45.45	41.67	38.46
15	88.24	83.33	78.95	75.00	71.43	68.18	65.22	62.50	60.00	55.56	51.72	48.39
20	90.91	86.96	83.33	80.00	76.92	74.07	71.43	68.97	66.67	62.50	58.82	55.56
25	92.59	89.29	86.21	83.33	80.65	78.13	75.76	73.53	71.43	67.57	64.10	60.98
30	93.75	**90.91**	88.24	85.71	83.33	81.08	78.95	76.92	75.00	71.43	68.18	65.22
35	94.59	92.11	89.74	87.50	85.37	83.33	81.40	79.55	77.78	74.47	71.43	68.63
40	95.24	93.02	90.91	88.89	86.96	85.11	83.33	81.63	80.00	76.92	74.07	71.43
45	95.74	93.75	91.84	90.00	88.24	86.54	84.91	83.33	81.82	78.95	76.27	73.77
50	96.15	94.34	92.59	90.91	89.29	87.72	86.21	84.75	83.33	80.65	78.13	75.76
55	96.49	94.83	93.22	91.67	90.16	88.71	87.30	85.94	84.62	82.09	79.71	77.46
60	96.77	95.24	93.75	92.31	90.91	89.55	88.24	86.96	85.71	83.33	81.08	78.95
65	97.01	95.59	94.20	92.86	91.55	90.28	89.04	87.84	86.67	84.42	82.28	80.25
70	97.22	95.89	94.59	93.33	92.11	90.91	89.74	88.61	87.50	85.37	83.33	81.40
75	97.40	96.15	94.94	93.75	92.59	91.46	90.36	89.29	88.24	86.21	84.27	82.42
80	97.56	96.39	95.24	94.12	93.02	91.95	90.91	89.89	88.89	86.96	85.11	83.33
85	97.70	96.59	95.51	94.44	93.41	92.39	91.40	90.43	89.47	87.63	85.86	84.16
90	97.83	96.77	95.74	94.74	93.75	92.78	91.84	90.91	90.00	88.24	86.54	84.91

	Before	After initial impact	After volume decrease	%
Income	€ 100.00	€ 100.00	€ 90.91	100.00
Dynamic Costs	€ 60.00	€ 57.00	€ 51.82	57.00
Gross Contribution	€ 40.00	€ 43.00	€ 39.09	43.00
Static Costs	€ 30.00	€ 30.00	€ 30.00	33.00
Dynamic Net Contribution	€ 10.00	€ 13.00	€ 9.09	10.00

If we decrease our volume by 9.09 per cent, we retain DNC% at 10 per cent – the level it was before any of the decisions were made. It is worthwhile considering the other dynamic indicators here. A volume decrease makes no difference to the GC% – it will be the same as it was after the initial impact. So we can quickly calculate the impact of the volume decrease on our BeGap%:

New BeGap% = New DNC% / New GC%

New BeGap% = 10.00% / 43.00% = 23.26%

The business is slightly more risky than before any change. As the volume has dropped, the value of the static costs have remained the same – an effective SC% increase. As mentioned in the discussions on cost structure in *Chapter 2: What are dynamic indicators?* this can make a business seem riskier in times when the externals are in decline.

You should also assess the impact on DNA%. If the only change is one of volume, then as a percentage of sales, the Stock%, Dr% and Cr% indicators should stay the same, that is, at the levels after the initial impact of the decrease in dynamic costs.

Looking at the strands of your SNA:

	Before	After initial impact	After volume decrease
Income	€ 100.00	€ 100.00	€ 90.91
Stock	€ 50.00	€ 47.50	€ 43.18
Debtors	€ 100.00	€ 100.00	€ 90.91
Creditors	€ 80.00	€ 78.00	€ 70.91
SNA	€ 70.00	€ 69.50	€ 63.18
Stock%	50.00%	47.50%	47.50%
Dr%	100.00%	100.00%	100.00%
Cr%	80.00%	78.00%	78.00%
SNA%	70.00%	69.50%	69.50%

The decrease in volume means we will actually decrease the value of SNA, from €70, the figure before anything happened, to €63.18.

So what does this mean for the DNA%?

DNA = SNA *after* Decision – SNA *before* Initial Impact

DNA = €63.18 – €70.00 = €(6.82)

Money has been released for the SNA time warp and as a percentage of the new level of income the DNA% calculates as:

$$\textbf{DNA\%} = \frac{€(6.82)}{€90.91} \times 100 = (7.50)\%$$

This seems to be a significant movement of cash out of the time warp of your SNA. This can be seen powerfully by looking at the overall impact on the DCM%:

DCM% = DNC% – DNA%

DCM% = 10.00% – (7.50)% = 17.50%

There is a real inflow of cash for the model business with this option. This option can be summarized as:

Eight dynamic indicators

	Before	After initial impact	After volume decrease
GC%	40.00%	43.00%	43.00%
DNC%	10.00%	13.00%	10.00%
BeGap%	25.00%	30.23%	23.26%
Stock%	50.00%	47.50%	47.50%
Dr%	100.00%	100.00%	100.00%
Cr%	80.00%	78.00%	78.00%
DNA%	0.00%	(0.50)%	(7.50)%
DCM%	10.00%	13.50%	17.50%

The bigger the decrease in DC% we can obtain, the higher the volume decrease we could allow. Controlling DC% in a shrinking or highly competitive market is a must. Efficiency is a key driver for these types of markets. However, we could decrease volume as an alternative, focusing on a smaller, more lucrative niche in the market.

> **Cause** DC down
> **Possible benefit** Decrease price
> **Method** Look-up/Calculation

The next possible action to look at is decreasing your price. You have not sold any less but every sale has made less money. A price decrease does not affect the value of dynamic costs. They stay the same. Therefore any decrease in price will go straight down to your bottom line – your DNC.

But how much can you allow to drop out of your bottom line while retaining your original DNC%? What you need to know, and what dynamic financial management tells you, is the actual price decrease you could allow in your business without reducing your original DNC%.

What does a decrease in price really mean? In a manufacturing, service or retail business it is fairly obvious – you put down the price of the products or services that you provide. However, when dynamic costs go down we often pass too much of this benefit on to our customers.

Back to our model business where we were looking at a decrease of 5 per cent in our DC. What price decrease could the model business need to implement in order to retain its original DNC% of 10 per cent? In dynamic financial management the formula for this is:

% Price Decrease = % DC Decrease × Dynamic Adjuster

But first we need to find the dynamic adjuster using a dynamic look-up table (*see* Table 10.6).

Table 10.6 ● Dynamic adjuster for price decrease after decrease in DC%

Existing DNC%	10	15	20	25	30	35	40	45	50	55	60	65	70	75	80
1	0.101	0.152	0.202	0.253	0.303	0.354	0.404	0.455	0.505	0.556	0.606	0.657	0.707	0.758	0.808
2	0.102	0.153	0.204	0.255	0.306	0.357	0.408	0.459	0.510	0.561	0.612	0.663	0.714	0.765	0.816
3	0.103	0.155	0.206	0.258	0.309	0.361	0.412	0.464	0.515	0.567	0.619	0.670	0.722	0.773	0.825
4	0.104	0.156	0.208	0.260	0.313	0.365	0.417	0.469	0.521	0.573	0.625	0.677	0.729	0.781	0.833
5	0.105	0.158	0.211	0.263	0.316	0.368	0.421	0.474	0.526	0.579	0.632	0.684	0.737	0.789	0.842
6	0.106	0.160	0.213	0.266	0.319	0.372	0.426	0.479	0.532	0.585	0.638	0.691	0.745	0.798	0.851
7	0.108	0.161	0.215	0.269	0.323	0.376	0.430	0.484	0.538	0.591	0.645	0.699	0.753	0.806	0.860
8	0.109	0.163	0.217	0.272	0.326	0.380	0.435	0.489	0.543	0.598	0.652	0.707	0.761	0.815	0.870
9	0.110	0.165	0.220	0.275	0.330	0.385	0.440	0.495	0.549	0.604	0.659	0.714	0.769	0.824	0.879
10	0.111	0.167	0.222	0.278	0.333	0.389	0.444	0.500	0.556	0.611	**0.667**	0.722	0.778	0.833	0.889
12	0.114	0.170	0.227	0.284	0.341	0.398	0.455	0.511	0.568	0.625	0.682	0.739	0.795	0.852	0.909
14	0.116	0.174	0.233	0.291	0.349	0.407	0.465	0.523	0.581	0.640	0.698	0.756	0.814	0.872	0.930
16	0.119	0.179	0.238	0.298	0.357	0.417	0.476	0.536	0.595	0.655	0.714	0.774	0.833	0.893	0.952
18	0.122	0.183	0.244	0.305	0.366	0.427	0.488	0.549	0.610	0.671	0.732	0.793	0.854	0.915	0.976
20	0.125	0.188	0.250	0.313	0.375	0.438	0.500	0.563	0.625	0.688	0.750	0.813	0.875	0.938	1.000
25	0.133	0.200	0.267	0.333	0.400	0.467	0.533	0.600	0.667	0.733	0.800	0.867	0.933	1.000	1.067
30	0.143	0.214	0.286	0.357	0.429	0.500	0.571	0.643	0.714	0.786	0.857	0.929	1.000	1.071	1.143
35	0.154	0.231	0.308	0.385	0.462	0.538	0.615	0.692	0.769	0.846	0.923	1.000	1.077	1.154	1.231
40	0.167	0.250	0.333	0.417	0.500	0.583	0.667	0.750	0.833	0.917	1.000	1.083	1.167	1.250	1.333
50	0.200	0.300	0.400	0.500	0.600	0.700	0.800	0.900	1.000	1.100	1.200	1.300	1.400	1.500	1.600

Referring to the model business, the DC% is currently 60 per cent and DNC% is 10 per cent. Using Table 10.6 gives you the highlighted figure of 0.667. With a dynamic cost decrease of 5 per cent we can use the formula:

% Price Decrease = Decrease in DC × Dynamic Adjuster

% Price Decrease = 5.00 × 0.667 = 3.34%

So if my current price is €100, the decrease will be €3.34 (a 3.34 per cent price decrease), therefore my new price will be €96.66. Let's see if it works:

	Before	After initial impact	After price decrease	%
Income	€100.00	€100.00	€96.66	100.00
Dynamic Costs	€60.00	€57.00	€57.00	58.97
Gross Contribution	€40.00	€43.00	€39.66	41.03
Static Costs	€30.00	€30.00	€30.00	31.03
Dynamic Net Contribution	€10.00	€13.00	€9.66	10.00

If we can achieve a DC decrease of 5 per cent we could afford to reduce our price by 3.34 per cent and still retain DNC% at 10 per cent – the level it was before any of the decisions were made. However, the price reduction you can afford is only 3.34 per cent, not 5 per cent as some managers believe.

We can quickly calculate the impact of the price decrease on our breakeven gap%:

New BeGap% = New DNC% / New GC%

New BeGap% = 10.00% / 41.03% = 24.37%

Not surprisingly this has reduced compared to the situation after the initial impact. We have retained our DNC% but the GC% has been reduced from 43 per cent to 41.03 per cent.

If the only change is one of price, then with the exception of debtors, as a value these indicators should stay the same. The Dr% should stay at the same percentage of income. We can therefore look at the impact on the strands of the SNA:

	Before	**After initial impact**	**After price decrease**
Income	€ 100.00	€ 100.00	€ 96.66
Stock	€ 50.00	€ 47.50	€ 47.50
Debtors	€ 100.00	€ 100.00	€ 96.66
Creditors	€ 80.00	€ 78.00	€ 78.00
SNA	€ 70.00	€ 69.50	€ 66.16
Stock%	50.00%	47.50%	49.14%
Dr%	100.00%	100.00%	100.00%
Cr%	80.00%	78.00%	80.70%
SNA%	70.00%	69.50%	68.44%

The change in value of the SNA represented by the DNA is:

DNA = SNA *after* Decision – SNA *before* Initial Impact

DNA = €66.16 – €70.00 = €(3.84)

Looking at this as a percentage of the new income figure, the DNA% is:

$$\text{DNA\%} = \frac{€(3.84)}{€96.66} \times 100 = (3.97)\%$$

So the DNA% is negative, meaning there has been a beneficial movement of money out of the time warp of the SNA due to the decrease in price. But again, when the movement is price – beware. This could simply be due to the value of debtors. Each one is now paying us relatively less income.

The final evaluation is to see the impact of this option on the DCM%:

$$DCM\% = DNC\% - DNA\%$$

$$DCM\% = 10.00\% - (3.97)\% = 13.97\%$$

This option has not substantially increased the DCM%. Summarizing this:

Eight dynamic indicators

	Before	After initial impact	After price decrease
GC%	40.00%	43.00%	41.03%
DNC%	10.00%	13.00%	10.00%
BeGap%	25.00%	30.23%	24.37%
Stock%	50.00%	47.50%	49.14%
Dr%	100.00%	100.00%	100.00%
Cr%	80.00%	78.00%	80.70%
DNA%	0.00%	(0.50)%	(3.97)%
DCM%	10.00%	13.50%	13.97%

Your DCM% is 13.97 per cent, which means you have released cash from your time warp equivalent to 13.97 per cent of your current period's income, more than the 10 per cent you were predicting before the change.

As a possible benefit from decreasing your dynamic costs, decreasing your price seems a favourable option given the shape of the model business. It could now reduce its price and, perhaps, gain a competitive advantage. What about your business? Would your dynamic indicators give you this positive result – the same DNC% and a greater DCM%?

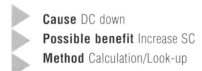

Cause DC down
Possible benefit Increase SC
Method Calculation/Look-up

If one set of costs go down, it is often the case that this has been the result of a change in the cost structure – a move from dynamic costs to static costs. What we need to know is the relationship between the two costs and what the compensating increase could be to maintain our original DNC% at this level of activity. (Of course, if our activity level changes we are back to our earlier discussions on cost structure, risk and reward in *Chapter 2: What are dynamic indicators?*)

We often know the amount by which we could increase the static costs, but we also need to know what percentage this represents so that we can again start to examine the changed shape of our business. We can look this up using Table 10.7, but first we need to calculate the dynamic adjuster using the following calculation:

Dynamic Adjuster = Decrease in DC × Original DC%

Dynamic Adjuster = 5.00 × 60.00%

Dynamic Adjuster = 3.00

We can now take this dynamic adjuster to use Table 10.7. Reading from the table, our original SC% was 30 per cent and our dynamic adjuster is 3.00. This means we could increase our static costs by 10 per cent and still retain our original DNC%. Let's see if it works:

	Before	After initial impact	After SC increase	%
Income	€ 100.00	€ 100.00	€ 100.00	100.00
Dynamic Costs	€ 60.00	€ 57.00	€ 57.00	57.00
Gross Contribution	€ 40.00	€ 43.00	€ 43.00	43.00
Static Costs	€ 30.00	€ 30.00	€ 33.00	33.00
Dynamic Net Contribution	€ 10.00	€ 13.00	€ 10.00	10.00

Table 10.7 ● **Increase in SC% to maintain same DNC% after a DC decrease**

Current SC%	Dynamic adjuster											
	2	3	4	5	6	7	8	9	10	12	14	16
10	20.00	30.00	40.00	50.00	60.00	70.00	80.00	90.00	100.00	120.00	140.00	160.00
15	13.33	20.00	26.67	33.33	40.00	46.67	53.33	60.00	66.67	80.00	93.33	106.67
20	10.00	15.00	20.00	25.00	30.00	35.00	40.00	45.00	50.00	60.00	70.00	80.00
25	8.00	12.00	16.00	20.00	24.00	28.00	32.00	36.00	40.00	48.00	56.00	64.00
30	6.67	**10.00**	13.33	16.67	20.00	23.33	26.67	30.00	33.33	40.00	46.67	53.33
35	5.71	8.57	11.43	14.29	17.14	20.00	22.86	25.71	28.57	34.29	40.00	45.71
40	5.00	7.50	10.00	12.50	15.00	17.50	20.00	22.50	25.00	30.00	35.00	40.00
45	4.44	6.67	8.89	11.11	13.33	15.56	17.78	20.00	22.22	26.67	31.11	35.56
50	4.00	6.00	8.00	10.00	12.00	14.00	16.00	18.00	20.00	24.00	28.00	32.00
55	3.64	5.45	7.27	9.09	10.91	12.73	14.55	16.36	18.18	21.82	25.45	29.09
60	3.33	5.00	6.67	8.33	10.00	11.67	13.33	15.00	16.67	20.00	23.33	26.67
65	3.08	4.62	6.15	7.69	9.23	10.77	12.31	13.85	15.38	18.46	21.54	24.62
70	2.86	4.29	5.71	7.14	8.57	10.00	11.43	12.86	14.29	17.14	20.00	22.86
75	2.67	4.00	5.33	6.67	8.00	9.33	10.67	12.00	13.33	16.00	18.67	21.33
80	2.50	3.75	5.00	6.25	7.50	8.75	10.00	11.25	12.50	15.00	17.50	20.00
85	2.35	3.53	4.71	5.88	7.06	8.24	9.41	10.59	11.76	14.12	16.47	18.82
90	2.22	3.33	4.44	5.56	6.67	7.78	8.89	10.00	11.11	13.33	15.56	17.78

However, we need to remember that dynamic costs vary with output while static costs stay the same. If the future sales are buoyant, this will mean we will get relatively more reward. But if the market is uncertain we will also have more risk if sales drop. Static costs are often more difficult to get rid of than people anticipate.

What about the impact on the other dynamic indicators? We can quickly calculate the impact of the static cost increase on our breakeven gap%:

New BeGap% = New DNC% / New GC%

New BeGap% = 10.00% / 43.00% = 23.26%

A slightly more risky business as might be expected with an increase in static costs.

In the section on managing changes in static costs we identify that the strands of our SNA are not affected by changes in the static costs. So, this secondary action of increasing static costs will have no additional impact on DNA%. However, there is still the change in SNA as a result of the initial impact to consider.

	Before	After initial impact	After SC increase
Income	€ 100.00	€ 100.00	€ 100.00
Stock	€ 50.00	€ 47.50	€ 47.50
Debtors	€ 100.00	€ 100.00	€ 100.00
Creditors	€ 80.00	€ 78.00	€ 78.00
DNA	€ 70.00	€ 69.50	€ 69.50
Stock%	50.00%	47.50%	47.50%
Dr%	100.00%	100.00%	100.00%
Cr%	80.00%	78.00%	78.00%
DNA%	70.00%	69.50%	69.50%

The movement in the time warp of your SNA is reflected in your DNA:

DNA = SNA *after* Decision − SNA *before* Initial Impact

DNA = €69.50 − €70.00 = €(0.50)

Then DNA% is:

$$\text{DNA\%} = \frac{€(0.50)}{€100.00} \times 100 = (0.50)\%$$

So the DNA% is now slightly negative, meaning there has been a marginal movement of money out of the strands of your SNA. The size and the direction of this movement will depend on the relationship between the Stock% and Cr% in your business. The overall effect on the DCM% is:

DCM% = DNC% – DNA%

DCM% = 10.00% – (0.50)% = 10.50%

We can summarize this option as follows:

Eight dynamic indicators

	Before	After initial impact	After SC increase
GC%	40.00%	43.00%	43.00%
DNC%	10.00%	13.00%	10.00%
BeGap%	25.00%	30.23%	23.26%
Stock%	50.00%	47.50%	47.50%
Dr%	100.00%	100.00%	100.00%
Cr%	80.00%	78.00%	78.00%
DNA%	0.00%	(0.50)%	(0.50)%
DCM%	10.00%	13.50%	10.50%

Moving costs within the cost structure of the model business has a positive effect, although the results after the initial impact were more favourable. You need to do the analysis on your cost structure to see if this is a possible benefit for you in your business.

chapter 11

Increases in your static costs

Why do static costs increase?

Increases in your static costs, as with all increases in a business, need to be managed, and there are two stages in understanding the impact on your business:

1   The initial impact of the increase.

2   The alternative actions you could take to proactively manage this increase.

The initial impact of any increase can be most successfully visualized using the eight dynamic indicators on the radar chart. The trends you will be monitoring using the dynamic breakeven graph and the dynamic cash graph will put these increases into context – do you need to react or is it simply a momentary blip?

However, we should be managing the increase dynamically. From our understanding of the increase, monitored in the three charts we are using to visualize the business, we can begin to select the most appropriate action to get the business back into shape.

An example of this for static costs could be responding to a proposed increase in the rent of your premises. A dynamic response would be to negotiate with your landlord for, say, holding the rent at the current level in exchange for taking on a longer-term lease commitment. Another example might be taking on another administrator to cope with the increasing legislation facing business. How do you get back into shape? Can you pass the increase on to your customers? If so, what price increase would this require? This chapter will give you the power to answer all of these questions. And you will not need to be a mathematician or an accountant to do it.

It is worth repeating that in dynamic financial management we have a specific way of defining dynamic management of these increases. In terms of our dynamic indicators we do not know what will happen as a result of these increases, but with dynamic financial management techniques we can predict very accurately what needs to be done to keep your business fit and healthy. And we have defined fit and healthy as returning the DNC% to the same level as it was before the initial management decision.

For example, let us look at the model business:

	%
Income	100
Dynamic Costs	60
Gross Contribution	40
Static Costs	30
Dynamic Net Contribution	10

If static costs go up to 35 per cent, the initial impact on the contribution statement would look like this:

	%
Income	100
Dynamic Costs	60
Gross Contribution	40
Static Costs	35
Dynamic Net Contribution	5

Your DNC% has been reduced to 5 per cent. We need to know what the alternative ways are of getting your DNC% back up to its original level of 10 per cent.

We will examine the two stages mentioned earlier, i.e. look at the initial impact of the increase in static costs and then the measures available to us to manage these dynamically and regain our level of fitness, i.e. regain our original DNC%. As managers we are often faced with a choice of decisions and changing cost structures is one of these alternatives.

Increases in your static costs

Let us begin with a summary of what could happen if your business suffered from an increase in its static costs. For the model business, if static costs increased by 5 per cent, the possible actions to compensate are:

Change		Appropriate action to regain DNC%	Amount
Increase in	⫸	Increase volume	By 5.00%
static costs	⫸	Increase price	By 1.67%
of 5%	⫸	Decrease dynamic costs	By 2.50%

The shape of your business after each of these changes is shown below.

Eight dynamic indicators

	Before any change	After initial impact SC increase 5%	After volume increase 5.0%	After price increase 1.67%	After DC decrease 2.50%
GC%	40.00%	40.00%	40.00%	40.98%	41.50%
DNC%	10.00%	8.50%	10.00%	10.00%	10.00%
BeGap%	25.00%	21.25%	25.00%	24.40%	24.10%
Stock%	50.00%	50.00%	50.00%	49.18%	48.75%
Dr%	100.00%	100.00%	100.00%	100.00%	100.00%
Cr%	80.00%	80.00%	80.00%	78.69%	79.00%
DNA%	0.00%	0.00%	3.33%	1.64%	(0.25)%
DCM%	10.00%	8.50%	6.67%	8.36%	10.25%

The decision is now yours:

● accept the new shape of your business after the initial impact and change your targets accordingly;

● work dynamically towards one of the above possible actions;

● somewhere in between.

Whatever your decision, you can predict its impact before you are committed to any changes – managing tomorrow today.

How did we get to these results? First we need to find out the result of the initial impact of the change in static costs, then we need to look at all the possible actions that could be taken to compensate for this increase.

The initial impact

When your static costs increase there are going to be a number of impacts on your eight dynamic indicators. These are shown in Fig 11.1.

The eight dynamic indicators	Change static costs
	Tool
GC%	
DNC%	Look-up and calculation
BeGap%	Calculation
Stock%	
Dr%	
Cr%	
DNA%	
DCM%	Calculation

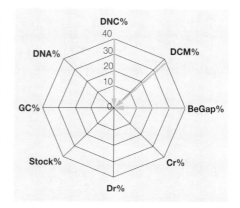

Fig 11.1 ●
Radar chart of dynamic indicators

Interestingly, there are not many of the dynamic indicators affected. In fact, with a decision to increase static costs, there are only three effects we need to consider: BeGap%, DNC% and DCM%. BeGap% and DNC% will both decrease as shown in Fig 11.1. As you already know, DCM% is calculated as DNC% less DNA%. In this change SNA has remained static, therefore the DNA% will not change. However, DNC% has gone down. Therefore DCM% will also go down.

We can now look at the magnitude of the initial impact on each of the eight dynamic indicators. As an example we will use the figures in the model business. Throughout this chapter we will assume that the static costs have increased by 5 per cent, i.e. they have increased from 30 per cent to 31.5 per cent. In the case of static costs the first effect we need to consider is the change to DNC%.

Cause SC up
Effect on DNC%
Method Look-up/Calculation

In the model business the existing DNC% was 10 per cent. What will be the impact of the 5 per cent increase in static costs? There are actually two ways to approach this one.

Adjuster method

The basic calculation for the new DNC% value is as follows:

New DNC% = Existing DNC% – 'Dynamic Adjuster'

The dynamic look-up table that gives this dynamic adjuster is shown in Table 11.1. Referring to the model business, the SC% is currently 30 per cent and we are going to increase our static costs by 5 per cent. Taking these figures and looking up in the table the dynamic adjuster, you will get 1.50.

Table 11.1 ● **Dynamic adjuster for new DNC% after an SC increase**

Current					% Increase in SC						
SC%	1	3	5	7	9	10	12	14	16	18	20
10	0.10	0.30	0.50	0.70	0.90	1.00	1.20	1.40	1.60	1.80	2.00
15	0.15	0.45	0.75	1.05	1.35	1.50	1.80	2.10	2.40	2.70	3.00
20	0.20	0.60	1.00	1.40	1.80	2.00	2.40	2.80	3.20	3.60	4.00
25	0.25	0.75	1.25	1.75	2.25	2.50	3.00	3.50	4.00	4.50	5.00
30	0.30	0.90	**1.50**	2.10	2.70	3.00	3.60	4.20	4.80	5.40	6.00
35	0.35	1.05	1.75	2.45	3.15	3.50	4.20	4.90	5.60	6.30	7.00
40	0.40	1.20	2.00	2.80	3.60	4.00	4.80	5.60	6.40	7.20	8.00
45	0.45	1.35	2.25	3.15	4.05	4.50	5.40	6.30	7.20	8.10	9.00
50	0.50	1.50	2.50	3.50	4.50	5.00	6.00	7.00	8.00	9.00	10.00
55	0.55	1.65	2.75	3.85	4.95	5.50	6.60	7.70	8.80	9.90	11.00
60	0.60	1.80	3.00	4.20	5.40	6.00	7.20	8.40	9.60	10.80	12.00
65	0.65	1.95	3.25	4.55	5.85	6.50	7.80	9.10	10.40	11.70	13.00
70	0.70	2.10	3.50	4.90	6.30	7.00	8.40	9.80	11.20	12.60	14.00
75	0.75	2.25	3.75	5.25	6.75	7.50	9.00	10.50	12.00	13.50	15.00
80	0.80	2.40	4.00	5.60	7.20	8.00	9.60	11.20	12.80	14.40	16.00
85	0.85	2.55	4.25	5.95	7.65	8.50	10.20	11.90	13.60	15.30	17.00
90	0.90	2.70	4.50	6.30	8.10	9.00	10.80	12.60	14.40	16.20	18.00

The current DNC% in the contribution statement is 10 per cent and to arrive at the new DNC% we use the following formula:

New DNC% = Existing DNC% – 'Dynamic Adjuster'

New DNC% = 10.00% − 1.50 = 8.50%

The dynamic adjuster allows you to identify your new DNC% as a result of this static cost increase. But for the more mathematical reader there is a short cut you could use for this indicator.

Mathematical method

New DNC% = Existing DNC% − (Increase in SC × SC%)

New DNC% = 10.00% − (5 × 30%)

New DNC% = 10.00% − 1.50% = 8.50%

Your DNC% is the most important dynamic indicator – it is the measure of your effectiveness, the amount of overall contribution you make on your activities.

Let us look at the new contribution statement for the model business:

	Before		After	
Income	€ 100.00	100.00%	€ 100.00	100.00%
Dynamic Costs	€ 60.00	60.00%	€ 60.00	60.00%
Gross Contribution	€ 40.00	40.00%	€ 40.00	40.00%
Static Costs	€ 30.00	30.00%	€ 31.50	31.50%
Dynamic Net Contribution	€ 10.00	10.00%	€ 8.50	8.50%

The next dynamic indicator of contribution this will affect is the BeGap%.

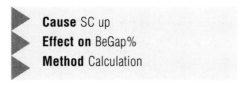

Cause SC up
Effect on BeGap%
Method Calculation

The basic calculation for the new BeGap% value is simple and is based upon the two previous results. With this change there is no effect on GC%, therefore new GC% is simply GC%.

$$\text{New BeGap\%} = \frac{\text{New DNC\%}}{\text{New GC\%}}$$

$$\text{New BeGap\%} = \frac{8.50\%}{40.00\%}$$

New BeGap% = 21.25%

This is a frightening result: with only a 5 per cent increase in your static costs, your business is 15 per cent more at risk – your BeGap% has dropped by 15 per cent (from 25 per cent to 21.25 per cent). A high price indeed for such a seemingly small change.

So, you know you have a static cost increase due, yet you can see immediately the impact of this on the dynamic indicators of contribution. No lengthy recalculations were needed – just the use of a few standard tools and techniques used throughout dynamic financial management.

In summary, the dynamic indicators of contribution are:

GC%	was	40.00%	is now	40.00%
DNC%	was	10.00%	is now	8.50%
BeGap%	was	25.00%	is now	21.25%

With changes in static costs we can relax a little bit. There is no impact on the structure of your DNA. But since your DNC% has changed there is a final impact to consider – the impact on DCM%.

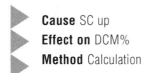

Cause SC up
Effect on DCM%
Method Calculation

The final dynamic indicator is now exceptionally easy to calculate:

$$DCM\% = DNC\% - DNA\%$$

$$DCM\% = 8.50\% - 0.00\% = 8.50\%$$

Your DCM% after the change is now only 8.5 per cent (the same as your new DNC%). Therefore, you have reduced the value of the dynamic cash coming into your business because you have reduced your overall contribution to the business.

The new shape of your business

The eight dynamic indicators before and after the increase in dynamic costs are:

Contribution statement

	Before	After
Income	€ 100.00	€ 100.00
Dynamic Costs	€ 60.00	€ 60.00
Gross Contribution	€ 40.000	€ 40.00
Static Costs	€ 30.00	€ 31.50
Dynamic Net Contribution	€ 10.00	€ 8.50

DNA statement

	Before	After
Income	€ 100.00	€ 100.00
Stock	€ 50.00	€ 50.00
Debtors	€ 100.00	€ 100.00
Creditors	€ 80.00	€ 80.00
Static Net Assets	€ 70.00	€ 70.00

Eight dynamic indicators

	Before	After
GC%	40.00%	40.00%
DNC%	10.00%	8.50%
BeGap%	25.00%	21.25%
Stock%	50.00%	50.00%
Dr%	100.00%	100.00%
Cr%	80.00%	80.00%
DNA%	0.00%	0.00%
DCM%	10.00%	8.50%

Figure 11.2 shows how this looks on the radar chart.

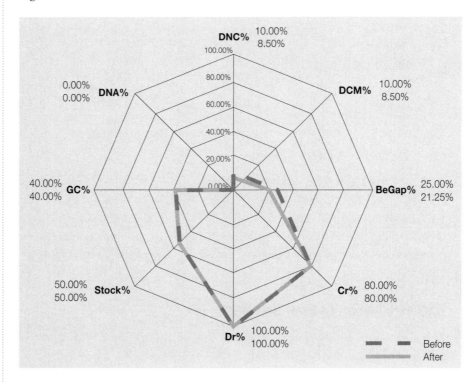

Fig 11.2 ● Model business radar chart

As you can see, the contribution indicators are shrinking – which has also led to a reduction in the DCM% and an increase in risk.

Actions for dynamic management of an increase in static costs

Change needs to be managed dynamically and with our assessment of the initial impact of the increase in static costs on our business we can do this effectively. The following techniques are designed to help you decide on the most appropriate action to take to get your business back into shape. And the dynamic financial management definition of back into shape is:

'returning the DNC% to the same level as it was before the change.'

So what are the appropriate actions to dynamically manage an increase in static costs?

Change		Appropriate action to regain DNC%
Increase	⫸	Increase volume
in static	⫸	Increase price
costs	⫸	Decrease dynamic costs

These may seem obvious things that you could do to regain your DNC%. Many of us are left knowing what needs to be done but we have no idea of the magnitude of the change we must seek to introduce. Dynamic financial management techniques will allow you to predict the magnitude of each of the changes that will be needed to compensate for the initial impact.

Again we can look at the impact of these using a series of dynamic look-up tables, dynamic adjusters and calculations.

Cause SC up
Possible action Increase volume
Method Calculation

If our SC increases by 5 per cent, the volume increase needed is an all too easy answer.

For a percentage increase in SC the percentage increase in volume needed is exactly the same as the percentage increase in SC.

For example, in the model business the SC increased by 5 per cent so the volume must also need to increase by 5 per cent:

	Before	After initial impact	After volume increase	%
Income	€ 100.00	€ 100.00	€ 105.00	100.00
Dynamic Costs	€ 60.00	€ 60.00	€ 63.00	60.00
Gross Contribution	€ 40.00	€ 37.00	€ 42.00	40.00
Static Costs	€ 30.00	€ 31.50	€ 31.50	30.00
Dynamic Net Contribution	€ 10.00	€ 8.50	€ 10.50	10.00

If we increase our volume by 5 per cent, we regain DNC% at 10 per cent – the level it was before any of the decisions were made. It is worthwhile considering the other dynamic indicators here. The volume increase has made no difference to the GC%.

We can quickly calculate the impact of the volume increase on our BeGap%:

New BeGap% = New DNC% / New GC%

New BeGap% = 10.00% / 40.00% = 25.00%

In fact, this is exactly the same BeGap% as you had before the change. And this should not be surprising. The initial change had no impact on GC% and our dynamic management has returned the DNC% to its original level. Like many of the answers revealed with dynamic financial management this may now seem like stating the obvious. But again, not a lot of managers realize these simple relationships – this really is value-added financial management.

What about the effect on DNA%? There was no effect on DNA% after the initial impact. From a change in volume there should be no change in the percentage of these; however, there will be an impact on the value of the components of the DNA. This can be seen below:

	Before	After initial impact	After volume increase
Income	€ 100.00	€ 100.00	€ 105.00
Stock	€ 50.00	€ 50.00	€ 52.50
Debtors	€ 100.00	€ 100.00	€ 105.00
Creditors	€ 80.00	€ 80.00	€ 84.00
SNA	€ 70.00	€ 70.00	€ 73.50
Stock%	50.00%	50.00%	50.00%
Dr%	100.00%	100.00%	100.00%
Cr%	80.00%	80.00%	80.00%
SNA%	70.00%	70.00%	70.00%

However, a change in the value of SNA will lead to change in DNA% and, as a consequence, the DCM%. What will be the impact on both of these? Comparing it with the situation before any change in the static costs this would be:

DNA = SNA *after* Decision – SNA *before* Initial Impact

DNA = €73.50 – €70.00 = €3.50

Then DNA% is:

$$\text{DNA\%} = \frac{€3.50}{€105.00} \times 100 = 3.33\%$$

So the DNA% is now positive, meaning that there has been a movement of money in the strands of the SNA due to the increase in volume. The final evaluation is to see whether this has been compensated for with the increase in DNC% and we will do this by looking at the DCM%:

DCM% = DNC% – DNA%

DCM% = 10.00% – 3.33% = 6.67%

This option has not eliminated the DCM% but it has reduced it. Summarizing this option:

Eight dynamic indicators

	Before	After initial impact	After volume increase
GC%	40.00%	40.00%	40.00%
DNC%	10.00%	8.50%	10.00%
BeGap%	25.00%	21.25%	25.00%
Stock%	50.00%	50.00%	50.00%
Dr%	100.00%	100.00%	100.00%
Cr%	80.00%	80.00%	80.00%
DNA%	0.00%	0.00%	3.33%
DCM%	10.00%	8.50%	6.67%

We now know the change in volume needed – we only need to know if that is really feasible in the current market environment. The bigger the increase in SC% we have to cope with, the higher the volume increase needed to compensate. Controlling SC% in a shrinking or highly competitive market is a must. Effectiveness should be a key driver for these types of markets. In fact, this is something we also need to be wary of when a market is growing. We often increase our static costs to cope with the growth – more administration is needed – so we need to ensure that the increase in static costs remains within the target SC% or we will end up in the unmanaged growth syndrome.

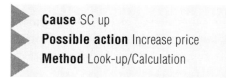

Cause SC up
Possible action Increase price
Method Look-up/Calculation

The next possible action to look at is increasing your price in order to increase your DNC%. Why will this work? Look at the following example.

Comparing this to the volume increase we talked about earlier, a price increase means you have not sold any more but every sale has made more money. If you look at the tables above, a price increase does not affect the value of dynamic or static costs. They stay the same. Therefore any increase in price will go straight down to your bottom line – your DNC.

Again we are faced with the question of how much. How much do you need to increase your price by in order to regain your DNC% after having to endure an increase in your static costs? What you need to know, and what dynamic financial management tells you, is the actual price increase you need in your business to regain your original DNC%.

When static costs go up, we are often tempted to pass on these increases to our customers. But we often pass on the wrong price and too high a price increase can result in a loss of customers.

Back to our model business where we were looking at an increase of 5 per cent in our SC. What price increase does the model business need to implement in order to regain its original DNC% of 10 per cent? In dynamic financial management this is calculated as:

% Price Increase = Increase in SC × Dynamic Adjuster

But first we need to find the dynamic adjuster using a dynamic look-up table (*see* Table 11.2). Referring to the model business the SC% is currently 30 per cent and the DNC% is 10 per cent. Simply knowing these few figures allows you to use the table to find the dynamic adjuster, and you will get 0.333.

Table 11.2 ● Dynamic adjuster for price increase after an SC increase

Existing DNC%	Existing SC%														
	10	15	20	25	30	35	40	45	50	55	60	65	70	75	80
1	0.101	0.152	0.202	0.253	0.303	0.354	0.404	0.455	0.505	0.556	0.606	0.657	0.707	0.758	0.808
2	0.102	0.153	0.204	0.255	0.306	0.357	0.408	0.459	0.510	0.561	0.612	0.663	0.714	0.765	0.816
3	0.103	0.155	0.206	0.258	0.309	0.361	0.412	0.464	0.515	0.567	0.619	0.670	0.722	0.773	0.825
4	0.104	0.156	0.208	0.260	0.313	0.365	0.417	0.469	0.521	0.573	0.625	0.677	0.729	0.781	0.833
5	0.105	0.158	0.211	0.263	0.316	0.368	0.421	0.474	0.526	0.579	0.632	0.684	0.737	0.789	0.842
6	0.106	0.160	0.213	0.266	0.319	0.372	0.426	0.479	0.532	0.585	0.638	0.691	0.745	0.798	0.851
7	0.108	0.161	0.215	0.269	0.323	0.376	0.430	0.484	0.538	0.591	0.645	0.699	0.753	0.806	0.860
8	0.109	0.163	0.217	0.272	0.326	0.380	0.435	0.489	0.543	0.598	0.652	0.707	0.761	0.815	0.870
9	0.110	0.165	0.220	0.275	0.330	0.385	0.440	0.495	0.549	0.604	0.659	0.714	0.769	0.824	0.879
10	0.111	0.167	0.222	0.278	**0.333**	0.389	0.444	0.500	0.556	0.611	0.667	0.722	0.778	0.833	0.889
12	0.114	0.170	0.227	0.284	0.341	0.398	0.455	0.511	0.568	0.625	0.682	0.739	0.795	0.852	0.909
14	0.116	0.174	0.233	0.291	0.349	0.407	0.465	0.523	0.581	0.640	0.698	0.756	0.814	0.872	0.930
16	0.119	0.179	0.238	0.298	0.357	0.417	0.476	0.536	0.595	0.655	0.714	0.774	0.833	0.893	0.952
18	0.122	0.183	0.244	0.305	0.366	0.427	0.488	0.549	0.610	0.671	0.732	0.793	0.854	0.915	0.976
20	0.125	0.188	0.250	0.313	0.375	0.438	0.500	0.563	0.625	0.688	0.750	0.813	0.875	0.938	1.000
25	0.133	0.200	0.267	0.333	0.400	0.467	0.533	0.600	0.667	0.733	0.800	0.867	0.933	1.000	1.067
30	0.143	0.214	0.286	0.357	0.429	0.500	0.571	0.643	0.714	0.786	0.857	0.929	1.000	1.071	1.143
35	0.154	0.231	0.308	0.385	0.462	0.538	0.615	0.692	0.769	0.846	0.923	1.000	1.077	1.154	1.231
40	0.167	0.250	0.333	0.417	0.500	0.583	0.667	0.750	0.833	0.917	1.000	1.083	1.167	1.250	1.333
50	0.200	0.300	0.400	0.500	0.600	0.700	0.800	0.900	1.000	1.100	1.200	1.300	1.400	1.500	1.600

Finally, to arrive at the actual price increase needed we can slot the adjuster into the formula below:

% Price Increase = Increase in SC × Dynamic Adjuster

% Price Increase = 5.00 × 0.333 = 1.67%

So if my current price is €100, the increase will be €1.67 (a 1.67 per cent price increase), therefore my new price will be €101.67.

Comparing the contribution statement now:

	Before	After initial impact	After price Increase	%
Income	€100.00	€100.00	€101.67	100.00
Dynamic Costs	€60.00	€60.00	€60.00	59.01
Gross Contribution	€40.00	€40.00	€41.67	40.99
Static Costs	€30.00	€31.50	€31.50	30.99
Dynamic Net Contribution	€10.00	€8.50	€10.17	10.00

So, in order to compensate for an SC increase of 5 per cent we need to increase our price by 1.67 per cent to regain DNC% at 10 per cent – the level it was before any of the decisions were made.

Again you need to consider the result of this action on the new shape of your business. Although the initial changes in static costs had no impact on GC%, the compensating price increase will have had an effect. You have already recalculated this in the contribution statement above. It is now at 40.99 per cent. With this information we can consider the impact of the price increase on our BeGap%:

New BeGap% = New DNC% / New GC%

New BeGap% = 10.00% / 40.99% = 24.40%

We must also consider the impact on DNA% as shown below:

	Before	After initial impact	After price increase
Income	€100.00	€100.00	€101.67
Stock	€50.00	€50.00	€50.00
Debtors	€100.00	€100.00	€101.67
Creditors	€80.00	€80.00	€80.00
SNA	€70.00	€70.00	€71.67
Stock%	50.00%	50.00%	49.18%
Dr%	100.00%	100.00%	100.00%
Cr%	80.00%	80.00%	78.69%
SNA%	70.00%	70.00%	70.49%

If the only change is price, then as a value, stock and creditors will stay the same. However, this means that the Stock% and Cr% go down as a percentage of the new income value. The Dr% will stay at the same percentage of income which means that the value has gone up. As the combined result of these changes, the SNA value and percentage will also change.

As there is an impact on the DNC% and DNA% there must also be an impact on DCM%.

> DNA = SNA *after* Decision – SNA *before* Initial Impact

> DNA = €71.67 – €70.00 = €1.67

Then DNA% remains as:

> $$DNA\% = \frac{€1.67}{€101.67} \times 100 = 1.64\%$$

So the DNA% is now positive, meaning that there has been a small movement of money into the strands of the DNA due to the increase in price. But again, when the movement is price – beware. This could simply be more debtors because each one is now paying us relatively more income. The final evaluation is to see whether this has been compensated for with the increase in DNC% and we will do this by looking at the DCM%:

> DCM% = DNC% – DNA%

> DCM% = 10.00% – 1.64% = 8.36%

This option has not eliminated the DCM% but it has reduced it. Let us summarize this option:

Eight dynamic indicators

	Before	After initial impact	After price increase
GC%	40.00%	40.00%	40.99%
DNC%	10.00%	8.50%	10.00%
BeGap%	25.00%	21.25%	24.40%
Stock%	50.00%	50.00%	49.18%
Dr%	100.00%	100.00%	100.00%
Cr%	80.00%	80.00%	78.69%
DNA%	0.00%	0.00%	1.64%
DCM%	10.00%	8.50%	8.36%

Your DCM% is 8.36 per cent, which means you have released cash from your time warp equivalent to 8.36 per cent of your current period's income.

You now know the price increase you need to pass on to your customers to compensate for an increase in static costs. It is up to you and your knowledge of the business and the market environment to assess the feasibility of such an increase.

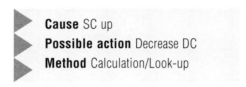

Cause SC up

Possible action Decrease DC

Method Calculation/Look-up

If one set of costs go up, it is often the case that you need to look for savings elsewhere. Often we need to become more efficient and the decreases have to come from reducing the dynamic costs. We often know the amount by which we need to reduce the dynamic costs, but we also need to know what percentage this represents so that we can again start to examine the changed shape of our business.

In order to do this we need to use the dynamic adjuster we looked at earlier:

Dynamic Adjuster = Increase in SC × Original SC%

Dynamic Adjuster = 5.00 × 30.00%

Dynamic Adjuster = 1.50

We can use this figure in Table 11.3. Our original DC% was 60 per cent and our dynamic adjuster is 1.50, so using halfway between the columns for 1 and 2 we get 2.50. This means we need to decrease our dynamic costs by 2.5 per cent to regain our DNC%.

Table 11.3 ● Decrease in DC% to maintain same DNC% after an SC increase

Current						Dynamic adjuster						
DC%	1	2	3	4	5	6	7	8	9	10	12	14
10	10.00	20.00	30.00	40.00	50.00	60.00	70.00	80.00	90.00	100.00	120.00	140.00
15	6.67	13.33	20.00	26.67	33.33	40.00	46.67	53.33	60.00	66.67	80.00	93.33
20	5.00	10.00	15.00	20.00	25.00	30.00	35.00	40.00	45.00	50.00	60.00	70.00
25	4.00	8.00	12.00	16.00	20.00	24.00	28.00	32.00	36.00	40.00	48.00	56.00
30	3.33	6.67	10.00	13.33	16.67	20.00	23.33	26.67	30.00	33.33	40.00	46.67
35	2.86	5.71	8.57	11.43	14.29	17.14	20.00	22.86	25.71	28.57	34.29	40.00
40	2.50	5.00	7.50	10.00	12.50	15.00	17.50	20.00	22.50	25.00	30.00	35.00
45	2.22	4.44	6.67	8.89	11.11	13.33	15.56	17.78	20.00	22.22	26.67	31.11
50	2.00	4.00	6.00	8.00	10.00	12.00	14.00	16.00	18.00	20.00	24.00	28.00
55	1.82	3.64	5.45	7.27	9.09	10.91	12.73	14.55	16.36	18.18	21.82	25.45
60	1.67	3.33	5.00	6.67	8.33	10.00	11.67	13.33	15.00	16.67	20.00	23.33
65	1.54	3.08	4.62	6.15	7.69	9.23	10.77	12.31	13.85	15.38	18.46	21.54
70	1.43	2.86	4.29	5.71	7.14	8.57	10.00	11.43	12.86	14.29	17.14	20.00
75	1.33	2.67	4.00	5.33	6.67	8.00	9.33	10.67	12.00	13.33	16.00	18.67
80	1.25	2.50	3.75	5.00	6.25	7.50	8.75	10.00	11.25	12.50	15.00	17.50
85	1.18	2.35	3.53	4.71	5.88	7.06	8.24	9.41	10.59	11.76	14.12	16.47
90	1.11	2.22	3.33	4.44	5.56	6.67	7.78	8.89	10.00	11.11	13.33	15.56

	Before	After initial impact	After DC decrease	%
Income	€ 100.00	€ 100.00	€ 100.00	100.00
Dynamic Costs	€ 60.00	€ 60.00	€ 58.50	58.50
Gross Contribution	€ 40.00	€ 40.00	€ 41.50	41.50
Static Costs	€ 30.00	€ 31.50	€ 31.50	31.50
Dynamic Net Contribution	€ 10.00	€ 8.50	€ 10.00	10.00

We have regained a DNC% of 10 per cent by achieving a compensating decrease in dynamic costs. But what about the impact on the eight dynamic indicators? We have shown above that GC% has gone up to 41.5 per cent. This was a direct result of the saving in dynamic costs. Calculating the impact on BeGap%:

New BeGap% = New DNC% / New GC%

New BeGap% = 10.00% / 41.50% = 24.10%

We could now go through the analysis of changes in DNA%. After all, this action has resulted in a decrease in our dynamic costs of 2.5 per cent. This should also result in a decrease in Stock% and Cr%. This requires going through the initial impact tables for a DC decrease in *Chapter 10: Decreases in your dynamic costs*. For brevity in this section we will show the result below. You can prove this for yourself at your leisure. The Stock% comes from Table 10.3 and the Cr% from Table 10.4.

	Before	After initial impact	After DC decrease
Income	€ 100.00	€ 100.00	€ 100.00
Stock	€ 50.00	€ 50.00	€ 48.75
Debtors	€ 100.00	€ 100.00	€ 100.00
Creditors	€ 80.00	€ 80.00	€ 79.00
SNA	€ 70.00	€ 70.00	€ 69.75
Stock%	50.00%	50.00%	48.75%
Dr%	100.00%	100.00%	100.00%
Cr%	80.00%	80.00%	79.00%
SNA%	70.00%	70.00%	69.75%

As price has not changed, the Dr% remains the same. The overall impact on DNA% can now be calculated along with the final dynamic indicator to consider, DCM%:

DNA = SNA *after* Decision – SNA *before* Initial Impact

DNA = €69.75 – €70.00 = €(0.25)

Then DNA% is:

$$\mathbf{DNA\% = \frac{€(0.25)}{€100.00} \times 100 = (0.25)\%}$$

So the DNA% is now slightly negative, meaning that there has been a marginal movement of money out of the strands of your DNA. The size and the direction of this movement will depend on the relationship between the Stock% and Cr% in your business.

The overall effect on the DCM% is:

DCM% = DNC% – DNA%

DCM% = 10.00% – (0.25)% = 10.25%

Your DCM% is 10.25 per cent, which means you have released cash from your time warp equivalent to 10.25 per cent of your current period's income.

Eight dynamic indicators

	Before	After initial impact	After DC decrease
GC%	40.00%	40.00%	41.50%
DNC%	10.00%	8.50%	10.00%
BeGap%	25.00%	21.25%	24.10%
Stock%	50.00%	50.00%	48.75%
Dr%	100.00%	100.00%	100.00%
Cr%	80.00%	80.00%	79.00%
DNA%	0.00%	0.00%	(0.25)%
DCM%	10.00%	8.50%	10.25%

As a possible management action, moving costs within the cost structure of the model business has had a positive effect. You need to do the analysis on your cost structure to see if this is a possible action for you in your business.

chapter 12

Decreases in your static costs

Why do static costs decrease?

Decreases in your static costs, as with all decreases in a business, need to be managed, and there are two stages in understanding the impact on your business:

1 The initial impact of the decrease.

2 The alternative actions you could take to proactively manage this decrease.

The initial impact of any decrease can be most successfully visualized using the eight dynamic indicators on the radar chart. The trends you will be monitoring using the dynamic breakeven graph and the dynamic cash graph will put these decreases into context – what freedom this has given you to develop your business.

However, we should be managing the decrease dynamically. From our understanding of the decrease, monitored in the three charts we are using to visualize the business, we can begin to select the most appropriate action to take to get the business back into shape.

It is worth repeating that, in dynamic financial management, we have a specific way of defining dynamic management of these decreases. In terms of our dynamic indicators we do not know what will happen as a result of these decreases, but with dynamic financial management techniques we can predict very accurately what needs to be done to keep your business fit and healthy. And we have defined fit and healthy as returning the DNC% to the same level as it was before the initial management decision.

For example, let us look at the model business:

	%
Income	100
Dynamic Costs	60
Gross Contribution	40
Static Costs	30
Dynamic Net Contribution	10

If static costs go down to 25 per cent, the initial impact on the contribution statement would look like this:

	%
Income	100
Dynamic Costs	60
Gross Contribution	40
Static Costs	25
Dynamic Net Contribution	15

Your DNC% has increased to 15 per cent. We need to know what the alternative ways are of getting your DNC% back to its original level of 10 per cent.

We will examine the two stages mentioned earlier, i.e. look at the initial impact of the decrease in static costs and then the measures available to us to manage these dynamically and retain our level of fitness, retain our original DNC%. As managers we are often faced with alternatives and changing cost structures is one of these alternatives.

Decreases in your static costs

For the model business, if static costs go down by 5 per cent from 30 per cent to 28.5 per cent, the possible actions to compensate are:

Change		Appropriate action to regain DNC%	Amount
Decrease in	⮕	Decrease volume	By 5.00%
static costs	⮕	Decrease price	By 1.67%
of 5%	⮕	Increase dynamic costs	By 2.50%

The table below shows the shape of the business after each of these changes:

Eight dynamic indicators

	Before any change	After initial impact SC decrease 5.00%	After volume decrease 5.00%	After price decrease 1.67%	After DC increase 2.50%
GC%	40.00%	40.00%	40.00%	38.98%	38.50%
DNC%	10.00%	11.50%	10.00%	10.00%	10.00%
BeGap%	25.00%	28.75%	25.00%	25.65%	25.97%
Stock%	50.00%	50.00%	50.00%	50.85%	51.25%
Dr%	100.00%	100.00%	100.00%	100.00%	100.00%
Cr%	80.00%	80.00%	80.00%	81.36%	81.00%
DNA%	0.00%	0.00%	(3.68)%	(1.69)%	0.25%
DCM%	10.00%	11.50%	13.68%	11.69%	9.75%

The decision is now yours:

● accept the new shape of your business after the initial impact and change your targets accordingly;

● work dynamically towards one of the above possible actions;

● somewhere in between.

Whatever your decision, you can predict its impact before you are committed to any changes – managing tomorrow today.

How did we get to these results? First we need to find the result of the initial impact of the decrease in static costs, then we need to look at all the possible actions that could be taken to compensate for this decrease.

The initial impact

Decreases in your static costs are always going to be welcome and are usually an indication of increasing effectiveness or improved economies of scale. What you need to know is the definitive impact of the decrease on your eight dynamic indicators so that you can decide how to reposition the business to take best advantage of this reduction. The first thing to appreciate is the direction of the impact of the change and this can be seen in Fig 12.1.

The eight dynamic indicators	Change static costs
	Tool
GC%	
DNC%	Look-up and calculation
BeGap%	Calculation
Stock%	
Dr%	
Cr%	
DNA%	
DCM%	Calculation

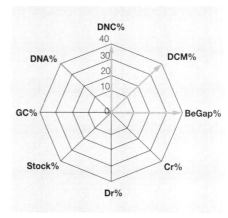

Fig 12.1 ●
Radar chart of dynamic indicators

With a decrease in static costs, there are only three effects we need to consider: DNC%, BeGap% and DCM%. DNC% and BeGap% will both increase as shown in the radar chart. As you already know, DCM% is DNC% less DNA%. In this change SNA has remained static, therefore DNA% is zero. However, DNC% has gone up. Therefore DCM% will also go up.

We can now look at the magnitude of the initial impact on each of the eight dynamic indicators. As an example we will use the figures in the model business. Throughout this chapter we will assume that the static costs have decreased by 5 per cent, i.e. they have decreased from 30 per cent to 28.5 per cent.

In the case of static costs, the first indicator we need to consider is the change to DNC%.

Cause SC down
Effect on DNC%
Method Look-up/Calculation

In the model business the existing DNC% was 10 per cent. What will be the impact of the 5 per cent decrease in static costs? There are two ways to approach this one.

Adjuster method

The basic calculation for the new DNC% value is as follows:

New DNC% = Existing DNC% + 'Dynamic Adjuster'

The dynamic look-up table that gives this dynamic adjuster is shown in Table 12.1.

Table 12.1 ● Dynamic adjuster for new DNC% after an SC decrease

Current	% Decrease in SC										
SC%	1	3	5	7	9	10	12	14	16	18	20
10	0.10	0.30	0.50	0.70	0.90	1.00	1.20	1.40	1.60	1.80	2.00
15	0.15	0.45	0.75	1.05	1.35	1.50	1.80	2.10	2.40	2.70	3.00
20	0.20	0.60	1.00	1.40	1.80	2.00	2.40	2.80	3.20	3.60	4.00
25	0.25	0.75	1.25	1.75	2.25	2.50	3.00	3.50	4.00	4.50	5.00
30	0.30	0.90	**1.50**	2.10	2.70	3.00	3.60	4.20	4.80	5.40	6.00
35	0.35	1.05	1.75	2.45	3.15	3.50	4.20	4.90	5.60	6.30	7.00
40	0.40	1.20	2.00	2.80	3.60	4.00	4.80	5.60	6.40	7.20	8.00
45	0.45	1.35	2.25	3.15	4.05	4.50	5.40	6.30	7.20	8.10	9.00
50	0.50	1.50	2.50	3.50	4.50	5.00	6.00	7.00	8.00	9.00	10.00
55	0.55	1.65	2.75	3.85	4.95	5.50	6.60	7.70	8.80	9.90	11.00
60	0.60	1.80	3.00	4.20	5.40	6.00	7.20	8.40	9.60	10.80	12.00
65	0.65	1.95	3.25	4.55	5.85	6.50	7.80	9.10	10.40	11.70	13.00
70	0.70	2.10	3.50	4.90	6.30	7.00	8.40	9.80	11.20	12.60	14.00
75	0.75	2.25	3.75	5.25	6.75	7.50	9.00	10.50	12.00	13.50	15.00
80	0.80	2.40	4.00	5.60	7.20	8.00	9.60	11.20	12.80	14.40	16.00
85	0.85	2.55	4.25	5.95	7.65	8.50	10.20	11.90	13.60	15.30	17.00
90	0.90	2.70	4.50	6.30	8.10	9.00	10.80	12.60	14.40	16.20	18.00

With a SC% of 30 per cent in the model business, and an anticipated decrease in these static costs by 5 per cent, we can look up our dynamic adjuster of 1.50. Placing this adjuster into our calculation gives:

New DNC% = Existing DNC% + 'Dynamic Adjuster'

New DNC% = 10.00% + '1.50' = 11.50%

So for a decrease in static costs of 5 per cent in the model business the resulting beneficial impact on DNC% is an increase to 11.5 per cent from the original figure of 10 per cent.

There is also a short-cut method to reach this answer.

Mathematical method

New DNC% = Existing DNC% + (Decrease in SC × SC%)

New DNC% = 10.00 + (5.00% × 30.00)

New DNC% = 10.00 + 1.50 = 11.50%

The new figure of 11.5 per cent represents an increase in effectiveness within the business, achieving more from a relatively smaller amount of static costs.

Let us look at the new contribution statement for the model business:

	Before		After	
Income	£100.00	100.00%	£100.00	100.00%
Dynamic Costs	£60.00	60.00%	£60.00	60.00%
Gross Contribution	£40.00	40.00%	£40.00	40.00%
Static Costs	£30.00	30.00%	£28.50	28.50%
Dynamic Net Contribution	£10.00	10.00%	£11.50	11.50%

The other dynamic indicator of contribution this will affect is the BeGap%.

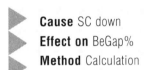

Cause SC down
Effect on BeGap%
Method Calculation

The basic calculation for the new BeGap% value is simple and is based upon the two previous results (new GC% is simply GC% in this case):

$$\text{New BeGap\%} = \frac{\text{New DNC\%}}{\text{New GC\%}}$$

$$\text{New BeGap\%} = \frac{11.50\%}{40.00\%}$$

$$\text{New BeGap\%} = 28.75\%$$

This is an improvement in the BeGap% from its original level of 25 per cent. Reducing the static costs has also resulted in a less risky business. We could now afford to lose 28.75 per cent of our volume before we start to make a loss (we would break even).

In summary, the dynamic indicators of contribution are:

GC%	was	40.00%	is now	40.00%
DNC%	was	10.00%	is now	11.50%
BeGap%	was	25.00%	is now	28.75%

The managers of the model business can now see the reward for their efforts to improve effectiveness reflected in the dynamic indicators of contribution. And with changes in static costs we can relax a little bit. There is no impact on the structure of your DNA. But when your DNC% has changed, there is a final impact to consider – the impact on DCM%.

Cause SC down
Effect on DCM%
Method Calculation

The final dynamic indicator is now exceptionally easy to calculate:

DCM% = DNC% – DNA%

DCM% = 11.50% – 0.00% = 11.5%

Your DCM% after the change is 11.5 per cent, exactly the same as your DNC%. You have increased the value of the dynamic cash moving into your business but you have done this directly by increasing your overall contribution to the business.

The new shape of your business

The eight dynamic indicators before and after the decrease in static costs are:

Contribution statement			DNA statement		
	Before	**After**		**Before**	**After**
Income	£100.00	£100.00	Income	£100.00	£100.00
Dynamic Costs	£60.00	£60.00	Stock	£50.00	£50.00
Gross Contribution	£40.00	£40.00	Debtors	£100.00	£100.00
Static Costs	£30.00	£28.50	Creditors	£80.00	£80.00
Dynamic Net Contribution	£10.00	£11.50	Static Net Assets	£70.00	£70.00

Eight dynamic indicators

	Before	**After**
GC%	40.00%	40.00%
DNC%	10.00%	11.50%
BeGap%	25.00%	28.75%
Stock%	50.00%	50.00%
Dr%	100.00%	100.00%
Cr%	80.00%	80.00%
DNA%	0.00%	0.00%
DCM%	10.00%	11.50%

How this looks on the radar chart is shown in Fig 12.2. As you can see, the contribution indicators for your business are stretching! As a result you have more cash to use in your future activities.

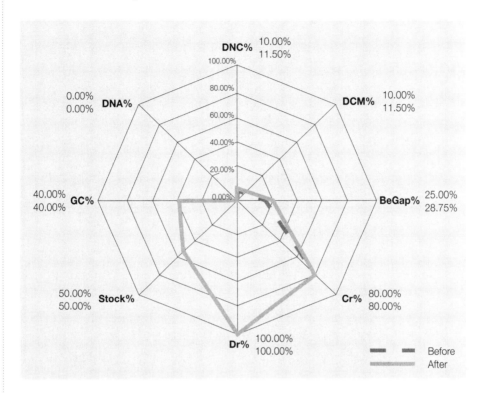

Fig 12.2 ● Model business radar chart

Actions for dynamic management of a decrease in static costs

As we have said, you need to manage change dynamically. Even beneficial changes can be taken advantage of. You now have the freedom to improve the quality of your business, or even to allow yourself to take more time off to relax.

So what are the appropriate actions to dynamically manage a decrease in static costs, to take advantage of the freedom presented by this change?

Change		Appropriate action to retain DNC%
Decrease	⟶	Decrease volume
in static	⟶	Decrease price
costs	⟶	Increase dynamic costs

These may seem obvious things that you could do to retain your DNC%. But when we have an advantage we need to make sure we do not just throw it all away. We need to know how much freedom we now have within the dynamics of our business.

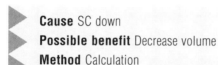

Cause SC down

Possible benefit Decrease volume

Method Calculation

If our SC decreases by 5 per cent, the volume decrease you could allow is an all too easy answer.

For a percentage decrease in SC the percentage decrease in volume allowed is exactly the same as the percentage decrease in SC.

For example, in the model business the SC decreased by 5 per cent so the volume can also decrease by 5 per cent. Let's see if it works:

	Before	After initial impact	After volume decrease	%
Income	£100.00	£100.00	£95.00	100.00
Dynamic Costs	£60.00	£60.00	£57.00	60.00
Gross Contribution	£40.00	£40.00	£38.00	40.00
Static Costs	£30.00	£28.50	£28.50	30.00
Dynamic Net Contribution	£10.00	£11.50	£9.50	10.00

If we decrease our volume by 5 per cent, we retain DNC% at 10 per cent – the level it was before any of the changes. It is worthwhile considering the other dynamic indicators here. The volume decrease has made no difference to the GC% so we can move straight to the recalculation of BeGap%:

New BeGap% = New DNC% / New GC%

New BeGap% = 10.00% / 40.00% = 25.00%

In fact, this is the same BeGap% as you had before the change. And this should not be surprising. The initial change had no impact on GC% and our dynamic management has returned the DNC% to its original level. Like many of the answers revealed with dynamic financial management this may now seem like stating the obvious. But again, not a lot of managers realize these simple relationships – this really is value-added financial management.

What about the effect on DNA%? There was no effect on DNA% after the initial impact. And from a change in volume there should be no change in the percentage of these. There will be an impact on the value of the components of the DNA to cope with the decreased level of activity. This can be seen in the table below:

	Before	After initial impact	After volume decrease
Income	£100.00	£100.00	£95.00
Stock	£50.00	£50.00	£47.50
Debtors	£100.00	£100.00	£95.00
Creditors	£80.00	£80.00	£76.00
SNA	£70.00	£70.00	£66.50
Stock%	50.00%	50.00%	50.00%
Dr%	100.00%	100.00%	100.00%
Cr%	80.00%	80.00%	80.00%
SNA%	70.00%	70.00%	70.00%

However, a change in the value of SNA will lead to change in DNA% and therefore DCM%. So what will be the impact on these? Comparing it with the situation before any change in the static costs this would be:

DNA = SNA *after* Decision – SNA *before* Initial Impact

DNA = £66.50 – £70.00 = £(3.50)

Then DNA% is:

$$\text{DNA\%} = \frac{£(3.50)}{£95.00} \times 100 = (3.68)\%$$

So the DNA% is now negative, meaning that there has been a significant movement of money in the strands of the SNA due to the decrease in volume. The final evaluation is to see the overall effect on the cash:

DCM% = DNC% – DNA%

$$DCM\% = 10.00\% - (3.68)\% = 13.68\%$$

This option has had a significant and positive effect on the DCM%. To summarize this option:

Eight dynamic indicators

	Before	After initial impact	After volume decrease
GC%	40.00%	40.00%	40.00%
DNC%	10.00%	11.50%	10.00%
BeGap%	25.00%	28.75%	25.00%
Stock%	50.00%	50.00%	50.00%
Dr%	100.00%	100.00%	100.00%
Cr%	80.00%	80.00%	80.00%
DNA%	0.00%	0.00%	(3.68)%
DCM%	10.00%	11.50%	13.68%

So, with a 5 per cent decrease in volume you will be no worse off than you were before if you have reduced your static costs by 5 per cent. Indeed, with regard to cash you will be better off. A more effective business can withstand variations in volume.

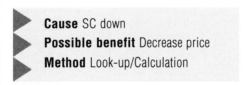

Cause SC down
Possible benefit Decrease price
Method Look-up/Calculation

When static costs go down we may want to pass on these decreases to our customers by lowering our prices in order to gain a competitive advantage. But we often pass on the wrong price decrease that actually results in a DNC% lower than it was before. We need to know exactly how much we can reduce our price yet retain our original DNC%.

The basic calculation for the %price decrease needed is:

% Price Decrease = Decrease in SC × Dynamic Adjuster

The dynamic look-up table that gives this dynamic adjuster is shown in Table 12.2. Referring to the model business, the SC% is currently 30 per cent and we have a DNC% of 10 per cent. Taking these figures and looking up in the table the dynamic adjuster, you will get 0.333. With an anticipated static cost

Table 12.2 ● Dynamic adjuster for price decrease after an SC decrease

Existing DNC%	Existing SC%														
	10	15	20	25	30	35	40	45	50	55	60	65	70	75	80
1	0.101	0.152	0.202	0.253	0.303	0.354	0.404	0.455	0.505	0.556	0.606	0.657	0.707	0.758	0.808
2	0.102	0.153	0.204	0.255	0.306	0.357	0.408	0.459	0.510	0.561	0.612	0.663	0.714	0.765	0.816
3	0.103	0.155	0.206	0.258	0.309	0.361	0.412	0.464	0.515	0.567	0.619	0.670	0.722	0.773	0.825
4	0.104	0.156	0.208	0.260	0.313	0.365	0.417	0.469	0.521	0.573	0.625	0.677	0.729	0.781	0.833
5	0.105	0.158	0.211	0.263	0.316	0.368	0.421	0.474	0.526	0.579	0.632	0.684	0.737	0.789	0.842
6	0.106	0.160	0.213	0.266	0.319	0.372	0.426	0.479	0.532	0.585	0.638	0.691	0.745	0.798	0.851
7	0.108	0.161	0.215	0.269	0.323	0.376	0.430	0.484	0.538	0.591	0.645	0.699	0.753	0.806	0.860
8	0.109	0.163	0.217	0.272	0.326	0.380	0.435	0.489	0.543	0.598	0.652	0.707	0.761	0.815	0.870
9	0.110	0.165	0.220	0.275	0.330	0.385	0.440	0.495	0.549	0.604	0.659	0.714	0.769	0.824	0.879
10	0.111	0.167	0.222	0.278	**0.333**	0.389	0.444	0.500	0.556	0.611	0.667	0.722	0.778	0.833	0.889
12	0.114	0.170	0.227	0.284	0.341	0.398	0.455	0.511	0.568	0.625	0.682	0.739	0.795	0.852	0.909
14	0.116	0.174	0.233	0.291	0.349	0.407	0.465	0.523	0.581	0.640	0.698	0.756	0.814	0.872	0.930
16	0.119	0.179	0.238	0.298	0.357	0.417	0.476	0.536	0.595	0.655	0.714	0.774	0.833	0.893	0.952
18	0.122	0.183	0.244	0.305	0.366	0.427	0.488	0.549	0.610	0.671	0.732	0.793	0.854	0.915	0.976
20	0.125	0.188	0.250	0.313	0.375	0.438	0.500	0.563	0.625	0.688	0.750	0.813	0.875	0.938	1.000
25	0.133	0.200	0.267	0.333	0.400	0.467	0.533	0.600	0.667	0.733	0.800	0.867	0.933	1.000	1.067
30	0.143	0.214	0.286	0.357	0.429	0.500	0.571	0.643	0.714	0.786	0.857	0.929	1.000	1.071	1.143
35	0.154	0.231	0.308	0.385	0.462	0.538	0.615	0.692	0.769	0.846	0.923	1.000	1.077	1.154	1.231
40	0.167	0.250	0.333	0.417	0.500	0.583	0.667	0.750	0.833	0.917	1.000	1.083	1.167	1.250	1.333
50	0.200	0.300	0.400	0.500	0.600	0.700	0.800	0.900	1.000	1.100	1.200	1.300	1.400	1.500	1.600

decrease of 5 per cent, to arrive at the percentage price decrease required we use the calculation given above.

% Price Decrease = Decrease in SC × Dynamic Adjuster

% Price Decrease = 5.00 × 0.333 = 1.67%

So if my current price is £100 the decrease will be £1.67 (a 1.67 per cent price decrease), therefore my new price will be £98.33. To see if it works:

	Before	After initial impact	After price decrease	%
Income	£100.00	£100.00	£98.33	100.00
Dynamic Costs	£60.00	£60.00	£60.00	61.02
Gross Contribution	£40.00	£40.00	£38.33	38.98
Static Costs	£30.00	£28.50	£28.50	28.98
Dynamic Net Contribution	£10.00	£11.50	£9.83	10.00

So the percentage price decrease we could pass on to the customers of the model business if we can achieve a decrease in static costs is 1.67 per cent if we wish to retain the DNC% at 10 per cent. Many managers mistakenly assume a decrease of 5 per cent in costs can allow a price reduction of 5 per cent – a one-to-one relationship. This is obviously untrue.

There are going to be effects on other dynamic indicators of contribution. Although the initial changes in static costs had no impact on GC%, the compensating price decrease will have a detrimental effect. You have already recalculated this in the contribution statement above. It is now at 38.98 per cent. With this information we can consider the impact of the price increase on our BeGap%:

New BeGap% = New DNC% / New GC%

New BeGap% = 10.00% / 38.98% = 25.65%

We must also consider the impact on DNA% as shown below:

	Before	**After initial impact**	**After price decrease**
Income	£100.00	£100.00	£98.33
Stock	£50.00	£50.00	£50.00
Debtors	£100.00	£100.00	£98.33
Creditors	£80.00	£80.00	£80.00
SNA	£70.00	£70.00	£68.33
Stock%	50.00%	50.00%	50.85%
Dr%	100.00%	100.00%	100.00%
Cr%	80.00%	80.00%	81.36%
SNA%	70.00%	70.00%	69.49%

If the only change is price, then as a value, stock and creditors will stay the same. However, this means that the Stock% and Cr% go up as a percentage of the new income value. The Dr% will stay at the same percentage of income, meaning the value has gone down. As the combined result of these changes the SNA value and percentage will also change. And with the way the strands of the DNA are made up in the model business, the overall effect on SNA is a slight decrease in value but a slight increase as a percentage of income. So what is the effect on the DNA%?

DNA = SNA *after* Decision – SNA *before* Initial Impact

DNA = £68.33 – £70.00 = £(1.67)

Then DNA% is:

$$\text{DNA\%} = \frac{\pounds(1.67)}{\pounds98.33} \times 100 = (1.69)\%$$

So the DNA% is now negative, meaning that there has been an apparent movement of money out of the strands of the SNA due to the decrease in price. But again, exercise caution here. This is due to debtors being lower because of the decrease in price.

The final evaluation is to see whether this has been compensated for with the increase in DNC% and we will do this by looking at the DCM%:

$$\text{DCM\%} = \text{DNC\%} - \text{DNA\%}$$

$$\text{DCM\%} = 10.00\% - (1.69)\% = 11.69\%$$

This option has improved the DCM%. Let us summarize this option:

Eight dynamic indicators

	Before	After initial impact	After price decrease
GC%	40.00%	40.00%	38.98%
DNC%	10.00%	11.50%	10.00%
BeGap%	25.00%	28.75%	25.65%
Stock%	50.00%	50.00%	50.85%
Dr%	100.00%	100.00%	100.00%
Cr%	80.00%	80.00%	81.36%
DNA%	0.00%	0.00%	(1.69)%
DCM%	10.00%	11.50%	11.69%

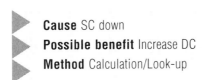

Cause SC down
Possible benefit Increase DC
Method Calculation/Look-up

If one set of costs go down, it is often the case that you have moved the costs into another category. We often know the amount by which we can afford to increase our dynamic costs, but we also need to know what percentage this represents so that we can again start to examine the changed shape of our business. In order to do this we need to use the dynamic adjuster we looked at earlier:

$$\text{Dynamic Adjuster} = \text{Decrease in SC} \times \text{Original SC\%}$$

$$\text{Dynamic Adjuster} = 5.00 \times 30.00\%$$

$$\text{Dynamic Adjuster} = 1.50$$

We can now use this figure in Table 12.3.

Table 12.3 ● Increase in DC% to maintain same DNC% after an SC decrease

Current	Dynamic adjuster											
DC%	1	2	3	4	5	6	7	8	9	10	12	14
10	10.00	20.00	30.00	40.00	50.00	60.00	70.00	80.00	90.00	100.00	120.00	140.00
15	6.67	13.33	20.00	26.67	33.33	40.00	46.67	53.33	60.00	66.67	80.00	93.33
20	5.00	10.00	15.00	20.00	25.00	30.00	35.00	40.00	45.00	50.00	60.00	70.00
25	4.00	8.00	12.00	16.00	20.00	24.00	28.00	32.00	36.00	40.00	48.00	56.00
30	3.33	6.67	10.00	13.33	16.67	20.00	23.33	26.67	30.00	33.33	40.00	46.67
35	2.86	5.71	8.57	11.43	14.29	17.14	20.00	22.86	25.71	28.57	34.29	40.00
40	2.50	5.00	7.50	10.00	12.50	15.00	17.50	20.00	22.50	25.00	30.00	35.00
45	2.22	4.44	6.67	8.89	11.11	13.33	15.56	17.78	20.00	22.22	26.67	31.11
50	2.00	4.00	6.00	8.00	10.00	12.00	14.00	16.00	18.00	20.00	24.00	28.00
55	1.82	3.64	5.45	7.27	9.09	10.91	12.73	14.55	16.36	18.18	21.82	25.45
60	1.67	3.33	5.00	6.67	8.33	10.00	11.67	13.33	15.00	16.67	20.00	23.33
65	1.54	3.08	4.62	6.15	7.69	9.23	10.77	12.31	13.85	15.38	18.46	21.54
70	1.43	2.86	4.29	5.71	7.14	8.57	10.00	11.43	12.86	14.29	17.14	20.00
75	1.33	2.67	4.00	5.33	6.67	8.00	9.33	10.67	12.00	13.33	16.00	18.67
80	1.25	2.50	3.75	5.00	6.25	7.50	8.75	10.00	11.25	12.50	15.00	17.50
85	1.18	2.35	3.53	4.71	5.88	7.06	8.24	9.41	10.59	11.76	14.12	16.47
90	1.11	2.22	3.33	4.44	5.56	6.67	7.78	8.89	10.00	11.11	13.33	15.56

Reading from the table, our original DC% was 60 per cent and our dynamic adjuster is 1.50. This means we can afford to increase our dynamic costs by 2.5 per cent and still retain our DNC%. To see if it works:

	Before	After initial impact	After DC increase	%
Income	£100.00	£100.00	£100.00	100.00
Dynamic Costs	£60.00	£60.00	£61.50	61.50
Gross Contribution	£40.00	£40.00	£38.50	38.50
Static Costs	£30.00	£28.50	£28.50	28.50
Dynamic Net Contribution	£10.00	£11.50	£10.00	10.00

We have retained our DNC% by allowing a static cost decrease of 5 per cent in the model business to be compensated for by a 2.5 per cent increase in the dynamic costs. But what about the impact on the other eight dynamic indicators? The table above shows that our GC% has gone down to 38.5 per cent. This was a direct result of the increase in dynamic costs. Calculating the impact on our BeGap%:

New BeGap% = New DNC% / New GC%

New BeGap% = 10.00% / 38.50% = 25.97%

We could now go through the analysis of changes in DNA%. After all this action has resulted in an increase in our dynamic costs of 2.5 per cent. This should also result in an increase in Stock% and Cr%. This requires going through the initial impact tables for an increase in dynamic costs. The Stock% comes from Table 9.3 (p. 222), and the Cr% comes from Table 9.4 (p. 223). Here we will show the result in the table below. You can prove this for yourself at your leisure.

	Before	**After initial impact**	**After DC decrease**
Income	£100.00	£100.00	£100.00
Stock	£50.00	£50.00	£51.25
Debtors	£100.00	£100.00	£100.00
Creditors	£80.00	£80.00	£81.00
SNA	£70.00	£70.00	£70.25
Stock%	50.00%	50.00%	51.25%
Dr%	100.00%	100.00%	100.00%
Cr%	80.00%	80.00%	81.00%
SNA%	70.00%	70.00%	70.25%

As price has not changed, the Dr% remains the same. The overall impact on DNA% can now be calculated. The final dynamic indicator to consider is DCM%:

DNA = SNA *after* Decision – SNA *before* Initial Impact

DNA = £70.25 – £70.00 = £0.25

Then DNA% is:

$$\text{DNA\%} = \frac{\text{£0.25}}{\text{£100.00}} \times 100 = 0.25\%$$

So the DNA% is now slightly positive, meaning that there has been a marginal movement of money into the strands of your DNA. The size and the direction of this movement will depend on the relationship between the Stock% and Cr% in your business.

The overall effect on the DCM% is:

$$DCM\% = DNC\% - DNA\%$$

$$DCM\% = 10.00\% - 0.25\% = 9.75\%$$

Your DCM% is 9.75 per cent, which means you have tied up a little more cash in your time warp, mostly due to the relationship between dynamic costs, stock and creditors.

Eight dynamic indicators

	Before	After initial impact	After DC increase
GC%	40.00%	40.00%	38.50%
DNC%	10.00%	11.50%	10.00%
BeGap%	25.00%	28.75%	25.97%
Stock%	50.00%	50.00%	51.25%
Dr%	100.00%	100.00%	100.00%
Cr%	80.00%	80.00%	81.00%
DNA%	0.00%	0.00%	0.25%
DCM%	10.00%	11.50%	9.75%

chapter 13

Meeting ever more demanding targets

Introduction

As the world becomes ever more competitive and demands upon businesses increase, a frequent imposition on managers is to increase the percentage dynamic net contribution of their company or department. These impositions can come from inside or outside influences. For example, stakeholders (the bank or the shareholders) may be demanding better performance. You may even be insisting on this increase yourself. This chapter will review the choices available to managers in responding to such impositions.

For the model business, a rise in DNC% from 10 per cent to 12 per cent means a 20 per cent increase in DNC%. The possible actions to achieve this were:

Change		Appropriate action to regain DNC%	Amount
Increase in	➡	Increase volume	By 7.14%
DNC% target	➡	Increase price	By 2.27%
by 20%	➡	Decrease dynamic costs	By 3.33%
	➡	Decrease static costs	By 6.67%

The shape of your business after these changes will be:

Eight dynamic indicators

	Before any change	After volume increase 1.14%	After price increase 2.27%	After DC decrease 3.33%	After SC decrease 6.67%
GC%	40.00%	40.00%	41.33%	42.00%	40.00%
DNC%	10.00%	12.00%	12.00%	12.00%	12.00%
BeGap%	25.00%	30.00%	29.03%	28.57%	30.00%
Stock%	50.00%	50.00%	48.89%	48.33%	50.00%
Dr%	100.00%	100.00%	100.00%	100.00%	100.00%
Cr%	80.00%	80.00%	78.22%	78.67%	80.00%
DNA%	0.00%	4.67%	2.22%	(0.34)%	0.00%
DCM%	10.00%	7.33%	9.78%	12.34%	12.00%

If you are asked to increase your DNC%, the choices available to you are:

● increase the level of activity in your department, unit or company;

● increase the value of your income by charging more for your activities or products;

● decrease your dynamic costs;

● decrease your static costs.

This is a different perspective from the changes we have examined so far. We have assumed changes within the structure of the business and looked at the initial impact on the dynamic indicators. We have then moved on to look at the options available to ensure we remain fit and healthy, i.e. retain our DNC%. We have now recognized that we are not fit and healthy enough. We need to be even fitter to compete in the new market place. The general level of fitness out there has increased and we need to regain our competitive edge. But we need to be faster, leaner, stronger. These can be seen as the four choices above that we are faced with and we will address each in turn.

But let us set the scene. In the model business we have been achieving a DNC% of 10 per cent. But let's say we are under increasing pressure to improve this, and we have been targeted to improve performance of the DNC% indicator by 20 per cent, i.e. we are targeted to increase it to 12 per cent. A DNC% of 12 per cent doesn't sound too much to ask. But what do we need to do to achieve this, and are some of the ways easier than others?

Choice one

Increasing activity levels to improve DNC%

Your activity levels can obviously go up or down. This section builds on the principle that you have to improve your DNC%, but also assumes you cannot increase your price at the moment. This also assumes that you are in a business where costs are difficult to change in the short term. Therefore the only option available to you is to increase your activity level (volume) to improve contribution. Service-based industries are often faced with these types of decisions.

This is also a common issue that many business unit or department heads are faced with: an ever increasing demand for a higher DNC% – a higher contribution. Your resources and costs are well established, therefore your only option is to increase your activity levels. The difficult question is: 'By how much do I need to increase my activity level to make my new DNC% target?' Again a series of easy tables and calculations can work this out for you.

But DNC% is not everything. At the same time, as ever, you need to keep your finger on the pulse of your eight dynamic indicators viewed through your radar chart. The effect on the eight dynamic indicators of an increase in activity level is shown in Fig 13.1.

The eight dynamic indicators	Increase activity level (volume)
GC%	
DNC%	Targeted
BeGap%	Calculation
Stock%	
Dr%	
Cr%	
DNA%	Calculation
DCM%	Calculation

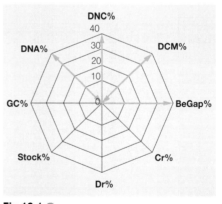

Fig 13.1 ●
Radar chart of dynamic indicators

Unlike many of the other decisions we have so far been faced with, this decision starts with a target for one of the eight dynamic indicators – DNC%. We are almost doing the decision in reverse. We know the DNC% target and now need to use a table to derive the activity level needed to achieve this target.

With the need to meet this DNC% through improved activity levels, only three of the eight dynamic indicators are affected. There will be many changes in the values of your other indicators, but as a percentage of income they should remain the same. Some of these may be affected in the short term as your decisions make their way through the time warp, but as you settle down to your new level of activity, these other dynamic indicators should come back into shape.

DNC% is changing because we have been set a new target DNC%. And the change is positive because that is the nature of targets. The BeGap% will change because the volume of activity has changed and therefore the income has changed. This will be a positive change in BeGap%. DCM% will improve but this effect may take time to work through the time warp of your business.

Going back to the original question, by how much will I need to increase my level of activity to meet this new target? As with many dynamic decisions this can be calculated exactly using a dynamic look-up table (*see* Table 13.1). All you need to know to use this table is your existing BeGap% and the percentage increase required in your DNC%. As you can see, the current BeGap% is 25 per cent and we are looking at an increase in DNC% of 20 per cent. Using the table below:

Table 13.1 ● **New Volume% to achieve new DNC%**

Existing BeGap%	% Increase in DNC% required								
	2.50%	5%	7.5%	10%	12.5%	15%	20%	25%	30%
5	100.13	100.26	100.40	100.53	100.66	100.80	101.06	101.33	101.60
10	100.28	100.56	100.84	101.12	101.41	101.69	102.27	102.86	103.45
15	100.44	100.89	101.34	101.80	102.26	102.72	103.66	104.62	105.59
20	100.63	101.27	101.91	102.56	103.23	103.90	105.26	106.67	108.11
25	100.84	101.69	102.56	103.45	104.35	105.26	**107.14**	109.09	111.11
30	101.08	102.19	103.32	104.48	105.66	106.87	109.38	112.00	114.75
35	101.36	102.77	104.21	105.69	107.22	108.79	112.07	115.56	119.27
40	101.69	103.45	105.26	107.14	109.09	111.11	115.38	120.00	125.00
45	102.09	104.27	106.54	108.91	111.39	113.99	119.57	125.71	132.53
50	102.56	105.26	108.11	111.11	114.29	117.65	125.00	133.33	142.86
55	103.15	106.51	110.09	113.92	118.03	122.45	132.35	144.00	157.89
60	103.90	108.11	112.68	117.65	123.08	129.03	142.86	160.00	181.82
65	104.87	110.24	116.18	122.81	130.23	138.61	159.09	186.67	225.81
70	106.19	113.21	121.21	130.43	141.18	153.85	187.50	240.00	333.33
75	108.11	117.65	129.03	142.86	160.00	181.82	250.00	400.00	1,000.00
80	111.11	125.00	142.86	166.67	200.00	250.00	500.00		
85	116.50	139.53	173.91	230.77	342.86	666.67			
90	129.03	181.82	307.69	1,000.00					

Reading from the table this would give you a required increase in volume of 107.14 per cent. Let's see if it works:

	Before	After	%
Income	£100.00	£107.14	100.00
Dynamic Costs	£60.00	£64.28	60.00
Gross Contribution	£40.00	£42.86	40.00
Static Costs	£30.00	£30.00	28.00
Dynamic Net Contribution	£10.00	£12.86	12.00

It works. Your DNC% is now 12 per cent of your new income level (assuming you can keep your static costs static). What has this done to the other dynamic indicators? As mentioned previously, GC% will not change, but because DNC% has changed, so will the BeGap%:

$$\text{New BeGap\%} = \frac{\text{New DNC\%}}{\text{New GC\%}}$$

$$\text{New BeGap\%} = \frac{12.00\%}{40.00\%} = 30.00\%$$

As you would expect, an increase in activity will widen the BeGap and make the business safer.

With a volume increase, the strands of the SNA will not change as a percentage of income but they will as a value. We need to increase their levels to support the new level of activity:

	Before	After
Income	£100.00	£107.14
Stock	£50.00	£53.57
Debtors	£100.00	£107.14
Creditors	£80.00	£85.71
SNA	£70.00	£75.00
Stock%	50.00%	50.00%
Dr%	100.00%	100.00%
Cr%	80.00%	80.00%
SNA%	70.00%	70.00%

So, in value the SNA has risen to £75. What does this mean for your DNA% – the movement in your SNA?

$$\text{DNA} = \text{SNA } after \text{ Change} - \text{SNA } before \text{ Change}$$

$$\text{DNA} = £75.00 - £70.00 = £5.00$$

Because of the increase in volume required you have had to invest an extra £5 in value in your SNA. Looking at this as a percentage of the new income:

$$\text{DNA\%} = \frac{£5.00}{£107.14} \times 100$$

$$\text{DNA\%} = 4.67\%$$

This means you have imprisoned 4.67 per cent of your new income in your time warp as a result of this growth. What impact will this have on DCM?

$$\text{DCM\%} = \text{DNC\%} - \text{DNA\%}$$

$$\text{DCM\%} = 12.00\% - 4.67\% = 7.33\%$$

Less cash has been generated than would have been without this required increase in DNC%. An increased target on contribution has had an adverse effect on cash, something which is often overlooked.

The new shape of your business

The eight dynamic indicators before and after the increase in activity levels are:

Contribution statement			DNA statement		
	Before	**After**		**Before**	**After**
Income	£100.00	£107.14	Income	£100.00	£107.14
Dynamic Costs	£60.00	£64.28	Stock	£50.00	£53.57
Gross Contribution	£40.00	£42.86	Debtors	£100.00	£107.14
Static Costs	£30.00	£30.00	Creditors	£80.00	£85.71
Dynamic Net Contribution	£10.00	£12.86	Static Net Assets	£70.00	£75.00

Eight dynamic indicators

	Before	After
GC%	40.00%	40.00%
DNC%	10.00%	12.00%
BeGap%	25.00%	30.00%
Stock%	50.00%	50.00%
Dr%	100.00%	100.00%
Cr%	80.00%	80.00%
DNA%	0.00%	4.67%
DCM%	10.00%	7.33%

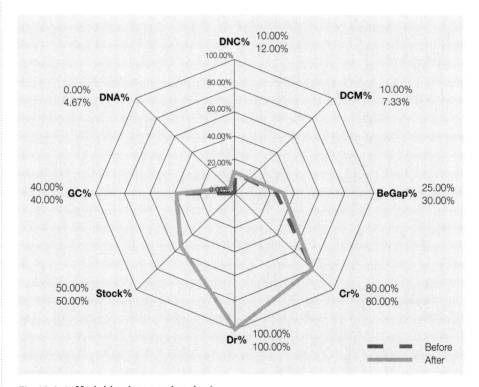

Fig 13.2 ● Model business radar chart

How this looks on the radar chart is shown in Fig 13.2.

As you can see, the contribution indicators for your business are increasing – after all, that was the intention of the target increase. The only negative is the money for the increase in the strands of your SNA needed to support this increased level of activity. If this is not available then increasing the level of activity as a way to improving DNC% is not an option for your business, i.e. do not grow unless you can afford it.

Choice two

Increasing the value of your income

In simple business terms this means increasing your price. If you are looking at a business as a whole this is a feasible option (depending on your customers' response, of course). If you are in charge of a department, especially if this is a service department, this may seem unrealistic. But we have said that budget allocation is the equivalent of income in this situation. You may be able to negotiate an increase in budget allocation. This is not as unusual as it seems. Surely any annual budget negotiation is a balance between controlling costs and securing a budget allocation. Most departmental managers would seek to have some sort of surplus – you may refer to it as a contingency fund. This is your effective DNC%.

The impact on the DNC% should be more dramatic if the change is one of price rather than activity. But we are still left with the question: 'By how much do I need to increase my price to achieve my new target DNC%?' And again, dynamic financial management can provide the answer.

But DNC% is not everything. At the same time, as ever, you need to keep your finger on the pulse of your eight dynamic indicators viewed through your radar chart. The effect on the eight dynamic indicators of an increase in price is shown in Fig 13.3.

The eight dynamic indicators	Increase price
	Tool
GC%	Calculation
DNC%	Targeted
BeGap%	Calculation
Stock%	Calculation
Dr%	
Cr%	Calculation
DNA%	Calculation
DCM%	Calculation

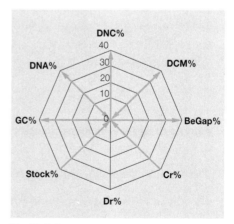

Fig 13.3 ●
Radar chart of dynamic indicators

With the need to meet this new DNC% target through an increase in price activity levels, only Dr% is not affected. But the value of debtors will be. As you would expect, with an increased target in DNC% and an increase in price, the other dynamic indicators of contribution – GC% and BeGap% – will increase. Stock% and Cr% will stay the same in value, but as your anchor point, income, has increased, these will decrease as a percentage.

Again, this decision starts with a target for one of the eight dynamic indicators – DNC%. We know the DNC% target and now need to calculate the price increase required. The answer can be read straight from one of our dynamic look-up tables (*see* Table 13.2).

Table 13.2 ● Price change to achieve new DNC%

Existing DNC%	New DNC% 1	2	3	4	5	6	7	8	9	10
1	0.00	1.02	2.06	3.13	4.21	5.32	6.45	7.61	8.79	10.00
2	−1.01	0.00	1.03	2.08	3.16	4.26	5.38	6.52	7.69	8.89
3	−2.02	−1.02	0.00	1.04	2.11	3.19	4.30	5.43	6.59	7.78
4	−3.03	−2.04	−1.03	0.00	1.05	2.13	3.23	4.35	5.49	6.67
5	−4.04	−3.06	−2.06	−1.04	0.00	1.06	2.15	3.26	4.40	5.56
6	−5.05	−4.08	−3.09	−2.08	−1.05	0.00	1.08	2.17	3.30	4.44
7	−6.06	−5.10	−4.12	−3.13	−2.11	−1.06	0.00	1.09	2.20	3.33
8	−7.07	−6.12	−5.15	−4.17	−3.16	−2.13	−1.08	0.00	1.10	2.22
9	−8.08	−7.14	−6.19	−5.21	−4.21	−3.19	−2.15	−1.09	0.00	1.11
10	−9.09	−8.16	−7.22	−6.25	−5.26	−4.26	−3.23	−2.17	−1.10	0.00
12	−11.11	−10.20	−9.28	−8.33	−7.37	−6.38	−5.38	−4.35	−3.30	−2.22
14	−13.13	−12.24	−11.34	−10.42	−9.47	−8.51	−7.53	−6.52	−5.49	−4.44
15	−14.14	−13.27	−12.37	−11.46	−10.53	−9.57	−8.60	−7.61	−6.59	−5.56
20	−19.19	−18.37	−17.53	−16.67	−15.79	−14.89	−13.98	−13.04	−12.09	−11.11
25	−24.24	−23.47	−22.68	−21.88	−21.05	−20.21	−19.35	−18.48	−17.58	−16.67
30	−29.29	−28.57	−27.84	−27.08	−26.32	−25.53	−24.73	−23.91	−23.08	−22.22
35	−34.34	−33.67	−32.99	−32.29	−31.58	−30.85	−30.11	−29.35	−28.57	−27.78
40	−39.39	−38.78	−38.14	−37.50	−36.84	−36.17	−35.48	−34.78	−34.07	−33.33
50	−49.49	−48.98	−48.45	−47.92	−47.37	−46.81	−46.24	−45.65	−45.05	−44.44

Table 13.2 ● **Continued**

Existing DNC%	12	14	16	18	New DNC% 20	25	30	35	40	50
1	12.50	15.12	17.86	20.73	23.75	32.00	41.43	52.31	65.00	98.00
2	11.36	13.95	16.67	19.51	22.50	30.67	40.00	50.77	63.33	96.00
3	10.23	12.79	15.48	18.29	21.25	29.33	38.57	49.23	61.67	94.00
4	9.09	11.63	14.29	17.07	20.00	28.00	37.14	47.69	60.00	92.00
5	7.95	10.47	13.10	15.85	18.75	26.67	35.71	46.15	58.33	90.00
6	6.82	9.30	11.90	14.63	17.50	25.33	34.29	44.62	56.67	88.00
7	5.68	8.14	10.71	13.41	16.25	24.00	32.86	43.08	55.00	86.00
8	4.55	6.98	9.52	12.20	15.00	22.67	31.43	41.54	53.33	84.00
9	3.41	5.81	8.33	10.98	13.75	21.33	30.00	40.00	51.67	82.00
10	2.27	4.65	7.14	9.76	12.50	20.00	28.57	38.46	50.00	80.00
12	0.00	2.33	4.76	7.32	10.00	17.33	25.71	35.38	46.67	76.00
14	−2.27	0.00	2.38	4.88	7.50	14.67	22.86	32.31	43.33	72.00
15	−3.41	−1.16	1.19	3.66	6.25	13.33	21.43	30.77	41.67	70.00
20	−9.09	−6.98	−4.76	−2.44	0.00	6.67	14.29	23.08	33.33	60.00
25	−14.77	−12.79	−10.71	−8.54	−6.25	0.00	7.14	15.38	25.00	50.00
30	−20.45	−18.60	−16.67	−14.63	−12.50	−6.67	0.00	7.69	16.67	40.00
35	−26.14	−24.42	−22.62	−20.73	−18.75	−13.33	−7.14	0.00	8.33	30.00
40	−31.82	−30.23	−28.57	−26.83	−25.00	−20.00	−14.29	−7.69	0.00	20.00
50	−43.18	−41.86	−40.48	−39.02	−37.50	−33.33	−28.57	−23.08	−16.67	0.00

In the model business, with an existing DNC% of 10 per cent and a targeted DNC% of 12 per cent we would need to increase prices by 2.27 per cent.

Let's see if it works:

	Before	After	%
Income	£100.00	£102.27	100.00
Dynamic Costs	£60.00	£60.00	58.67
Gross Contribution	£40.00	£42.27	41.33
Static Costs	£30.00	£30.00	29.33
Dynamic Net Contribution	£10.00	£12.27	12.00

What has this done to the other dynamic indicators? As mentioned previously, a price change will also result in a change in your GC% and this can be read from the contribution statement above. As the DNC% and the GC% have both changed, there is going to be an impact on the BeGap%:

$$\text{New BeGap\%} = \frac{\text{New DNC\%}}{\text{New GC\%}}$$

$$\text{New BeGap\%} = \frac{12.00\%}{41.33\%} = 29.03\%$$

As you would expect, an increase in price will widen the BeGap – we have improved both GC% and DNC% and made the business safer.

The strands of the SNA will be affected. Stock% and Cr% will not change in terms of value but they will do as a percentage. Dr% is the other way round. It will not change in terms of percentage, but as the income has increased, it will change in terms of value.

	Before	After
Income	£100.00	£102.27
Stock	£50.00	£50.00
Debtors	£100.00	£102.27
Creditors	£80.00	£80.00
SNA	£70.00	£72.27
Stock%	50.00%	48.89%
Dr%	100.00%	100.00%
Cr%	80.00%	78.22%
SNA%	70.00%	70.67%

So, in value the SNA has increased slightly. What does this mean for your DNA% – the movement in your SNA?

DNA = SNA *after* Change – SNA *before* Change

DNA = £72.27 – £70.00 = £2.27

Because of the increase in price it looks like you have had to invest an extra £2.27 in value in your SNA. But with a price change you need to think about the interpretation. Much of the change is money you are entitled to for the first time because of the increase in price reflected through the increase in debtors. Looking at this as a percentage of the new income:

$$\text{DNA\%} = \frac{£2.27}{£102.27} \times 100$$

DNA% = 2.22%

This means you have imprisoned 2.22 per cent of your new income in your time warp due to this increase in the value of your debtors, but if you manage these well, the rewards of this action today will be seen tomorrow.

What impact will this have on DCM?

$$DCM\% = DNC\% - DNA\%$$

$$DCM\% = 12.00\% - 2.22\% = 9.78\%$$

A decrease in this period therefore, but the benefits will come.

We now have the final piece of information and can reassess the shape of our business on the radar chart.

The new shape of your business

The eight dynamic indicators before and after the increase in price are:

Contribution statement			DNA statement		
	Before	**After**		**Before**	**After**
Income	£100.00	£102.27	Income	£100.00	£102.27
Dynamic Costs	£60.00	£60.00	Stock	£50.00	£50.00
Gross Contribution	£40.00	£42.27	Debtors	£100.00	£102.27
Static Costs	£30.00	£30.00	Creditors	£80.00	£80.00
Dynamic Net Contribution	£10.00	£12.27	Static Net Assets	£70.00	£72.27

Eight dynamic indicators

	Before	**After**
GC%	40.00%	41.33%
DNC%	10.00%	12.00%
BeGap%	25.00%	29.03%
Stock%	50.00%	48.89%
Dr%	100.00%	100.00%
Cr%	80.00%	78.22%
DNA%	0.00%	2.22%
DCM%	10.00%	9.78%

How this looks on the radar chart is shown in Fig 13.4.

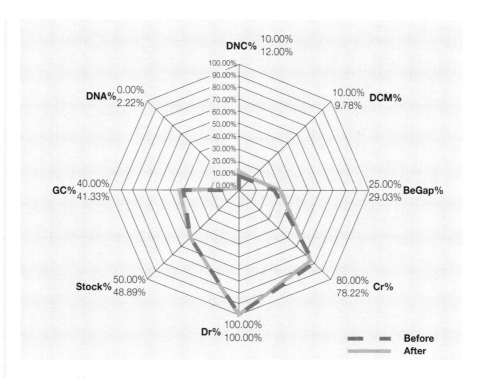

Fig 13.4 ● Model business radar chart

Choice three

Decreasing your dynamic costs

This is one of the two most obvious options for managers to take when faced with a more challenging target – 'If stakeholders want more DNC then I'm going to have to make some cuts around here'. The problem most managers face is where to make the cuts – can we be more efficient (cutting dynamic costs) or can we be more effective (cutting static costs)? Each of these choices will have a different impact on the shape of the business, and the results will also be different from those discussed so far.

The answer to this option is easy – whatever we need to put on the bottom line we need to take off one of the cost lines. Therefore 2 per cent on the bottom means DC% needs to drop by 2 percentage points, from 60 per cent to 58 per cent. It could not be more simple. Let's see if it works:

	Before	After	%
Income	£100.00	£100.00	100.00
Dynamic Costs	£60.00	£58.00	58.00
Gross Contribution	£40.00	£42.00	42.00
Static Costs	£30.00	£30.00	30.00
Dynamic Net Contribution	£10.00	£12.00	12.00

But how much of a drop in your dynamic costs does this represent in percentage terms (rather than in percentage points)? 2/60 is the same as a 3.33 per cent decrease in our dynamic costs. Again this does not sound too hard to achieve. But in a business like the model business, where the dynamic costs are a significant proportion of the total costs, reducing them may be difficult.

What has this done to the other dynamic indicators? A change in dynamic costs will also result in a change in your GC% and this can be read from the contribution statement above. As the DNC% and the GC% have both changed, there is going to be an impact on the BeGap%:

$$\text{New BeGap\%} = \frac{\text{New DNC\%}}{\text{New GC\%}}$$

$$\text{New BeGap\%} = \frac{12.00\%}{42.00\%} = 28.57\%$$

The strands of the SNA will also be affected. Stock% and Cr% will change because one of the components within these must have changed. The magnitude of these changes can be found by referring back to *Chapter 10: Decreases in your dynamic costs*. Using the tables from this section to estimate this proposed change of a 3.33 per cent decrease in the dynamic costs, we get the following figures for the strands in the DNA:

	Before	After
Income	£100.00	£100.00
Stock	£50.00	£48.33
Debtors	£100.00	£100.00
Creditors	£80.00	£78.67
SNA	£70.00	£69.66
Stock%	50.00%	48.33%
Dr%	100.00%	100.00%
Cr%	80.00%	78.67%
SNA%	70.00%	69.66%

So in value the SNA will decrease slightly – some money has been released from the time warp. What does this mean for your DNA% – the movement in your SNA?

DNA = SNA *after* Change – SNA *before* Change

DNA = £69.66 – £70.00 = £(0.34)

Because of the decrease in dynamic costs you have released £0.34 from your SNA. Looking at this as a percentage of income:

$$DNA\% = \frac{£(0.34)}{£100.00} \times 100 = (0.34)\%$$

What impact will this have on DCM?

DCM% = DNC% – DNA%

DCM% = 12.00% – (0.34)% = 12.34%

We now have the final piece of information and can reassess the shape of our business on the radar chart.

The new shape of your business

The eight dynamic indicators before and after the decrease in dynamic costs are:

Contribution statement			DNA statement		
	Before	**After**		**Before**	**After**
Income	£100.00	£100.00	Income	£100.00	£100.00
Dynamic Costs	£60.00	£58.00	Stock	£50.00	£48.33
Gross Contribution	£40.00	£42.00	Debtors	£100.00	£100.00
Static Costs	£30.00	£30.00	Creditors	£80.00	£78.67
Dynamic Net Contribution	£10.00	£12.00	Static Net Assets	£70.00	£69.66

Eight dynamic indicators

	Before	After
GC%	40.00%	42.00%
DNC%	10.00%	12.00%
BeGap%	25.00%	28.57%
Stock%	50.00%	48.33%
Dr%	100.00%	100.00%
Cr%	80.00%	78.67%
DNA%	0.00%	(0.34)%
DCM%	10.00%	12.34%

This is shown on the radar chart in Fig 13.5.

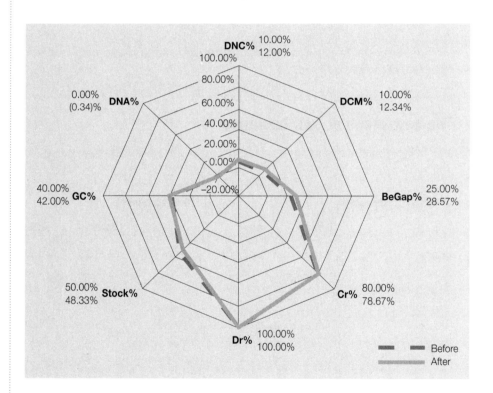

Fig 13.5 ● Model business radar chart

A slightly more healthy business, therefore, but in today's competitive advantage those extra few inches off the waist line can make all the difference.

Choice four

Decreasing your static costs

The other most obvious options for managers to take when faced with a more challenging target is to reduce the static costs – become more effective. Again the choice will have a different impact on the shape of the business, and the results will also be different from those discussed so far.

It is easy – whatever we need to put on the bottom line we need to take off one of the cost lines, so 2 per cent on the bottom means SC% needs to drop by 2 percentage points, from 30 per cent to 28 per cent. That sounds too easy, but it works:

	Before	After	%
Income	£100.00	£100.00	100.00
Dynamic Costs	£60.00	£60.00	60.00
Gross Contribution	£40.00	£40.00	40.00
Static Costs	£30.00	£28.00	28.00
Dynamic Net Contribution	£10.00	£12.00	12.00

But how much of a drop is this in percentage terms (rather than in percentage points)? 2/30 is the same as a 6.67 per cent decrease in our static costs. Because of the cost structure for the model business this is higher than the decrease needed in the dynamic costs. This also sounds a bit harder to achieve. It is not simply decreasing static costs from 30 per cent to 28 per cent – it means trimming the static costs by 6.67 per cent.

What has this done to the other dynamic indicators? You will be aware by now that a change in the static cost will have no impact on the GC%. But we have changed the DNC%, so there will be some impact on the BeGap%:

$$\text{New BeGap\%} = \frac{\text{New DNC\%}}{\text{New GC\%}}$$

$$\text{New BeGap\%} = \frac{12.00\%}{40.00\%} = 30.00\%$$

As we discovered in *Chapter 12: Decreases in your static costs*, with these types of changes we can relax a little bit. There is no impact on the strands of your SNA. Therefore the DNA and DNA% are nil. But if your DNC% has changed, there will be a final impact to consider – the impact on DCM%.

$$DCM\% = DNC\% - DNA\%$$

$$DCM\% = 12.00\% - 0.00\% = 12.00\%$$

The full benefit of the increase in DNC% is seen in cash as well.

The new shape of your business

The eight dynamic indicators before and after the decrease in dynamic costs are:

Contribution statement	Before	After	DNA statement	Before	After
Income	£100.00	£100.00	Income	£100.00	£100.00
Dynamic Costs	£60.00	£60.00	Stock	£50.00	£50.00
Gross Contribution	£40.00	£40.00	Debtors	£100.00	£100.00
Static Costs	£30.00	£28.00	Creditors	£80.00	£80.00
Dynamic Net Contribution	£10.00	£12.00	Static Net Assets	£70.00	£70.00

Eight dynamic indicators

	Before	After
GC%	40.00%	40.00%
DNC%	10.00%	12.00%
BeGap%	25.00%	30.00%
Stock%	50.00%	50.00%
Dr%	100.00%	100.00%
Cr%	80.00%	80.00%
DNA%	0.00%	0.00%
DCM%	10.00%	12.00%

We now have the final piece of information and can reassess the shape of our business on the radar chart (*see* Fig 13.6).

There is very little change to the radar chart, but the changes are all positive and again, the fittest will survive. A slightly more healthy business, therefore, but in today's competitive environment those extra few inches of the waist line can make all the difference.

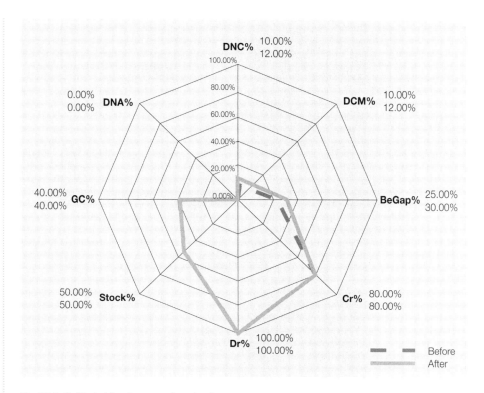

Fig 13.6 ● **Model business radar chart**

Summary

So the model business has four choices to meet its new target DNC% of 12 per cent (a 20 per cent increase):

● increase volume by 7.14 per cent

● increase price by 2.27 per cent

● decrease dynamic costs by 3.33 per cent

● decrease static costs by 6.67 per cent.

As ever, the choice is not about a mathematical solution. The managers of the model business would need to consider the internal and external factors affecting their businesses in order to make the right choice.

Conclusion

You have now achieved the status of a dynamic financial manager.

You will have now mastered new tools and techniques to help you better understand and manage your business. By using the information already available to you, you can now not only manage today but also because you now firmly have your finger on the pulse of the business you can influence tomorrow – managing tomorrow today.

We have shown you how to choose your dynamic indicators, set dynamic targets, and manage the gaps. These techniques allow you to keep your business in shape.

With dynamic decisions you can now predict the mathematical results of your possible actions and so choose the most commercially feasible one to implement as well as understand the outcome for your business. If your accountant says 'it's your decision – it's up to you!') – it really is – now you can manage these decisions with the knowledge that you are making an informed choice and can predict the implications of that choice.

You will now be able to answer the questions raised in 'What's it all about?' Indeed you will now be able to confidently answer most questions about your business and have thought of many more yourself – creating more choices to improve your business.

You have been on a journey with us, learning a new way to view your operations and to understand their past, their present and their future performance – *Managing Tomorrow Today*.

Thank you for joining us on this journey, good luck!

Bill Snaith and Jane Walker

Abbreviations and glossary

Abbreviations

GC%   Gross contribution expressed as a percentage of income.

DNC%   Dynamic net contribution expressed as a percentage of income.

BeGap% Breakeven gap expressed as a percentage of income.

Stock% Stock expressed as a percentage of income.

Dr%   Debtors expressed as a percentage of income.

Cr%   Creditors expressed as a percentage of income.

DNA%   Dynamic net assets expressed as a percentage of income.

DCM%   Dynamic cash movement expressed as a percentage of income.

DFM   Dynamic financial management.

Glossary

Activity   The level of chargeable activity that generates your income. In manufacturing and retail businesses this will be the volume of things sold. In service businesses – whether in the private sector, public sector or of charitable status – this will be the amount of service provided.

Anchor   Income is the anchor point for all the dynamic indicators as it gives the monetary compensation for the activity in your business.

Breakeven   The amount of income you need to cover all your costs – to make neither a negative nor a positive dynamic net contribution.

Breakeven gap   The difference between your income and the breakeven income.

Breakeven Gap%   Breakeven gap expressed as a percentage of income.

Business   The term we have used to describe any organization or department that is using dynamic financial management to measure and monitor its performance.

Contribution   The difference between income and costs. This can be found as gross contribution and dynamic net contribution.

Creditors   People who have provided you with goods or services for which you have not yet paid. This indicates the future money you need to release from your time warp, and is the third, and last, strand of your DNA.

Creditor%   Creditors expressed as a percentage of income.

Debtors   People to whom you have sold goods or services that have not yet been paid for. This indicates the money from income still in the hands of your customers and therefore imprisoned in the time warp of your business and is the second strand of your DNA.

Debtor%   Debtors expressed as a percentage of income.

DNA statement   A summary statement showing the values of the stock, debtors and creditors at one moment in time – the components of the static net assets.

Dynamic   Reflects things that change due to the level of activity and the decisions made within the organization.

Dynamic adjuster   A figure to be used in a calculation or dynamic look-up table.

Dynamic breakeven graph   A visual portrayal of the breakeven income compared with the actual income at various points in time. The difference between the two lines is the breakeven gap.

Dynamic cash graph   A visual portrayal of the trends in the DNC% and the DNA% showing DCM% as the difference between the two lines.

Dynamic cash movement   A product of the dynamic net contribution plus or minus dynamic net asset movement. This indicates the net amount of money you have imprisoned or released from the time warp plus money generated from DNC.

Dynamic cash movement%	The dynamic cash movement expressed as a percentage of income.
Dynamic contribution statement	A summary statement showing the values of income, dynamic costs, gross contribution, static costs and dynamic net contribution.
Dynamic costs	Costs that vary with the activity of the business, for example, the time spent on a project, or the materials used in production.
Dynamic indicators	The figures that should be used to analyze your business in order to really understand what is happening inside your business.
Dynamic look-up table	A simple look-up table to help you evaluate your dynamic decisions.
Dynamic net assets	The movements in stock, debtors and creditors as a response to the activity and management of your business. Dynamic net assets show the movement in the money tied up in this time warp.
Dynamic net contribution	The money left from your income after all costs (dynamic and static) have been deducted. In a business this indicates the potential cash from each sale that could be invested back into your business.
Dynamic net contribution%	Dynamic net contribution expressed as a percentage of the income figure.
Dynamic payback	The number of periods needed to repay the investment in your static net assets to support growth.
Effectiveness	Doing the right thing. Managing the static costs at their optimum level to support the activities of the business. Maximizing your DNC%.
Efficiency	Doing the thing right. Managing the income level and the dynamic costs to achieve your maximum GC%.
Gap	The difference between the actual figures and the target figures for any of your dynamic indicators.
Gap%	The difference between the actual figures and the target figures for any of your dynamic indicators expressed as a percentage of income. Gaps can be positive or negative.

Gross contribution	Gross contribution is income less dynamic costs. It indicates the efficiency of your organization, how well you are able to control your dynamic costs or your income stream.
Gross contribution%	Gross contribution expressed as a percentage of income.
Income	The sales figure, budget allocation or contributions that determine or reflect the level of activity in your business. Income is the anchor for all dynamic indicators.
Initial impact	The new shape of your business after a change in income or costs. This does assume no other changes have taken place. The platform from which you can make decisions to dynamically manage these changes.
Period	The relevant time interval for measuring and monitoring your business. This may be a day, a week, a month, a quarter or a year. The more frequently you can measure and monitor your business, the more in control you will be.
Possible business benefits	The freedom that comes from making decisions that increase your income or reduce your costs.
Possible management actions	The actions you could take to dynamically manage decreases in your income or increases in your costs.
Radar chart	A graphical representation of all your dynamic indicators for the current period. A radar chart shows several values on different axes. Arranging the dynamic indicators around a radar chart gives you the shape of your business. This is based on a standard chart available in many computer spreadsheet packages.
Signpost	A method of navigating through the dynamic decision making in *Part Two*.
Static	Refers to looking at the business at a moment in time – freezing the shot.
Static costs	Regular costs that occur even if there is no activity, for example, rent and rates on your premises, or salaries. Static costs are often *lumpy* in that they change in big steps rather than in direct relation to activity, for example, recruiting one more person will increase your static costs in one step.
Static net assets	A snapshot of stock, debtors and creditors at a moment in time.

Stock	The value of unsold goods or services in your business. This is made up of raw materials in manufacturing businesses, work in progress in manufacturing and service organizations, and finished goods in manufacturing and retail organizations. This indicates the money invested in stock but still imprisoned in the time warp of your business and is the first of three strands building up your DNA.
Stock%	Stock expressed as a percentage of income.
Target	The expected value of a dynamic indicator.
Time warp	The delay between cause and effect experienced by a business. The money trap.

Index